WILLING TO CHOOSE

VOLITION *&* STORYTELLING IN SHAKESPEARE'S MAJOR PLAYS

WILLING TO CHOOSE

VOLITION & STORYTELLING IN
SHAKESPEARE'S MAJOR PLAYS

Essays by

Robert Pack

LOST HORSE PRESS
Sandpoint · Idaho

Acknowledgments

An early version of "Macbeth: The Anatomy of Love" first appeared in *The Yale Review.*

An earlier version of "King Lear and the Book of Job" first appeared in Robert Pack's book, *The Long View,* published by the University of Massachusetts Press.

Cover Art by Cristina Reinoso
Author Photo by Pamela Pack
Book Design by Christine Holbert

FIRST EDITION

ISBN 978-0-9762114-4-0

This and other fine Lost Horse Press titles
may be viewed online at *www.losthorsepress.org.*

Library of Congress Cataloguing-in-Publication Data

Pack, Robert, 1929-
   Willing to choose : volition and storytelling in Shakespeare's major plays / by Robert Pack.—1st ed.
      p. cm.
   ISBN 978-0-9762114-4-0 (alk. paper)
   1. Choice (Psychology) in literature. 2. Shakespeare, William, 1564-1616—Criticism and interpretation. 3. Shakespeare, William, 1564-1616—Characters. 4. Will in literature. 5. Psychology in literature. 6. Characters and characteristics in literature. 7. Storytelling in literature. I. Title.
   PR3069.C45P33 2007
   822.3'3—dc22
                              2006100144

Author's Note to the Reader

This book is intended for the reader and theatergoer who loves Shakespeare's plays and enjoys contemplating them in their complexity: the richness of metaphorical language, the characters' psychological depths and dimensions, the philosophical implications of the plays as organic dramatic entities that testify to the nature of human limitation and human freedom.

I assume that the reader has the patience to delight in the minute details of Shakespeare's patterns of imagery as well as to admire the overall structure of the plays. What most interests me is how these plays cohere and how they can be read from different perspectives which nevertheless complement each other. Thus, I have not adopted any single critical approach, but have responded to each play's individual identity with what seem to me appropriate and fruitful interpretative points of view.

Blessed in having been enfranchised by my profession to teach Shakespeare for half a century, I wish to share with my readers the humane vision I find everywhere in Shakespeare's incomparable plays—a vision empathetic to human suffering and moral aspiration, tempered by his acute awareness of human frailty, which has immeasurably enriched my own life.

Other Books by Robert Pack

Table of Contents

"He makes me lie awake o'nights and laugh . . .
And I say now, as I shall say again,
I love the man this side idolatry."

Life and death I set before you, the blessing
and the curse, and you shall choose life so that
you may live, you and your seed.

Since my dear soul was mistress to her choice
And could of men distinguish, her election
Hath seal'd thee for herself; for thou hast been
As one, in suffering all, that suffers nothing.

CHAPTER ONE

INTRODUCTION: WILL, CHOICE & STORYTELLING

I Motivation & Inevitability

Shakespeare's representation of human character usually assumes that each person's behavior is comprehensible in terms of his or her individual psychological motivation. In this sense, Shakespeare is primarily a determinist: a character's actions follow from that character's given or inherited nature as manifested through some form of appetite or desire, which Shakespeare often calls "will." A direct causal connection can be seen between the desires of Shakespeare's characters and the domestic, social, or political manifestation of those desires. It follows that Shakespeare's representation of human nature is open to analysis which, even when complex, is reductive in that it is informed by laws that are, in modern terms, biologically grounded or genetically programmed; so, too, is the behavior of Shakespearean characters conducive to psychological analysis in that Oedipal conflicts, particularly between son and father, abound in Shakespeare's plays. When we see a character caught up in a fundamental passion that determines a particular relationship, as Hamlet's obsessive hatred of Claudius or Othello's jealousy of Desdemona, an apparent inevitability of behavior becomes manifest that will lead this character to what we, the audience, are likely to regard as a fated conclusion.

While the necessities of their natures drive Shakespeare's characters to their seemingly inevitable fates according to psychological laws, nevertheless, either in action or in attitude, they sometimes appear to leap out of their behavioral molds, to will themselves to be other than what their earlier behavior revealed about them, and, in so doing, they demonstrate a capacity for radical freedom or transcendence based on a surprising choice. The moments in which these characters make manifest the freedom of their wills, in which they choose their actions or their attitudes within the circumstances or conditions in which they find themselves, are beyond predictability precisely because they are in some ultimate sense free of the psychological and behavioral laws that seem to determine their actions. Shakespeare, with his uncanny ability to make even extreme forms of behavior believable, is able to convince us of the credibility of these astonishing transformations, these discontinuities between what a character has been and what he or she suddenly chooses to be. In these circumstances, the word "will" takes on an opposite meaning from that of compelling desire; here the word connotes responsible and self-generated choice. Even if this choice does not take place until the moment before death—as if the certain knowledge of death had a miraculously liberating effect—the choice of a renewed self-identity reveals a power that somehow had been latent in the character all along. To present his characters as essentially determined yet capable of breaking free of the apparently fixed aspect of their natures, Shakespeare must find some paradoxical way of portraying the reality of both necessity and freedom, of behavioral determinism and the assertions of radical will that allow determinism to be transcended, even if only fleetingly in the moments before death, and even if this transcendence cannot change anything other than the attitude with which the character confronts his or her fate.

II Cawdor

I will examine acts of radical choice in five minor characters—Cawdor in *Macbeth*, Edmund in *King Lear*, Emilia in *Othello*, Laertes in *Hamlet*, Caliban in *The Tempest*, and Theseus in *A Midsummer Night's Dream*—and then make a comparative examination of the protagonists of these same plays, showing how the choices made by these minor characters underscore and illuminate those of the major characters. In some special cases—as when, in a state of madness, a character expresses a moral urging or attitude that is the opposite of his or her willed behavior—I will consider this attitude to be a choice that is made at an unconscious level, even though normally the concept of choice in describing Shakespeare's characters involves conscious will and deliberate volition on their parts. I will only do so when the unconscious choice, expressed through madness, reverses a deliberate earlier conscious choice which would violate that character's moral nature, as is true, for example, of Macbeth's decision to murder Duncan.

The Thane of Cawdor, a "disloyal traitor" who has betrayed the trusting King Duncan, is captured in battle by the armies of Macbeth, and he is sentenced to execution. The report to Duncan of Cawdor's death is as follows:

> . . . *he confessed his treasons,*
> *Implor'd your highness' pardon and set forth*
> *A deep repentance. Nothing in his life*
> *Became him like the leaving of it.* (I. iv. 4-8)

There is no hint here that Cawdor's confession contains an ulterior or strategic motive, such as the wish that his confession might bring about the sparing of his life or that suddenly he fears divine judgment and punishment. Cawdor's repentance, rather, is made wholly for its inherent virtue so that Cawdor can establish his final identity as a loyal man in the concluding moments of his life by choosing to reinvent himself, thus becoming the opposite of what he had been as a rebel. Such a decision is beyond explanation and could not have been anticipated; it is a gesture, though circumscribed by the fate of his execution, of radical freedom.

From the audience's point of view, the realization that such a radical choice of self-transformation is possible takes on immense significance since this awareness suffuses the entire play. When Macbeth says, for example, "I am in blood / Stepp'd in so far, that, should I wade no more, / Returning were as tedious as go o'er," meaning that it is too late for him to reverse his rebellious and murderous course of action, we know from the model of Cawdor's repentance that Macbeth's fatalism is self-selected rather than determined by outside forces. Macbeth always has the option of recanting and seeking forgiveness, but to the end he continues to reject this option. From the beginning, Macbeth knows with absolute clarity that the consequences of killing King Duncan—apart from whatever judgment occurs in the afterlife—will provoke judgment "here" in this life:

> But in these cases
> We still have judgment here; that we but teach
> Bloody instructions, which, being taught, return
> To plague the inventor; this even-handed justice
> Commends the ingredients of our poison'd chalice
> To our own lips. (I. vii. 7-12)

Macbeth knows that the morality of "even-handed justice" is so deeply ingrained in human nature that he cannot escape from his own conscience; thus, murder becomes a form of suicide. With a moral clarity that surpasses any self-understanding possessed by Hamlet, Othello, or Lear, Macbeth, even while contemplating the act of murder, already mourns the commission of the crime as an act in his imagination: "And pity, like a naked new-born babe, / Striding the blast . . . / Shall blow the horrid deed in every eye, / That tears shall drown the wind." We can see from the images of Macbeth's imagination that he is capable of remorse, as was Cawdor, and yet, mysteriously, beyond any rational explanation, Macbeth chooses not to abide by what he knows with such certitude. Never has a character entered into crime with more reason, based on self-awareness, not to do so. Although the forces acting upon Macbeth are formidable, such as the supernatural influences of the witches and the persuasiveness of Lady Macbeth, the contradiction between Macbeth's knowledge and his subsequent behavior is so extreme that Macbeth's evil finally must be understood as a form of absurdity: negation for the sake of negation.

When Macbeth, inquiring about his wife's sleeplessness, asks the Doctor, "Can'st thou not minister to a mind diseas'd?" and is told by the Doctor that "Therein the patient / Must minister to himself," Macbeth chooses to reject any prescription that demands self-confrontation and exclaims: "Throw physic to the dogs; I'll none of it." This rejection of the Doctor's cure can be comprehended as Macbeth's decision not to choose and thus to remain, unlike Cawdor, beyond forgiveness and redemption. But when confronted by Macduff, Macbeth's urgent words, "But get thee back, my soul is too much charg'd / With blood of thine already," reveal that he remains capable of remorse even though he is still unwilling to act according to the dictates of his conscience and the option of repentance.

What I have described as the absurdity of Macbeth's suicidal choosing, his negation for the sake of negation, is articulated by Macbeth when, in reviewing his life, he calls it "a tale / Told by an idiot, full of sound and fury, / Signifying nothing." Unlike Hamlet, Othello, and Lear, all of whom wish to have their stories told because, at some level, they realize that their lives do have significance, Macbeth, with ultimate irony, is driven to express that what he is expressing is not worth expressing. Such self-abnegation, of course, from the audience's point of view, contradicts itself because it makes us aware of the horror of Macbeth's choice, the option to live a life without meaning. As Macbeth had said earlier:

> . . . my way of life
> Is fall'n into the sear, the yellow leaf;
> And that which should accompany old age,
> As honour, love, obedience, troops of friends,
> I must not look to have. (V. iii. 22-26)

Like the Satanic "I will not serve," the prototype of rebelliousness, Macbeth's final speech, which begins, "I will not yield," locks him eternally into the identity he had created for himself when, against even his own reasoning, he had decided to murder Duncan. Macbeth's decision not to choose repentance, and thus, in effect, to reject his own humanity, is, in its way, as astonishing as Cawdor's final reversal, even though, at one level, it is consistent with the rebellious and murderous person he has become. Still, we must remember that Macbeth's identity as a traitor was an artificial creation in that its fabrication was contrary to Macbeth's earlier nature, which we have seen as including a vivid conscience and which Lady Macbeth had described as being "full o' the milk of human kindness."

The enigma of Macbeth's final refusal to "yield" is carried by Shakespeare even into Macbeth's last words, "Lay on Macduff, / And damn'd be him that first cries, 'Hold, enough!'" Although Macbeth intends these words to apply to Macduff, he himself, in this utterance, is the first to cry "Hold, enough!" and, in doing so, he damns himself, fulfilling his earlier prophecy of the "even-handed justice / [that] Commends the ingredients of our poison'd chalice / To our own lips." Like Lady Macbeth, who acknowledges her guilt and repents through her madness in spite of herself, Macbeth, at an unconscious level, affirms the morality that he had chosen again and again to defy. Divided against himself in his own kind of defiant madness, Macbeth, in his final moment, makes the same choice of self-judgment that Cawdor had made. Macbeth, however, makes his moral assertion in spite of himself, his nature still in rebellion against his will.

III Edmund

Like Cawdor, Edmund in *King Lear* also makes a radical choice to reverse himself into a new identity as he confronts his own death at the play's end. He, too, does so without an ulterior motive since there is no possibility of any reprieve for him. Having ordered that Lear's faithful daughter, Cordelia, be taken away for execution, and having been mortally wounded in a duel with his brother Edgar who had remained loyal to their father, Edmund spontaneously creates a new attitude toward the welfare of others and tries to save Cordelia. As if from nowhere, Edmund's words leap forth: "Some good I mean to do / Despite of mine own nature." This decision to do good for its own sake, through an act of will, returns Edmund, like Cawdor, to the empathetic bond upon which all human community must be based. Furthermore, Edmund's reversal contrasts with the absence of any recantation by Goneril or Regan. Earlier in the play Edmund made a conscious choice to do evil and could then reverse that choice, while Goneril and Regan make no such choice because they are unaware of the evil nature of their deeds and personalities. Without self-awareness, the choice to reverse a choice is impossible.

Although Edmund's choice to do good is essentially a free act, one that could not have been predicted from Edmund's past, it is not without some element of causation. Two events contribute to the transformation of

Edmund's nature. After Edgar had mortally wounded Edmund, Edgar says to his brother, "Let's exchange charity," and then he goes on to recount their father's death: "his flawed heart . . . / 'Twixt two extremes of passion, joy and grief, / Burst smilingly." This paradoxical description of Gloucester's death—in which opposite extremes of emotion are reconciled—has a profound effect on Edmund who responds: "This speech of yours hath mov'd me, / And perchance shall do some good." The second event, which also carries with it new information, comes when Edmund learns that both Goneril and Regan have died because of their jealous love for him. As if astonished that anyone really could love him, Edmund declares: "Yet Edmund was belov'd. The one the other / Poison'd for my sake, and after slew herself." Before this moment of realization, Edmund had seen love merely as lust, a passion that could be manipulated for political purposes, as Edmund, so he confesses, had manipulated Goneril and Regan in being "contracted to them both."

We must, however, return to the emphasis of Edmund's radical transformation in which he chooses to do good for no worldly gain. Early in the play Edmund listens to his father explain the breaking of familial bonds between brothers and between fathers and sons as being fated, caused by astronomical forces: "These late eclipses of the sun and moon." Edmund in the following soliloquy expresses his contempt for his father's deterministic view:

> *This is the excellent foppery of the world, that, when*
> *we are sick in fortune—often the surfeits of our own*
> *behavior—we make guilty of our disasters the sun,*
> *the moon, and the stars; as if we were villains on ne-*
> *cessity, fools by heavenly compulsion, knaves, thieves,*
> *and treachers by spherical predominance, drunk-*
> *ards, liars, and adulterers by an enforced obedience*
> *of planetary influence, and all that we are evil in*
> *by a divine thrusting on: an admirable evasion of*
> *whoremaster man, to lay his goatish disposition on*
> *the charge of a star.* (I. ii. 121-130)

Although it may appear that Edmund is disputing a deterministic view of human behavior, suggesting that if we become villains we do so out of choice, not out of necessity, Edmund's speech ends, not with a further assertion of individual responsibility, but, with another version of deterministic causation: "I should have been that I am had the maidenliest star in the firmament twinkled on my bastardizing." Edmund is claiming that he was determined to be what he is, not because of the position of the stars at his birth, but because of his inherited nature. Outer causation is replaced by inner causation, as if, in modern terms, one argued that one grew up to be a criminal because of one's genetic inheritance. Edmund here is eschewing any element of will or choice as an explanation for his treacherous behavior. It is, therefore, of particular significance at the play's end that (Edmund's choice to do something good is made, as he says, "Despite of mine own nature," a statement that contains the assumption that one's will can overcome one's nature or that one can create one's own nature through an act of will.)

The transformed Edmund, speaking to Albany, has a new sense of the urgency of time as he tries to undo his evil command to have Cordelia and Lear executed: "Quickly send, / (Be brief in it!) to th' castle, for my writ / Is on the life of Lear and on Cordelia. / Nay, send in time." But it is too late. Edmund cannot change events; he can only change himself. Though Albany's response to the messenger's announcement that "Edmund is dead" is a terse "That's but a trifle here," the audience may feel otherwise, just as moments later the audience may feel it matters immensely that Lear, too, unable to save Cordelia, dies with love for her in his heart. Lear's parental love—love without condition—is the opposite of Lear's earlier hatred for Cordelia when at the play's beginning he demanded that she declare her love for him and, when she refused, disowned her: "Here I disclaim all my paternal care." (Thus the strange parallel between the conversions of Edmund and Lear is completed, and once again Shakespeare shows that the only power human beings have over their fates lies not in events but in the attitude they take to what is beyond their control. The realm in which the will is sovereign may be only in the mind.)

Lear's banishment of Cordelia at the play's beginning is analogous to Macbeth's murder of Duncan in that both characters in these actions violate some fundamental force of humanity inherent within them, a humanity without which, in its social extension, moral law would be an impossibility. The great difference between them is that Macbeth is fully aware of the violation that he is about to commit, that in defying his conscience he will destroy himself, while Lear is blind to his own motives and to the consequences that will follow from his behavior. Macbeth's moral imagination, as when he visualizes the imaginary knife he will use to kill Duncan, is to Macbeth as Kent's (and later the fool's) advice and taunting are to Lear. Just as Macbeth rejects the dictates of his conscience, so, too, does Lear reject Kent's judgment of Lear's banishment of Cordelia as "hideous rashness," and when the furious Lear says to Kent, "Out of my sight!" Kent's reply, "See better, Lear," establishes the metaphor of blindness as fundamental to the entire play.)

As Lear comes to understand the consequences of disowning his daughter, a crime against the natural bond of familial love and paternal protectiveness, "O Lear, Lear, Lear! / Beat at this gate that let thy folly in / And thy dear judgment out!" the choices left to him—now that he has rejected self-justifying rationalization—become quite narrow and quite specific. Lear can either remain self-indulgently obsessed by guilt and remorse, "I did her wrong," or he can achieve a sufficient measure of self-forgiveness through a process of purgative madness that will, in due time, allow him to ask for Cordelia's forgiveness. Kent says of him: "A sovereign shame so elbows him: his own unkindness, / That stripp'd her from his benediction . . .—these things sting / His mind so venomously that burning shame / Detains him from Cordelia." But after the battle when Lear wakes up in his own kingdom in the presence of Cordelia, still half mad, thinking that if he is with his daughter he must have risen from the grave and now must be in heaven, Lear begins to speak in a language of utter simplicity, free of self-indulgent self-castigation, and with genuine humility: "I am a very foolish fond old man." And then in response to Cordelia's identifying herself as his child, a transfigured Lear is able, without equivocation, to implore his daughter, "Pray you now, forget and forgive." Like Cawdor's repentance, Lear's humbling of himself before his daughter must be seen as a radical act of choice, reversing his earlier image of himself as potent king and then as royal victim to a new image of himself as the supplicating father, unlike Macbeth who continues to disdain "the boy Malcolm," and continues to do generational battle (first with Duncan as father, then with Malcolm as son). Macbeth's "I will not yield, / To kiss the ground before young Malcolm's feet," can be seen as a gesture opposite to Lear's reconciliation with Cordelia, and in particular, Lear's acknowledgment and acceptance of his emotional dependency on his own child, thus resolving the generational struggle for dominance and power.

Lear makes three more remarkable choices—two are visionary choices of attitude, one remaining choice is an action—yet only the choice of attitude seems really to matter. The first choice is contained in Lear's speech to Cordelia just before they are about to be taken to prison:

> *Come, let's away to prison.*
> *We two alone will sing like birds i' th' cage.*
> *When thou dost ask me blessing, I'll kneel down,*

And ask of thee forgiveness. So we'll live,
And pray, and sing, and tell old tales, and laugh
At gilded butterflies, and hear poor rogues
Talk of court news; and we'll talk with them too:
Who loses and who wins, who's in, who's out;
And take upon's the mystery of things,
As if we were God's spies; and we'll wear out,
In a wall'd prison, packs and sects of great ones
That ebb and flow by th' moon. (V. iii. 8-19)

An amazing aspect of this speech is its double level of abstraction through Lear's impersonalizing of himself and his individual circumstances. When Lear says to Cordelia, "When thou dost ask me blessing, I'll kneel down, / And ask of thee forgiveness," nothing is specified, neither Lear's transgressions nor the content of Cordelia's blessing. Lear and Cordelia have become universalized in an archetypal exchange; it is as if we see them fixed forever in this moment of reconciliation in some rich tapestry. Lear envisions the two of them as having been removed from the medium of time; from an eternal perspective as "God's spies," they bear detached witness to court gossip so that all sorrow and tragedy take on the aesthetic quality of an "old tale." This capacity for detachment, even from one's own life, one's own imprisoning fate, is what Lear means by the "mystery of things." The incredible choice that Lear has made here—through an act of visionary will—is to transform his tears and his political fortune as a defeated king by releasing the power of laughter—laughter at something as ordinary and mundane as "gilded butterflies." Lear transforms himself by shifting his primary self-identification from the particular and fated circumstances of his life to an identity as observer, not only as witness of his own life, but of the flow of historical time as well. Paradoxically, Lear finds himself through his choice to depersonalize himself as a spectator, rather than as the tragic hero in his own play, and such a choice, it seems to me, is as radical and surprising as any we find in Shakespeare.

This vision of the flow of time, as if sorrow can be redeemed by song, is not, however, the final vision Shakespeare gives to Lear. Although Lear's taking on the "mystery of things" seems to have a culminating quality, the wheel of fortune turns again, and finally, as audience, we are compelled to bear witness to Lear as he bends over the dead body of Cordelia. As he does so, he informs the onlookers that "I kill'd the slave that was a-hanging thee," and the reality of this final action by Lear is confirmed by the attending Captain: "'Tis true, my lords, he did." And yet, strangely, this action seems hardly to matter. Lear's choice of an overt action has little effect on those who surround him; neither Kent nor Edgar even comments upon a feat so physically remarkable for an old man. The only thing that matters now is how Lear feels and how we feel in empathizing with him.

Earlier in the play, Gloucester had described the sort of man "that will not see / Because he does not feel," and, later, when the blinded Gloucester encounters Lear who says, "Yet you see how this world goes," Gloucester replies, "I see it feelingly." Now, at the play's end, it is Lear, having been emotionally blind, who sees things feelingly, and we, as audience, cannot be certain that what is literally true is more real than what is felt to be true. As Lear kneels over the dead body of Cordelia, he holds a feather just above her mouth and cries, "This feather stirs; she lives! If it be so, / It is a chance which does redeem all sorrows / That ever I have felt." In this moment, Lear believes that Cordelia is alive, but his belief is conditional; he has not entirely escaped the cold grip of reality. Seconds later, it is the apparently inescapable reality of her death that assumes ascendancy in Lear's mind: "Why should a dog, a horse, a rat, have life / And thou no breath at all? Thou'lt come no more." But Lear's perception of the absoluteness of Cordelia's death is immediately followed by another vision which Lear has at the instant of his own death—the illusion that Cordelia is alive: "Do you see this? Look on her! Her lips! / Look there, look there!"

Perhaps Lear is inviting the onlookers to bear witness to the last in a series of almost unthinkably terrible events, but if it is correct to read this moment as a break in Lear's hold on reality, what are we as audience to make of this illusion? Must we respond to it as an ultimate irony: Lear who has endured so much has come to a human limit and can endure no more. Gloucester's death, brought on by his reconciliation with Edgar just as his son asks for his father's blessing, had been described by Edgar as follows: "his flaw'd heart / . . . Twixt two extremes of passion, joy and grief, / Burst smilingly." This description can apply with equal accuracy to Lear's death, for we cannot tell whether it is grief at Cordelia's death or joy in thinking that she is alive that bursts Lear's heart and releases him, as Kent says, from "the rack of this tough world." Perhaps the cruelty of nature, as depicted relentlessly in this play, also has its limit in allowing illusion to be part of some larger structure of reality, and we may wish to remember here that Prometheus's great gift to humankind, in addition to fire, was "blind hope."

We cannot say that Lear's illusion at the end is an act of choice unless we extend the idea of choice-making from the conscious to the unconscious level, but perhaps we can consider Lear's illusion, based on feeling, his deep love for Cordelia, to be made manifest and deliberate in his successor, Edgar, whose words link feeling and truthfulness in his chosen memorial to Lear's life: "The weight of this sad time we must obey; / Speak what we feel, not what we ought to say." Here, too, Gloucester's earlier words that describe the man who "will not see / Because he does not feel" prove to be prophetic, for finally what Lear's feelings enable him to see is the infinite value of human love—this value is his undying truth. The nature of Shakespearean tragedy, its very essence, is that, paradoxically, it affirms and possesses what is most precious through the sorrow of loss.

IV Emilia

Emilia is well-suited to be Iago's wife in that she shares his profound skepticism both about sexual relations and about money. It is typical of Iago to generalize about women:

> *You are pictures out o' doors,*
> *Bells in your parlors, wild cats in your kitchens,*
> *Saints in your injuries, devils being offended,*
> *Players in your housewifery, and housewives in your beds.*
> (II. i. 109-112)

And when Emilia generalizes about men, one can detect Iago's influence upon her:

> *'Tis not a year or two shows us a man.*
> *They are all but stomachs, and we all but food.*
> *They eat us hungerly, and when they are full*
> *They belch us.* (III. iv. 101-104)

Both Iago and Emilia tend to see people in stereotypical categories, as automata to be programmed and manipulated. Given Emilia's fundamental cynicism, it is astonishing that she is, until the play's end, so blind to her husband's Satanic ways even though Iago is sufficiently adroit in his machinations to be able to deceive everyone he selects to plot against.

Iago's exploitation of Roderigo is well-served by convincing him that Desdemona will tire of Othello, and talking to the despairing Roderigo about Desdemona and Othello, Iago is most deft in expressing his views on the subject of love by talking about money:

> *When she is sated with his body, she will find the er-*
> *ror of her choice. She must have change, she must.*
> *Therefore put money in thy purse. If thou wilt needs*
> *damn thyself, do it a more delicate way than drown-*
> *ing. Make all the money thou canst. If sanctimony*
> *and a frail vow betwixt an erring barbarian and*
> *a supersubtle Venetian be not too hard for my wits*
> *and all the tribe of hell, thou shalt enjoy her: there-*
> *fore make money.* (I. iii. 351-359)

So, too, when Emilia is talking to Desdemona about adultery, she expresses herself in terms of worldly commerce, the price of things; money is
evoked as part of the currency of sexual exchange. Again, we see how profoundly Iago's influence has affected her attitude toward human relationships.

> DESDEMONA: *Dost thou in conscience think (tell me, Emilia)*
>   *That there be women do abuse their husbands*
>   *In such gross kind?*
> EMILIA: *There be some such, no question.*
> DESDEMONA: *Wouldst thou do such a deed for all*
>   *the world?*
> EMILIA: *Why, would not you?*
> DESDEMONA: *No, by this heavenly light.*
> EMILIA: *Nor I neither by this heavenly light. I might*
>   *do't as well i' th' dark.*
> DESDEMONA: *Wouldst thou do such a deed for all*
>   *the world?*
> EMILIA: *The world is a huge thing. It is great price*
>   *or a small vice.* (IV. iii. 61-70)

Emilia is quick-witted, cynical about male sexual behavior, practical,
and obedient to Iago: she complies, though not without misgivings, when
he orders her to filch Desdemona's handkerchief. We see nothing in Emilia
that anticipates her radical change into a kind of martyrdom and her
shift into an entirely different tone and style of address in her final brief
speeches.

Emilia clings to her belief that Iago is not a liar and a murderer as long
as she can. "Thou'rt not such a villain," she says to him. But when the
fact of Iago's treachery no longer can be denied, Emilia, shocked out of

the defensive structure of her earlier cynicism, boldly accuses Iago without further equivocation: "You told a lie, an odious damned lie: / Upon my soul, a lie, a wicked lie." A worldly and sophisticated person knows, of course, that people tell lies, yet in this moment Emilia realizes, as she has not before, what devastation lying can cause. She acknowledges, too, that she herself was partly complicit in Iago's lying because she had lied to herself in refusing to admit that she had suspected Iago's villainy much earlier. "I thought so then," Emilia blurts out, and then Emilia's sorrow for Desdemona obliterates all other concerns: "I'll kill myself for grief," she says. Iago, infuriated by her defiance, commands her," get you home," but Emilia, addressing Montano, the governor of Cyprus, and the other present noblemen, continues to assert herself: "'Tis proper I obey him, but not now, / Perchance, Iago, I will ne'er go home." In these heartbreaking lines, Emilia, in effect, divorces herself from Iago, and moments later Iago mortally stabs her.)

In her dying moments, freed at last from Iago's influence, Emilia symbolically marries Desdemona. "O lay me by my mistress' side," she implores, and she repeats the refrain, "Willow, willow, willow," of the song Desdemona sang before being strangled by Othello so that the two women merge in words, as well as in sacrificial identities. Emilia's last words to Othello, unlike anything else she says before this final scene, make her an apostle of truthfulness in which she speaks, not merely for herself, but in behalf of an ideal that expresses the longing of all humanity for honesty in human communication. ("She loved thee, cruel, Moor," Emilia says, "So come my soul to bliss as I speak true. So speaking as I think, I die, I die." Like Edgar's pledge at the very end of *King Lear*, "The weight of this sad time we must obey; / Speak what we feel, not what we ought to say," Emilia's last words constitute her leaving an inheritance by willing herself to speak with personal honesty. Her words resound beyond her own life, her own character, articulating a commitment to communal truthfulness that, surely, expresses a value Shakespeare himself, as his plays repeatedly reveal, treasured in his own heart.

Emilia's sacrificial gesture, "I'll kill myself for grief," and her final words, which emphasize the extreme importance of speaking the truth, "So come my soul to bliss as I speak true," are of immense significance to how the play ends. Emilia, unlikely as it may seem, becomes the model whom Othello tries to emulate. Othello will kill himself for grief, and Othello, too, will attempt, as Emilia declares, to "speak true." Addressing Lodivico, Othello says, "When you shall these unlucky deeds relate, / Speak of them as they are. Nothing extenuate," and although one can argue that Othello is being overly generous in describing himself when he goes on to say, "Then must you speak / Of one that lov'd not wisely but too well," it is an honest attempt on Othello's part at the restoration of language, an attempt that can be seen clearly as such in contrast to Iago's last utterance, "From this time forth I never will speak word."

Othello's final choice to commit suicide as a way of destroying his recent identity as a wife-killer and replacing it with his earlier identity as a servant of the state, is made manifest in Othello's final recollection of his role as a Venetian officer before his marriage to Desdemona:

> *Set you down this;*
> *And say besides, that in Aleppo once,*
> *Where a malignant and turban'd Turk*
> *Beat a Venetian and traduc'd the state,*
> *I took by the throat the circumcised dog,*
> *And smote him thus. (He stabs himself.)* (V. ii. 351-356)

In his mind, Othello merges two identities into one: the Turk who "traduc'd the state" and his current self who has murdered Desdemona in the perverted name of justice and thus usurped what he considers to be his true identity as statesman and loving husband. Othello then reenacts the past execution of the Turk by stabbing himself, and, in doing so, he kills the usurper self and restores his earlier identity. Since it was his past identity as the upholder of Venetian civilization upon which Othello could make his claim as wooer of Desdemona, Othello can, in his last couplet, also restore his self-image as a lover: "I kiss'd thee ere I killed thee. No way but this, / Killing myself to die upon a kiss."

Here, too, as is typical in Shakespearean tragedy, a character makes a final choice which will have no practical effect. Othello cannot bring Desdemona back to life, nor can he do anything to make future life possible for himself. His final act of killing himself and then kissing Desdemona changes his image of himself in his own mind, and probably in ours as well; we are likely to give assent to Cassio's valedictory remark: "For he was great of heart." Ultimately, Othello's fate is not entirely in his own hands; it is the result also in part of Iago's manipulations. Unlike Macbeth who was not deluded even by himself, knowing that "we still have judgment here," Othello to a great extent suffers because of forces acting upon him, diabolical forces that indeed strain credibility. Since it is the Satanic power of lying that has defeated Othello, only the counterforce of truth-telling, embodied by Emilia, is capable of offering the audience an uplifting element of hope.

The proper telling of Othello's story, therefore, contains the potential power of possible redemption. Othello understands this and makes his attempt, his most meaningful final choice, to participate in the telling of his story: "Set you down this," he says to those who bear witness to his tragedy. In this spirit of recording what has transpired in the hope that true storytelling, based on feeling, can redeem the plague of lying, Lodovico speaks the final words of the play: "Myself will straight aboard, and to the state / This heavy act with heavy heart relate."

V Laertes

We see Laertes first in Hamlet as a shallow and hypocritical young man and later as a brutal and mendacious murderer, the partner in conspiracy with the villainous Claudius. Before Laertes leaves home at the play's beginning, he advises his sister, Ophelia, to remain chaste, but Ophelia sees through his glib sermonizing and replies:

> *But, good my brother,*
> *Do not, as some ungracious pastors do,*
> *Show me the steep and thorny way to heaven,*
> *Whiles, like a puff'd and reckless libertine,*
> *Himself the primrose path of dalliance treads,*
> *And recks not his own rede.* (I. iii. 46-51)

Laertes cannot remove himself from his father Polonius quickly enough after fulfilling the mandatory propriety of returning for Hamlet's father's funeral; thus, his return later to avenge the death of Polonius can be seen ironically in the context of his ongoing hypocrisy. Laertes's excessive claims of filial love and loyalty are revealed in the grossly melodramatic language he uses in public to simulate outrage:

> *To hell allegiance! Vows to the blackest devil!*
> *Conscience and grace, to the profoundest pit!*
> *I dare damnation. To this point I stand,*
> *That both the worlds I give to negligence.*
> *Let come what comes! Only I'll be reveng'd*
> *Most thoroughly for my father.* (IV. i. 131-136)

So, too, when Laertes leaps into Ophelia's grave, his language is dubious in its ostentation, and his sincerity is in question:

> *Now pile dust upon the quick and the dead,*
> *Till of this flat a mountain you have made*
> *T' o'er-top old Pelion or the skyish head*
> *Of blue Olympus.* (V. i. 257-260)

Hamlet falls into the emotional trap of imitating Laertes's hyperbolic language, but he catches himself and rightly describes such speechmaking as rant. Hamlet grumbles, "Nay, an thou'lt mouth, / I'll rant as well as thou."

When goaded on by Claudius to join the plot against Hamlet's life by arranging a duel, Laertes will use a poisoned sword. He responds to Claudius's proposition to kill Hamlet with almost incredible crudeness: "[I'll] cut his throat i' th' church," and he expresses his willingness, "I will do't," to exploit even Hamlet's virtues as the King describes them for their treacherous purposes:

> *He* [Hamlet] *being remiss,*
> *Most generous, and free from all contriving,*
> *Will not peruse the foils; so that with ease,*
> *Or with a little shuffling, you may choose*
> *A sword unbated, and in a pass of practice*
> *Requite him for your father.* (IV. iii. 133-138)

Laertes's conscienceless dishonesty reaches its peak just before the duel with Hamlet begins. The contrite Hamlet makes an appeal for reconciliation to Laertes: "Give me your pardon, sir. I've done you wrong; / But pardon 't, as you are a gentleman." Confessing that some of his past behavior was the unfortunate result of his madness, Hamlet concludes his speech:

> *Let my disclaiming from a purpos'd evil*
> *Free me so far in your most generous thoughts,*
> *That I have shot my arrow o'er my house,*
> *And hurt my brother.* (V. ii. 245-248)

Hamlet's brotherly appeal is met with total hypocrisy as Laertes replies, "I do receive your offer'd love like love, / And will not wrong it," but he continues to act out the fatal plot as concocted by Claudius. Laertes's claim of accepting Hamlet's love is so blatantly false that it assumes an Iago-like credibility, and the generous Hamlet possesses nothing within himself that enables him to see through such extreme dissembling.

After the initial round of the duel when Hamlet hits Laertes, Laertes says to Claudius, "My Lord, I'll hit him now," and when the King replies, "I do not think 't," Laertes wavers in his intention to kill Hamlet with the poisoned sword. He says, "And yet it is almost against my conscience." But it is not until Hamlet wounds Laertes after they exchange rapiers in a scuffle and Laertes knows with certainty that he is about to die that Laertes's emerging conscience fully takes hold when he proclaims, "I am justly kill'd with mine own treachery." At this point, through an act of self-recognition which becomes an act of will, the reversal of Laertes's character is completed, and from that reversal follows a transformation as well of Laertes's style of speaking from his earlier hyperbole to conciseness, simplicity, sincerity, and directness:

> Exchange forgiveness with me, noble Hamlet:
> Mine and my father's death come not upon thee,
> Nor thine on me. (V. ii. 332-334)

The radical changes in character that take place in Cawdor, Edmund, Emilia, and Laertes occur at the point of death and with the full realization that their lives are about to end. It is as if the certain knowledge of death unlocks some totally hidden capacity for choice, some mysterious power of the will, that was inherent within them. Our awareness that this is so might lead us, who "are but mutes or audience to this act," to wonder if the knowledge of death—should we be able to take such knowledge to heart even before death is actually upon us—could empower us in transformative ways as it has done for these characters when they come to their conclusive reckoning.

In comparing Hamlet's final sense of himself, and his culminating choice of perspective with which to face death, with Laertes's reversal, we need to acknowledge two major differences in their circumstances: Laertes, unlike Hamlet, does not have to deal with a remarried mother, and Laertes's father has not been replaced by another father. The case for Hamlet's Oedipal motivation has been made fully by Ernest Jones (2) and embellished by many other Freudian critics, and it is convincing as the basis for a psychological analysis of the play: Hamlet's reluctance to kill Claudius is due in part to his identification with Claudius, just as Hamlet's suicidal impulses are partly caused by Hamlet's unconscious wish to punish himself for this same identification.

It is important, however, to avoid ultimate reductiveness while maintaining a belief in the essential relevancy of a psychoanalytic reading, to acknowledge that aspects of Hamlet's personality cannot be explained by any system which is neatly causal in relating motivation to certain manifestations of Hamlet's speech and behavior. Hamlet's Christian upbringing, for example, can also be seen as a cause for Hamlet's reluctance to commit murder. Just as the "Everlasting had fix'd / His canon 'gainst self-slaughter," so, too, had God fixed another commandment against murder—a commandment exactly opposite to Hamlet's father's cry for revenge to which Hamlet responds, "And thy commandment all alone shall live / Within the book and volume of my brain."

Hamlet is similar to Sophocles's *Oedipus Rex* (3) in that each is aware of a sickness in the community that somehow he is obligated to cure. The plague in Thebes is analogous to Hamlet's awareness that "There is something rotten in the state of Denmark." Oedipus comes to understand that he himself is the cause of the malady in his community, and Hamlet is aware, though in a confused way, that there is some deep correspondence between his own melancholy and the "rottenness" that he perceives as a social condition. Of paramount significance in Shakespeare's play is the fact that Hamlet knows that there is something about himself that he does not know, and that not knowing what it is will have fatal results. Thus Hamlet becomes the exemplary literary character to become aware of the power of his own unconscious mind—a power capable of harming himself as well as others. We can take Hamlet's words, "I have of late lost all my mirth, but wherefore I know not," to be his quintessential paradoxical knowledge—the knowledge that he does not know, that he is a stranger to his own mind.

Knowing that he cannot know is synonymous for Hamlet with knowing that he cannot make a significant choice to act, and knowing that he cannot act to "set things right" is synonymous with the realization that his destiny is to suffer. Hamlet's attitude toward suffering, therefore, will become his most defining feature, and, paradoxically, the style and tone of Hamlet's passivity, his "Let be," will result in the only act of choosing, other than the "To be or not to be" of suicidal negation, over which Hamlet has full control.

In Hamlet's elusive speech to Horatio, midway in the play, Hamlet apprehends a quality in Horatio that Hamlet himself does not possess but with which he can identify. Here, Hamlet is in part inventing Horatio by projecting onto him what Hamlet himself desires to feel, but cannot feel at this point in the play:

. . . for thou hast been
As one, in suffering all, that suffers nothing,

> *A man that fortune's buffets and rewards*
> *Hast ta'en with equal thanks; and bless'd are those*
> *Whose blood and judgment are so well co-mingled*
> *That they are not a pipe for fortune's finger*
> *To sound what stop she please. Give me that man*
> *That is not passion's slave, and I will wear him*
> *In my heart's core, ay, in my heart of heart,*
> *As I do thee.* (III. ii. 65-74)

Hamlet sees in Horatio a stoicism that he himself has lacked and a capacity for reason, a balance between passion and intellect, that allows one
to choose and thus, in some sense, determine one's own fate. The play later will reveal that Hamlet is partially accurate in his depiction of Horatio.
When Hamlet broods obsessively about death and decay beside Yorick's
grave, Horatio admonishes him by saying, "'Twere to consider too curious-
ly, to consider so." But when Horatio sees that Hamlet is dying of poison,
and Hamlet asks Horatio to "report me and my cause aright / To the unsatisfied," Horatio, with passionate abandon, snatches the cup of poison from
Hamlet to follow him in death. Identifying with Hamlet, and thus not
wishing to survive him, Horatio says, "Here's yet some liquor left." Hamlet
then wrests the cup from Horatio and gives him the reason why he must reject the "felicity" of death and survive:

> *If thou did'st ever hold me in thy heart,*
> *Absent thee from felicity awhile*
> *And in this harsh world draw thy breath in pain*
> *To tell my story.* (V. ii. 349-352)

Horatio will be true to the bond in which each, through empathetic identification, holds the other in his "heart's core."

The story must be told, and it must fulfill Hamlet's wishful projection
of himself onto Horatio "as one, in suffering all, that suffers nothing." For
this wish to be realized, at least in part, Hamlet's capacity for identification
with others must continue to expand, and indeed it does as when we later
hear Hamlet tell Horatio that "I am sorry, good Horatio, / That to Laertes
I forgot myself, / For by the image of my cause I see / The portraiture of
his." In dying, Hamlet becomes the story of Hamlet, passing beyond his
own suffering into an imaginative state of artistic wonder and speculation.
Hamlet does not suggest a moral for this story; it is the story itself that
matters, and beyond the story there is only silence. Hamlet's final words,

"The rest is silence," take us to that realm where human sorrow, human consciousness, and human identity pass back into the unspeaking matter of which the universe is composed, the "elements" to which Ariel returns when Prospero finally releases him into his own version of freedom.

There is nothing more mysterious in all of Shakespeare, I believe, than Hamlet's concept of "one, in suffering all, that suffers nothing." This concept is essentially similar to what Lear means when he speaks of taking on "the mystery of things." In both instances, we see characters in acts of imagination who for a moment step out of their own lives to become witnesses to their lives so that they then can see their lives as tales or stories. In this sense, they are quite literally in a state of ecstasy—outside themselves. Hamlet's final concerns and his two final choices turn away from his earlier obsession with killing Claudius, just as Lear's killing of the "slave" who killed Cordelia instantly fades from significance. Hamlet responds to Laertes's dying plea, "Exchange forgiveness with me, noble Hamlet: / Mine and my father's death come not upon thee, / Nor thine on me," with the generous and unequivocal reply, "Heaven make thee free of it." Nothing in the physical world is changed by Hamlet's response, yet nothing more meaningful happens in the entire play: a sense of values is restored. Forgiveness cannot change the past, but it can change the way in which the past is regarded.

Hamlet's final action, though it is entirely verbal, is his ultimate act of acceptance: "But let it be." Hamlet's impulse is to tell his story to the surviving members of the court:

> *You that look pale and tremble at this chance,*
> *That are but mutes or audience to this act,*
> *Had I but time (as this strict sergeant, death,*
> *Is strict in his arrest) O, I could tell you—*
> *But let it be.* (V. ii. 337-343)

Just as it was not given to Hamlet to control the circumstances of his own life or even to understand the complexities of his own emotions and motivation, so, too, Hamlet must accept that there is not enough time left for him to tell his own story. If his enigmatic story is indeed his only inheritance, it is for Horatio to tell it: "Horatio, I am dead; / Thou liv'st. Report me and my cause aright / To the unsatisfied." Only as Hamlet passes from his life into the story of his life is his earlier prophetic imagining of "one, in suffering all, that suffers nothing," fully realized. Since Fortinbras, as Hamlet realizes, will seize power in Denmark, Hamlet tells Horatio that Fortinbras "has my dying voice. / So tell him, with th' occurrents, more and less, / Which have solicited." Whether Horatio is capable of telling this story or Fortinbras capable of understanding it is another question, a question not to be answered within the parameters of the play since "The rest is silence."

VI Caliban

The transformation of Caliban in *The Tempest* is the most unlikely (and most open to speculation) of the examples I have chosen from secondary characters. Although Caliban's potential for reformation does not appear at a moment before death, this potential does reveal itself when the entire structure of his life, as heretofore determined by Prospero, is about to change. Either Caliban will remain on the island alone, or he will be taken back to Milan with Prospero. Caliban is a liar, a would-be rapist, and a would-be murderer; only Prospero's supervision prevents him from enacting his intention to commit such crimes. When Prospero confronts Caliban with the history of his ungrateful behavior,

> *Thou most lying slave,*
> *Whom stripes may move, not kindness! I have us'd thee,*
> *Filth as thou art, with human care; and lodged thee*
> *In mine own cell, till thou didst seek to violate*
> *The honor of my child.* (I. ii. 344-348)

Caliban replies, not with shame or remorse, but with unabashed delight in the very thought of raping Miranda: "Oh ho! Oh ho!—would it had been done! / Thou didst prevent me; I had peopled else / This isle with Calibans."

Caliban's conspiracy with Stephano and Trinculo to murder Prospero remains an abiding threat, and Prospero is in danger of repressing the knowledge of such evil, particularly when he is reveling in his art, his production of the visionary masque. Prospero has to interrupt himself from the performance of the masque with the reminder, "I had forgot that foul conspiracy / Of the beast Caliban, and his confederates / Against my life," and so the masque's "graceful dance" of the nymphs vanishes from sight. Artistic pleasure and indulgence, the human need for "dreams," must be put aside to make way for the stark awareness of reality: human aggression and murderousness are always lurking in the shadows. The knowledge of the omnipresence of such danger, epitomized by Caliban, is expressed by Prospero in his summary description of Caliban:

A devil, a born devil, on whose nature
Nurture can never stick; on whom my pains,
Humanely taken, all, all lost quite lost. (IV. i. 188-192)

Caliban appears to be the paradigmatic example of genetic determinism, a creature who is fixed in and by his own nature, impervious to any of the softening influences of civilization and the main agency of civilization, the family. Caliban represents primal desire in the forms of lust and aggression, desire which can best be understood at the basic level of food in which aggression and eating come together, at least metaphorically, as cannibalism, the word Caliban's name evokes as a grim pun. For Shakespeare, the word "appetite" always carries a sexual meaning. Not to understand Caliban for what he is—the compelling force of human appetite for dominance and sexual conquest—puts one in mortal peril; Caliban can be controlled but it would seem that he cannot be reformed. When, shortly later, Prospero says of Caliban, "this thing of darkness I / Acknowledge mine," he likewise acknowledges his responsibility for the control of Caliban, and, on a deeper level, he acknowledges that there is some element of Caliban in everyone, surely in his brother, and no doubt in himself as well. On this momentous day, appetite and the wish for control must be curtailed or forsworn; thus, Prospero must relinquish his daughter and give up even the power inherent in his art.

Before further examination of Prospero's remarkable act of will and renunciation, however, I will discuss Caliban's reaction to Prospero's final command: "Go sirrah, to my cell; / Take with you your companions: as you look / To have my pardon, trim it handsomely." Despite Prospero's earlier statement about Caliban, "a devil, on whose nature / Nurture cannot stick," Prospero offers to Caliban the possibility of "pardon." To our astonishment, Caliban's response is positive, and—something we have not seen before—it even contains an element of critical self-awareness:

Ay, that I will; and I'll be wise hereafter,
And seek for grace. What a thrice-double ass
Was I, to take this drunkard for a god,
And worship this dull fool! (V. i. 294-297)

Although it is possible to read this speech ironically, as if Caliban merely has learned to be placating and circumspect, his voice reveals a new tone of sincerity, and his surprising choice of the abstract word "grace" suggests that his thinking has moved into a higher realm of moral comprehension.

In realizing, too, that Stephano and Trinculo are just drunkards and fools, Caliban is able to distinguish appearances from actualities, and thus to detach himself from his own behavior so that he is now capable of being critical about himself and perhaps also of reforming his character. Just as Prospero's judgment had been mistaken earlier in Naples when he trusted his brother, so, too, he may be mistaken now in assuming that Caliban is incapable of any reform.

The exercise of free will and the condition of freedom within natural limits ultimately distinguish our humanity at any level, as we see both in Caliban and Ariel, his opposite. Prospero's final command to Ariel, "to the elements / Be free," returns Ariel to the nature from which he first emerged, a nature, however, which is free of the burdens and constraints of consciousness and conscience, of self-awareness and morality. It is as if Shakespeare, through Ariel, has imagined nature in its pristine and wordless form without human presence to interrupt the innocence of its silence just as Caliban had perverted the potential blessing of speech as taught to him by Prospero: "You taught me language; and my profit on't / Is, I know how to curse: the red plague on you, / For learning me your language."

But Prospero is not free to return to the unconscious state of nature as is Ariel, nor is Prospero free to relinquish language. Like Hamlet's "draw thy breath in pain to tell my story," and Othello's "Set you down this," and Edgar's "Speak what we feel," Prospero also knows the importance of telling his tale, "the story of my life / And the particular accidents gone by." Storytelling in Shakespeare's universe prevails as the power of language to redeem itself from lying and cursing. Alonso replies to Prospero's offer to tell his story with enthusiasm: "I long / To hear the story of your life, which must / Take the ear strangely," and Prospero affirms Alonso's affirmation with the promise that "I'll deliver all."

Telling his story, Prospero's culminating choice, must serve as the counterbalance to Prospero's great final renunciations: setting his beloved Ariel free, giving up his daughter in marriage, relinquishing his wish for revenge against his brother and forgiving him, forswearing any further use of his art—"this rough magic / I here abjure," and accepting the inevitability of death. Choice essentially makes nothing happen; it is an act of letting be, yet an act of will can change the character's and the audience's attitude toward everything that has gone before. The passivity of acceptance, expressed with mysterious evocativeness in Hamlet's "the readiness is all" and in Edgar's "ripeness is all," may finally be seen as the ultimate triumph of the human will within the mortal limits of what is possible.

VII Theseus

There are no major protagonists in *A Midsummer Night's Dream* as in the other plays discussed here, only a major theme—the folly of romantic love—which is exemplified by virtually everyone. Behavior determined by the passion of love is seen in all the characters, and the possibility of the transcendence of one's character is focused on a single concept or option: will a person caught up in amorous desire be able to maintain fidelity to that person or not. Put even more specifically, will the romantic lover be able to overcome what we will call an instinct for infidelity through the making of a vow, thus preparing him or her for marital and parental commitment with the "blessed" result of having healthy children?

Though Bottom may be the character that most engages the theatergoer, perhaps, ironically, because he is what he is and remains so no matter how his overt appearance changes during the play, yet Theseus may well be regarded as the character who undergoes the greatest transformation in the play as the result of what I have been calling radical choice. At the beginning of the play Theseus is an advocate of Athenian law and thus supports Egeus's claim that he, as father, in effect owns his daughter and has the right to decide whom she will marry and what the penalties will be if she disobeys his wishes. Toward the end of the play, however, at a crucial moment, Theseus renounces that law and turns against Egeus's wishes, making it possible for Hermia, Egeus's daughter, to marry someone of her own choosing. This ability of Theseus to reverse himself appears so suddenly in the play, almost, so it seems, without preparation, that we may hardly notice it as a transformation at all, and, surely we do not know out of what resources in Theseus it springs. We cannot "pluck out the heart of his mystery" to use Hamlet's phrase in making claim to his own unfathomable mystery. This is another manifestation of the mystery of will power to break free of the deterministic aspects of what seemed to be the limitations of a character's given nature.

Theseus's transformation is just as radical as those we have seen in other characters, both major and minor, but differs only in that the effects of his radical change have such huge social consequences: Theseus's radical change of views enable the play to end happily with multiple marriages, rather than tragically with violence and perhaps death resulting from jealousy and competitiveness. If in tragedy the emotion of jealousy, for example, leads to death; in comedy, as in *A Midsummer Night's Dream*, the emotion will not have such dire consequences, but will be alleviated by some principle of laughter that seems to be part of cosmic reality, as represented in this play by Puck who introduces himself as "I am that merry wanderer of the night." Puck's effect on everyone is to make them "hold their hips and loffe, / And waxen in their mirth." This spirit of comedy is equally represented by music—which appears as the spiritual extension of laughter—as represented by Ariel in *The Tempest* whose presence is described in the stage direction, "strange music." On hearing this music, Alonso asks, "What harmony is this? my good friends, hark!" to which Gonzalo replies, "Marvelous sweet music!"

But just as laughter and music are the expressive essence of comedy, the inevitability of suffering is the essence of tragedy as Edgar in *King Lear* states so succinctly: "We must endure our coming hence even as our going hither." In both the realms of comedy and tragedy, however, choice matters, since an act of will can change either how events will turn out and relationships be resolved, or else—of equal importance—what a character will make of his or her own trials and suffering.

VIII Will Power

In "Sonnet 136," addressed to a beloved person (and to us, his readers) Shakespeare, with obvious delight, puns egregiously on the word "will." Two basic, yet antithetical, meanings are inherent in this compacted word: "will" means desire and thus connotes the aspect of a human being that is driven by emotional compulsion; and "will" also means an act of mind which makes manifest volition and freedom of choice. These indeed are the great contending forces within every human being which make up his or her moral life and constitute the essence of their stories. The central paradox of Shakespeare's representation of human character, found throughout his plays, is that we are both fated or destined and at the same time capable of making free choices that affect our lives and fortunes. I can think of no better comparison, though seemingly far afield, to make at this point than to refer to the fundamental "weirdness" of quantum physics, that photons of light are simultaneously both waves and particles, depending on how they are observed. (4) How can this be? Well, that's just how it is!

The third meaning of the word "will" suggests the leaving of an inheritance, and the fourth suggests the person, named "Will," whose identity includes and encompasses all four levels of meaning. Desire as a form of necessity, choice as an expression of freedom, storytelling as the offering of his inheritance—these concerns constitute the heart of Shakespeare's identity as a human being with moral concerns as revealed impersonally in his fictions, and Shakespeare invites us to accept him, to empathize with him, to love him, even to make the choice to share his name as if in marriage, in these most tempting terms: "Make but my name thy love, and love that still, / And then thou lovest me, for my name is Will."

CHAPTER TWO

HAMLET: THE HEART OF THE MYSTERY

I Accountability

Although a psychoanalytic reading of *Hamlet* is essential to an understanding of the play, and has been well provided by Ernest Jones and others, such a reading is not complete and calls for additional forms of inquiry. Moral issues and the mystery of the transcendence of suffering cannot be reduced to psychoanalytic formulations. Although the validity of the Oedipus complex as having universal application has been challenged, yet the most substantial recent research, as put forth in Allen Johnson's, *Oedipus Ubiquitous*, (1) provides abundant evidence for its worldwide relevance as made manifest through myths and folk tales, particularly in its primary form in which the son feels competitive with his father and amorous toward his mother. Such a reading is profoundly helpful in an examination of Hamlet's unconscious motivation, the inaccessibility of which Hamlet himself is fully aware. As he says, "I do not know why yet I live to say this thing's to do." Hamlet knows that he does not know; this paradoxical awareness of self-ignorance lies at the heart of the play and raises the question of Hamlet's capacity for free choice and thus the possibility of his assuming responsibility for his puzzling actions. Any substantial reading of the play therefore must be based on Hamlet's unconscious identification with Claudius and with the figure of Nero. Hamlet's remarkable capacity for empathetic identification is also a central feature of his character and has crucial consequences.

The paradox of the simultaneity of freedom based on willful choice and of fatedness, based on unconscious motivation which, being unconscious, is not open to deliberate modification or rejection, has its paradigmatic model in Sophocles' *Oedipus Rex*. In that amazingly explicit play, Oedipus is fated to kill his father and marry his mother, and, although the cause of that fatedness is ascribed to Apollo, Sophocles gives us the psychological equivalent of divine destiny, as written in the stars, when he has Jocasta unintentionally reveal a truth, through denial, when she says to Oedipus, "Have no more fear of sleeping with your mother / How many men, in dreams, have lain with their mothers! / No reasonable man is troubled by such things," (2) thus proving the unreasonableness of what she calls "the reasonable man."

Oedipus could well claim that he cannot be held accountable for anything he does that has been fated by the gods. Oedipus cries out, "What has god done to me?" The Choragos asks him, "What god was it drove you to rake black / Night across your eyes?" Oedipus responds decisively, "Apollo, Apollo . . . He brought my sick sick fate upon me." Rather than simply excusing himself by blaming Apollo, Oedipus adds, "But the blinding hand was my own." (3) In so saying, Oedipus takes responsibility for his own self-punishment, and, in effect, accepts that he is guilty for the crimes he has committed, even though they were fated. The inescapable paradox here is that Oedipus is both innocent and guilty simultaneously. And the same is true of Hamlet who, like Oedipus, commits crimes with unconscious intent; also like Oedipus, he assumes responsibility for his fated actions. As Hamlet acknowledges, everything he does is determined by virtue of who he is according to a design beyond his choosing: "There is special providence in the fall of a sparrow." The passivity in not being able to control one's fate can yet be transformed into an activity of the will by choosing to hold oneself responsible even for one's destined behavior. It is not Apollo but Oedipus who determines his punishment: "This punishment / That I have laid upon myself is just," Oedipus declares, thus creating for himself a kind of personal freedom where there had been only mechanical and impersonal causation.

This creation of freedom, along with the assertion of morality in the place of deterministic compulsion, exists in many places in *Hamlet*. In the scene which follows Hamlet's unintentional killing of Polonius, Hamlet thinks that Claudius is hidden behind the arras, though it is not likely that Claudius could have gotten there so quickly. In any case, it is significant that Hamlet can only thrust his sword into the curtain because he cannot see the person behind it, who remains therefore a figment of his imagination, and because he is in his mother's bedroom. This is a scene in which Hamlet is under the sway of fate, yet his reaction to what he has done reveals a choice that he is free to make. After seeking to exchange blessings with his mother, Hamlet turns his attention to the body of the dead Polonius and declares:

> For this same lord,
> I do repent; but heaven hath pleased it so,
> To punish me with this, and this with me,

That I must be their scourge and minister.
I will bestow him, and will answer well
The death I gave him. (III. iv. 172-177)

Hamlet does not excuse himself by claiming that it was just a mistake [*Polonius scil. be with*] that he killed Polonius; rather, he assumes responsibility in the form of repentance even though, in another sense, this action is the result of some inscrutable plan of heaven's making. When Hamlet says, therefore, that he "will answer well / The death I gave him," he assumes responsibility for the punishment—his own death—which he takes to be the appropriate punishment for the crime as if he, not heaven, were the author.

Before I discuss the less reductive (than the psychoanalytic) explanation for Hamlet's motivation and behavior—the mystery of the transcendence of suffering in this play—I'll review the basic argument that Hamlet is indeed motivated by Oedipal desires on the unconscious level, and, that being the case, Hamlet cannot kill Claudius because Claudius has acted out Hamlet's very wishes of killing his father and marrying his mother. After observing disapprovingly to Horatio that Claudius likes to go carousing in town, Hamlet observes that "it is a custom / More honor'd in the breech than the observance," and complains that such drunken behavior gives Denmark an international bad name. Hamlet says "This heavy-headed revel east and west / Makes us traduc'd and taxed of other nations; / They call us drunkards." And then, suddenly, Hamlet goes into a kind of philosophical trance; the sarcastic tone of his voice changes, and he delivers his thoughts in an oracular manner as if expressing some universal truth:

> *So oft it chances in particular men,*
> *That for some vicious mole of nature in them,*
> *As in their birth, (wherein they are not guilty*
> *Since nature cannot choose his origin),*
> *By the o'er growth of some complexion,*
> *Oft breaking down the pales and forts of reason,*
> *Or by some habit that too much o'er-leavens*
> *The form of plausive manners; that these men,*
> *Carrying, I say, the stamp of one defect,*
> *Being nature's livery, or fortune's star,—*
> *His virtues else, be they as pure as grace,*
> *As infinite as man may undergo,*
> *Shall in the general censure take corruption*
> *From that particular fault.* (I. iv. 23-35)

Hamlet has been talking about Claudius, and it would seem that Claudius is still the subject of Hamlet's discourse when he says, "So oft it chances in particular men"; yet what Hamlet says, seemingly about Claudius, does not fit Claudius at all. Hamlet would not be exonerating Claudius by claiming that he is "not guilty / Since nature cannot choose his origin." Rather, Hamlet, as if talking about Claudius, seems really to be talking about himself, but without awareness of the identification that he is making or what he is revealing about himself as having "some vicious mole in nature" by which he himself is defined. What might that be? The identification with Claudius suggests that Claudius's actions correspond to Hamlet's own unconscious desires. And yet there is the sense that Hamlet cannot be held responsible, and therefore cannot be guilty, of what he does not consciously know, just as Oedipus is innocent of the destiny laid upon him by Apollo. But the opposite also is true, since both Oedipus and Hamlet at some level assume responsibility for their actions, and therefore Hamlet can blame Claudius as well as say that he "is not guilty," so that both Claudius and Hamlet fall under the same category of "particular men," and both therefore "take corruption / From that particular fault," a fault that Hamlet cannot name or specify.

The closest that Hamlet comes to acknowledging and disclosing his "particular fault" is in his soliloquy before he goes to sees his mother who has summoned him. Hamlet's soliloquy swings back and forth between the philosophically detached and the hysterically manic, and in this speech we hear Hamlet at his wildest and most ferocious. He is at the edge of madness, but it is his awareness of this fact, and his expression of his angry passion, that prevent him from being consumed by madness. He cries out in a possessed and demonic voice:

> 'Tis now the very witching time of night,
> When churchyards yawn and hell itself breathes out
> Contagion to this world. Now could I drink hot blood,
> And do such bitter business as the day
> Would quake to look on. Soft! now to my mother!
> O heart, lose not thy nature; let not ever
> The soul of Nero enter this firm bosom.
> Let me be cruel, not unnatural;
> I will speak daggers to her, but use none.
> My tongue and soul in this be hypocrites. (III. ii. 391-400)

Hamlet is aware that he is tempted to kill his mother, despite his father's earlier injunction to "leave her to heaven." From a moral point of view, Hamlet knows that this demonic temptation is not called for by Hamlet's pledge to avenge the death of his father. The cause of such a temptation, however, is powerfully suggested by Hamlet's comparison of himself with Nero who was guilty of having incest with his mother as reported explicitly by Tacitus:

> *Cluvius relates that Agrippina* [Nero's mother] *in her eagerness to retain her influence went so far that more than once at midday, when Nero, even at that hour, was flushed with wine and feasting* [behavior also exhibited by Claudius] *she presented herself attractively attired to her half intoxicated son and offered him her person, and that when kinsfolk observed wanton kisses and caresses, portending infamy . . . a freed girl, alarmed at her own peril by Nero's disgrace, told* [Seneca] *that the incest was notorious, as his mother boasted of it . . . Fabius Rusticus tells us that it was not Agrippina, but Nero who lusted for the crime.* (4)

In addition to committing incest with his mother, legend has it, as Hamlet well knows, Nero also killed her. Hamlet's identification with Nero reveals Hamlet's guilty disgust with his own incestuous and murderous desires, which result in his wish to kill his mother as an act of both atonement and denial. But Hamlet is fully aware that to do so would be "unnatural," and he is split between his natural and unnatural self: to "speak daggers to her, but use none." Hamlet, even in his impassioned state, is nevertheless aware of this division within himself, when he concludes, "My tongue and soul in this be hypocrites." Hamlet, as his name suggests, is a house divided: "And if a house be divided against itself, that kingdom cannot stand." (Mark 3:25)

When Hamlet arrives in his mother's chambers, his demeanor is so threatening that she is palpably afraid that he will kill her, and she cries out, "What wilt thou do? thou wilt not murther me? / Help, help, ho!" When Polonius echoes her cry for help, Hamlet runs him through with his sword. Gertrude then confronts Hamlet with "O me, what hast thou done?" and Hamlet, in his most representative mode of knowing that he does not know, responds: "Nay, I know not," and, bewildered as to who is who, adds, "Is it the king?" When Hamlet looks behind the arras and sees it is Polonius that he has killed, he makes another revealing remark: "I took thee for thy better." Although that comment might only mean that the king is of a higher rank than Polonius, this inadvertent comment also suggests that Hamlet has a strange and compelling admiration for Claudius.

The queen is wearing a locket which contains the picture of Claudius, and Hamlet is wearing a locket with the picture of his father. He holds up the two pictures before Gertrude's eyes, comparing the two kinds of loves and the two love objects, "the counterfeit presentment of two brothers." In doing so, Hamlet splits the figure of the father, toward whom ambivalence would be normal, into two diametrically opposite halves, one divine with "Hyperion's curls, the front of Jove himself," and the other degraded and disgusting, "like a mildewed ear." Both of these depictions are, of course, reductive simplifications. Hamlet's father died with all "his sins upon his head," and resides in purgatory; and Claudius, unlike Iago, is not without some attractive attributes like his genuine love for Gertrude and his honesty, when praying, in acknowledging why he cannot ask heaven for forgiveness while he still is in possession of the crown and of Gertrude.

When Hamlet says to Gertrude about the motivation for her marriage to Claudius, "You cannot call it love, for at your age / The heyday of the blood is tame," he is absolutely wrong, for it is apparent that there is a strong sexual attraction between them even at their age. What is revealed here is Hamlet's denial of the power and extension of sexual desire even to areas where seemingly it does not belong. The passionate exchanges between Hamlet and his mother are interrupted by the sudden appearance of the ghost. But this time the ghost can be seen only by Hamlet and must be thought of as Hamlet's guilty hallucination, a reversed version of the "primal scene" in which the child comes upon his parents making love and a further elaboration of the theme of spying and mistrust that spreads throughout the play. The concluding exchange of blessing and forgiveness in this scene between mother and son is also highly significant in that it anticipates the exchange of forgiveness between Hamlet and Laertes at the play's end.

II Two Moralities

Hamlet is torn by Oedipal wishes at a mostly unconscious level, but also Hamlet is torn between two moralities. One is the morality of his father, come back as a ghost, who espouses vengeance, "If thou didst ever thy dear father love . . . Revenge his foul and most unnatural murther," and Christian morality which is based first on the Hebrew Bible's commandment "Thou shalt not kill," and then extended into the New Testament's morality of forgiveness. When Hamlet says to the ghost, "And thy commandment all alone shall live within the book and volume of my brain," we are reminded of the biblical commandments which are being rejected:

> *Dearly beloved, avenge not yourselves, but rather give place unto wrath: for it is written, Vengeance is mine; I will repay saith the Lord. Therefore, if thine enemy hunger, feed him; if he thirst, give him drink. . . . Be not overcome with evil, but overcome evil with good.* (Romans 12: 19-21) (5)

Hamlet is never overtly aware that in rousing himself to obey his father's commandment of revenge, he is repressing or denying an alternative Christian morality, yet that morality is a deep part of Hamlet's character as his speeches so often reveal. For example, considering suicide as a guilt that he is not able to name, Hamlet rejects that option on the grounds that the law of God, "the Everlasting," has "fix'd / His canon 'gainst self-slaughter." Christian law, authored by a divinity of love, is in opposition to Hamlet's father's morality of revenge. Although his father also makes an appeal to Hamlet in the name of love, later in the play the morality of forgiveness will decisively win out over the morality of revenge though Hamlet does not overtly assert this choice in any philosophical formulation.

The play is replete with Christian references, such as Marcellus's description of the appearance of the ghost: "It faded on the crowing of the cock, / Some say that ever 'gainst that season comes / Wherein our saviour's birth is celebrated, / This bird of dawning singeth all night long," and these references remind us of the prevalence of the Christian morality against which Hamlet's father's morality of revenge is in complete opposition. It is remarkable that Hamlet does not comment on this opposition, which must therefore exist, given the excruciating pain it causes Hamlet, on an unconscious level. Hamlet appears to have opted for his father's morality and pledged himself to revenge his murder, yet it is reasonable to assume that Hamlet's famous delay and procrastination, though partly explicable according to Oedipal theory and the concept of repression, can also be explained in terms of the internalized conflict between two divergent moral systems. Although Hamlet at times professes a commitment to revenge, "From this time forth my thoughts be bloody or be nothing worth," it is even more powerfully true that Hamlet believes in and is motivated by the concept of "forgiveness" that is rooted in Hamlet's deep and distinguishing capacity for empathy and the identification with others.

III Suffering All

Beyond the explanations, for which there is much evidence, that Hamlet is driven by Oedipal forces and that Hamlet is torn between two divergent moralities, there is a third, and most mysterious, possible explanation both for Hamlet's behavior and his puzzled attitude toward himself and what appears to be his given destiny: "The time is out of joint. O cursed spite, / That ever I was born to set it right." The fatalism expressed here implies that some providential force has singled Hamlet out to achieve a particular task—the lifting of a curse from Denmark by killing Claudius—as Oedipus was assigned the task to lift the curse from Thebes. In both cases, the criminal who is the cause of the curse or plague turns out to be the would-be hero, Oedipus and Hamlet. Although at the beginning of the play Hamlet resents being given this responsibility, by the end he will fully accept whatever role he has been assigned to play: "There is special providence in the fall of a sparrow." The role, however, turns out to be not just the killing of Claudius, but also for Hamlet himself to suffer and to die.

Hamlet, so we come to see, is wrong in thinking that he has been assigned the mission to "set it right" as if some external action, like revenge, will achieve the desired result. The play will end, not with things set right, but with the unscrupulous Fortinbras in control of the kingdom of Denmark, like the cruel Creon's ascension to kingship in Thebes. Fortinbras' taking charge accompanied by the sound of firing cannons bodes no improvement over the rule of Claudius. The ancestral wars between Norway and Denmark, no doubt, will continue. What Hamlet is given to do, as he will come to understand, is to suffer, as if suffering somehow were an end in itself or existed for the sake of the story to be told about how suffering was endured. Here, too, Hamlet is like Sophocles's Oedipus who, after his crime has been revealed and he has blinded himself, proclaims to the chorus: "Of all men, I alone can bear this guilt." The most significant actions taken by Hamlet, surprisingly, are not his killing of Claudius or saving Denmark through political reform or through defensive battle, as at first he thinks, but through the exchanging of forgiveness with Laertes, accepting his role as sufferer ("But let it be") and exhorting Horatio to tell his story.

One of the most elusive and mysterious scenes in all of Shakespeare comes when Hamlet, disillusioned about court hypocrisy and conniving, happily greets Horatio who, Hamlet believes, is free of such vices as obsequiousness: "Nay, do not think I flatter; / For what advancement may I hope from thee, / That no revenue hast but thy good spirits / To feed and clothe thee?" Hamlet continues in this skeptical vein, and then says to Horatio, whom he has been addressing directly, and says, "Dost thou hear?" Of course, Horatio has heard, but it is as if Hamlet has been talking to himself and catches himself up with the awareness of his own distraction. What Hamlet says next is spoken in one of his philosophical trances, as in his speech about Claudius's not being guilty, and here, too, it is hard to identify the subject of Hamlet's discourse. Although ostensibly he is talking about Horatio, nothing in the play suggests or confirms that what Hamlet says applies to Horatio, nor, strictly speaking, can we say that it applies to Hamlet. Rather, strangely, Hamlet appears to be projecting onto Horatio an image of what he wishes he were like or what he wishes he might yet become. Hamlet articulates here his ideal identity—an identity quite at odds with one caught up in the passion of revenge:

> *for thou hast been*
> *As one, in suffering all, that suffers nothing,*
> *A man that fortune's buffets and rewards*
> *Hast ta'en with equal thanks; and bless'd are those*
> *Whose blood and judgment are so well co-mingled*
> *That they are not a pipe for fortune's finger*
> *To sound what stop she please. Give me that man*
> *That is not passion's slave, and I will wear him*
> *In my heart's core, ay, in my heart of heart,*
> *As I do thee.* (III. ii. 65-74)

The line "As one, in suffering all, that suffers nothing" is profoundly enigmatic and both entices and resists speculation. A pessimistic reading would be that suffering renders the world meaningless and that therefore suffering cannot transform what is meaningless, "nothing," into something meaningful. (But an optimistic reading, the one I prefer, might be that one can pass through suffering to some kind of a state of detachment in which the world is seen impersonally as a spectacle. Wordsworth's ending of his "Intimations of Immortality" ode, where he speaks of thoughts "that do lie too deep for tears," expresses and clarifies such an idea. But it is the passage in which King Lear, accepting the misfortune of their defeat in battle and their being taken off to prison, says to Cordelia, "We'll take upon 's the mystery of things as if we were god's spies," that most resembles Hamlet's line in its apparent acceptance and serenity.)

This momentarily serene Hamlet, who imagines himself as one who accepts fortune with equanimity and is thus not "passion's slave," is the antithesis of the ranting Hamlet who seeks to blot out everything "from the table of his memory" and exhorts himself with curses and oaths to kill his stepfather: "I should have fatted all the region kites / With this slave's offal. Bloody, bawdy, villain! / Remorseless, treacherous, lecherous, kindless villain! / O vengeance!" The Hamlet who is capable of transcending suffering, and who sees historical reality as if through the eyes of providence, as if he were one of God's spies, possesses the identity of Hamlet's deepest aspiration. His sense of the mystery of things, not his ability to change events or circumstances, makes Hamlet the master of fortune rather than its slave. This at the deepest level is Hamlet's wished-for self, the description of which is projected onto Horatio; this ideal is the one that Hamlet holds to be most precious in his heart.

IV Brothers

The theme of Hamlet's suffering as caused by Claudius's primal crime and Hamlet's identification with Claudius will ultimately be resolved through Hamlet's relationship with Laertes as Hamlet's surrogate brother. The plot of *Hamlet* commences with the replacement of one brother by another, and we soon learn that this is not a natural succession, but the result of Claudius's having murdered Hamlet's father. Hamlet says that it has the "primal eldest curse upon't," reminding us of the beginning of human violence in its reference to the murder of Abel by Cain. Later, when watching the grave digger throw up a skull, Hamlet compares it to "Cain's jawbone, that did the first murther." Hamlet's father's ghost exhorts Hamlet, "If thou did'st ever thy dear father love . . . / Revenge his foul and most unnatural murther"; indeed, Hamlet becomes obsessed with fulfilling this command and is puzzled by his own delay in achieving the goal of revenge. Almost without notice, however, the issue of revenge slips over into the issue of forgiveness though not in respect to Claudius. In the play's final scene when Hamlet finally kills the king, almost as an afterthought, and prodded on by Laertes with the cry of "The king, the king's to blame," there is no mention at all of Hamlet's father or of the killing of the king as a fulfillment of Hamlet's promise. It is as if Hamlet has forgotten that the king's treachery has been the cause of so many deaths, including those of the Queen, Laertes, and Hamlet himself. Hamlet's question after killing Claudius, "Is thy union here?" is puzzling and equivocal. The "union" that Hamlet refers to might be with death itself, or, since this question is followed immediately with the statement, "Follow my mother," it might suggest that the sexual consummation Claudius sought with Gertrude, Hamlet ironically believes, will be found only in death. In either case, it is astonishing that no immediate thought of Hamlet's father appears to be in Hamlet's mind.

There are, however, two things that do still overtly concern Hamlet. The first is the completion of an exchange of forgiveness that he had initiated earlier just before the duel was to begin when Hamlet proclaimed to Laertes:

> Let my disclaiming from a purpos'd evil
> Free me so far in your most generous thoughts,
> That I have shot my arrow o'er my house,
> And hurt my brother. (V. ii. 245-248)

Despite Hamlet's good will and obvious sincerity in seeking reconciliation, Laertes lies when he responds to Hamlet, "I do receive your offer'd love like love, / And will not wrong it." The duel begins and quickly heats up until inadvertently their rapiers are exchanged. Hamlet wounds Laertes with the poisoned rapier and Laertes realizes that he will shortly die. In this momentary pause, Laertes is transformed and newly filled with a sense of justice, "I am justly killed with mine own treachery." Like Cawdor in *Macbeth* who dies with only repentance as his motive, Laertes with his last breath pronounces judgment on Claudius, "he is justly served," and responds genuinely at last to Hamlet's offer of brotherly reconciliation: "Exchange forgiveness with me, noble Hamlet: / Mine and my father's death come not upon thee, / Nor thine on me." Hamlet's response, "Heaven make thee free of it," brings their reconciliation to its completion. It is not Hamlet's killing of Claudius, therefore, that offers some measure of resolution to this play, but the reconciliation between (surrogate) brothers that even in the moment of their deaths restores something like the good health of nature that preceded the first murder and its repetition as "something rotten in the state of Denmark," Claudius's Cain-like killing of Hamlet's father.

The second of Hamlet's terminal concerns is that Horatio lives to tell Hamlet's story, and when Horatio tries to drink from the poisoned cup, declaring, "I am more an antique Roman than a Dane," in the ancient heroic mode, Hamlet snatches the cup from his lips:

> O good Horatio, what a wounded name
> (Things standing thus unknown) shall live behind me.
> If thou didst ever hold me in thy heart,
> Absent thee from felicity awhile,
> And in this harsh world draw thy breath in pain,
> To tell my story. (V. ii. 347-353)

Hamlet's ultimate wish that his story be told needs to be considered against the background of the theme of lying and the failure of language, and thus of communication in general, including self-knowledge, that suffuse the play. This theme of mendacity is epitomized in the two scenes where Rosencrantz and Guildenstern, having been employed by the King to see what information they can get from Hamlet about his plans and his motivation, are making conversation with Hamlet. Previously they were his trusted friends; thus, Hamlet greets their arrival warmly with "My excellent good friends!" But Hamlet quickly suspects that they are now serving the king, so he makes an appeal to them, "be even and direct with me, whether you were sent for or no." Hamlet realizes that his appeal is in vain, and his speech becomes enigmatical and evasive even as it retains a genuine confessional aspect, one, however, not likely to be understood by the two betrayers. So when Hamlet says, "I have of late,—but wherefore I know not,—lost all my mirth," he acknowledges a profound truth—that he is indeed a mystery to himself, and yet he knows the relevance of this remark will not be comprehended in its full import.

In a later scene when Rosencrantz tries again to probe Hamlet's mind with a phony appeal, "You do surely bar the door upon your own liberty, if you deny your griefs to your friend." Hamlet answers with an explanation of his "griefs" that reveals his suspiciousness: "Sir, I lack advancement," a disclosure that despite its plausibility is nevertheless only peripheral to Hamlet's state of mind, and thus functions as a tactical distraction. Rosencrantz falls into the trap of trying to counter Hamlet's explanation: "How can that be when you have the voice of the king himself for your succession in Denmark?" Hamlet, again tactically, abruptly changes the subject and now addresses Guildenstern with what appears to be a random segue: "Will you play upon this pipe?" Hamlet surely knows that Guildenstern cannot play the recorder, and when Guildenstern protests, "My Lord, I cannot," Hamlet continues to insist that he do so. "I know no touch of it, my Lord," says Guildenstern, to which Hamlet replies with acerbic bitterness, "It is as easy as lying." This pithy statement contains the sum of Hamlet's disappointment and disillusionment, for if language is essentially a medium in which to mislead and lie, trust becomes impossible. Without veracity, the essential connective tissue of communication between human beings is broken.

When the above scene ends with the arrival of Polonius to inform Hamlet that his mother wishes to see him, the following surreal exchange takes place:

HAMLET: *Do you see yonder cloud that's almost*
in shape of a camel?
POLONIUS: *By the mass, and 'tis like a camel, indeed.*
HAMLET: *Methinks it is like a weasel.*
POLONIUS: *It is backed like a weasel.*
HAMLET: *Or like a whale?*
POLONIUS: *Very like a whale.*
HAMLET: *Then I will come to my mother by and by . . .*
POLONIUS: *I will say so.*
HAMLET: *By and by is easily said.* (III. ii. 380-389)

In this ironic passage, objectivity falls away, and anything can appear as anything else. Polonius agrees with Hamlet's impressionistic description of the clouds out of deference to Hamlet's position of power. But not only is visual discernment dissipated here, the sharing of the same physical world, but also sequential logic collapses, for Hamlet's statement "Then I will come to my mother by and by" has no relationship to Polonius's comment that precedes it. And Hamlet's concluding "By and by is easily said" echoes his earlier "It is as easy as lying" which makes all speech seem frivolous and insubstantial. Polonius takes his leave, and as Hamlet prepares to go to his mother's chambers, he speaks in a debased and demonic language that we can hardly recognize as his own: "Tis now the witching time of night. / When churchyards yawn and hell itself breathes out / Contagion to the world. / Now could I drink hot blood." Hamlet now thinks of language as a weapon, "I will speak daggers to her, but use none," but he has not entirely lost the distinction between the reality of language and action in the physical world.

Hamlet's disillusionment with language, therefore, cannot be regarded as complete after his farewell "adieu" to his deceased mother when Hamlet turns to the witnesses remaining on the stage:

You that look pale and tremble at this chance,
That are but mutes or audience to this act,
Had I but time (as this fell sergeant, death,
Is strict in his arrest) O I could tell you—
But let it be. Horatio, I am dead;
Thou liv'st. Report me and my cause aright
To the unsatisfied. (V. ii. 336-342)

At this moment, when Horatio reaches for the cup of poison, we see in the urgency of Hamlet's plea to Horatio not to commit suicide and find "felicity" in death, but to stay alive and tell Hamlet's story, that Hamlet's ultimate faith that language can have some kind of positive or healing effect in the world has not been lost. Despite all the betrayals that Hamlet has suffered—his mother's adultery and incest with Claudius, Ophelia's cowardly rejection of him at the whim of Polonius, the bribed sellout of his friendship with Rosencrantz and Guildenstern, the treachery of Laertes, all through lying and deceit—Hamlet still trusts Horatio to tell his story and bear accurate witness to his life.

V Acceptance

We can consider the main arcs of this play to move from the murder of one brother by another, to the exchange of forgiveness between brother figures who, like Hamlet senior and Claudius, share competitive feelings toward a woman, and the movement from the wish to actively "set things right" to acceptance and "readiness." These arcs are concordant with each other in that forgiveness needs to be regarded as a form of acceptance. In the scene where Ophelia is buried, Hamlet leaps into her grave and claims "I lov'd Ophelia. Forty thousand brothers / Could not with all their quantity of love / Make up my sum." The implication here is that Hamlet's love for Ophelia, unlike Laertes's love, is not tinged with incestuous desire, as was Claudius's love for Gertrude. Hamlet's "rant" over Ophelia's grave must give way to a quieter and more accepting Hamlet who can say to Laertes, "I lov'd you ever—but it is no matter. / Let Hercules himself do what he may, / The cat will mew and dog will have his day."

Thus the great sweep of this play takes Hamlet from the assumption that an action, such as revenge, can resolve what is wrong in Denmark, to acceptance in the will of Providence to accomplish the decree of fate, just as Apollo will see to it that the prophecy of the Delphic oracle, which foretold that Oedipus would kill his father and marry his mother, would be fulfilled. Hamlet's early "To be or not to be" soliloquy will achieve a transformation in the ringing phrase, "Let be," which precedes Hamlet's decision, despite Horatio's qualms about fighting the duel with Laertes:

> *There is special providence in the fall of a sparrow. If it be not now, 'tis not to come; if it be not to come, it will be now; if it be not now, yet it will come: the readiness is all. Since no man hath aught of what he leaves, what is't to leave betimes? Let be.* (V. ii. 223-228)

"Let be" and "the readiness is all," both oracular phrases, are closely linked as statements of acceptance of the will of Providence. Shakespeare continues the echo of these phrases almost to the end when Hamlet realizes that he will not live long enough to tell his own story: "O, I could tell you— / But let it be, Horatio, I am dead."

Preceded by Hamlet's first thoughts of suicide, "O that this too too solid flesh would melt, / Thaw and resolve itself into a dew," the "To be or not to be" speech, in which Hamlet abstracts the idea of his committing suicide into a philosophical conundrum, raises the further question of what causes Hamlet to have suicidal feelings at all. Why should the contemplation of killing his uncle in revenge for his father or the hasty remarriage of his mother somehow turn him against himself? Oedipal theory would hold that according to the law of talion, the fundamental human sense of reciprocity upon which all law and commercial trade is based, Hamlet must identify himself with Claudius on the unconscious level. Hamlet feels that he has wished for and willed the death of his own father. If this is part of Hamlet's psychological reality, then indeed he deserves to die—he must avenge his father against himself.

But it is not his father's morality of revenge that prevents him from suicide; rather, it is a Christian god who fixes "his canon 'gainst self-slaughter." Nevertheless, the temptation to bring about one's death according to one's own will and decision will be revised, beyond any unconscious psychological motivation: to replace his will with God's will in the form of the acceptance of what is fated, Hamlet's final "But let it be." This acceptance, though apparently passive, is better understood paradoxically as an active passivity in that it is the result of a positive choice, a sense of readiness, and a willingness to accept the unknown in his final ambiguous words, "the rest is silence." Earlier, Hamlet had challenged Guildenstern, "you would pluck out the heart of my mystery," but in the end, Hamlet's mystery is equally the mystery of Providence, and no doubt it is this sense of bearing witness to the unknown that led Hamlet to want to have Horatio tell his story.

VI History—Political & Personal

In the first scene of the play, when Marcellus, one of the guards, asks if anyone can explain the appearance of the ghost, "Who is't that can inform me?" Horatio confidently replies, "That can I," and he gives a full account of the political history that precedes the action of the play, a history of ongoing enmity and warfare in which Hamlet's father killed in battle young Fortinbras' father who as a result "by a seal'd compact, / Well ratified by law and heraldry, / Did forfeit with his life all those his lands / Which he stood seiz'd of, to the conqueror." Confident in his role as storyteller and historian, Horatio goes on to describe young Fortinbras' determination to "recover of us by strong hand" the land that his father lost, despite the illegality of this enterprise. The entire play is thus framed by Horatio's historical accounts of Hamlet's father as conqueror of Fortinbras and of Hamlet who has been succeeded as potential ruler of Denmark by young Fortinbras who has invaded the kingdom and taken charge.

Shortly after Horatio's opening account, we learn from Claudius that young Fortinbras's uncle, Norway, is "impotent and bed-rid," and thus has no control over Fortinbras. This is in significant contrast to the assertive and confident Claudius who has successfully assumed the throne despite Hamlet's legitimate claim to that position. In narrating this chronicle of ongoing and seemingly endless violent contention and warfare in dispute over the possession of land, Horatio envisions these conflicts as representative of a universal pattern that reflects cosmic disorder of "heaven and earth together." Horatio sees the current conditions in Denmark as resembling the time in Rome "a little ere the mightiest Julius fell," another example of rebellious disruption, in which the moon, "the moist star / Upon whose influence Neptune's empire stands / Was sick almost to doomsday with eclipse." Shakespeare thus establishes Horatio as the kind of historian who sees immediate and local events not simply as peculiar and unique, but as exemplary and revelatory: the disruption in the state of Denmark, as manifest in the appearance of the ghost, indicates to Horatio the breakdown of the inherent moral order of the universe. We may therefore surmise that Hamlet's wish at the end of the play to have Horatio tell his story is motivated by Hamlet's instinctive sense that his story also has worldly, even cosmic, implications. Whether or not Horatio is equal to the task assigned to him by Hamlet is a question to which I will return.

VII Force & Madness

The sense of the play as revealing political and historical causes and patterns is ironically extended through Hamlet's description of Fortinbras as he leads his army in an invasion of Poland. This depiction is at odds with Horatio's representation of Fortinbras as a lawless opportunist, which, indeed, is confirmed by the captain in Fortinbras' army who acknowledges that "We go to gain a little patch of ground / That hath in it no profit but the name." Hamlet, however, mistakenly sees Fortinbras not as a military thug and adventurer, but, rather, as "a delicate and tender prince," and Hamlet's definition of honor, "greatly to find quarrel in a straw / When honor's at the stake," is nothing more than an egregious form of rationalization for killing Claudius as Fortinbras would do if the opportunity presented itself to someone like him. By means of this rationalization, Hamlet contradicts and betrays all his previous praise for reason as when he said to Horatio "Give me that man / That is not passion's slave, and I will wear him / In my heart's core, ay, in my heart of heart, / as I do thee," and as he claims earlier in this very speech that we have not been given "That capability and godlike reason / To fust in us unus'd." And so this very speech, with still further irony, concludes with a cry, "O, from this time forth, / My thoughts be bloody or be nothing worth," a speech that negates the primacy of the gift of reason that Hamlet most prizes in himself. Bloody thoughts, should they usurp Hamlet's mind, would leave no room for the mentality of forgiveness, in opposition to the code of revenge, a mentality that Hamlet will embrace in his reconciliation with Laertes and will, I believe, define his final identity. The question that remains with us is whether bloody thoughts and overt action, rather than the less visible gestures of remorse and forgiveness, are the essence of historical pattern.

Throughout the play, Laertes, much like Fortinbras, who is virtually his double in that both of them have ineffective fathers (or father figures), also is presented as a callow and superficial young man. Unlike Hamlet, both Laertes and Fortinbras lack moral compunction and a capacity for genuine empathy. When we first see Laertes, preparing to depart from Denmark after the funeral (no doubt to escape from the snooping watch of Polonius), he is giving condescending and self-serving advice to Ophelia to avoid any amorous advances from Hamlet. Laertes cynically assumes that Hamlet's interest in Ophelia can only be driven by lust and that Hamlet could not have honorable marital intentions toward her. "Best safety lies in fear" is Laertes' negative message of suspicion, but Ophelia, who is not without discernment and spunk, directly challenges him:

> But, good my brother,
> Do not, as some ungracious pastors do,
> Show me the steep and thorny way to heaven,
> Whiles, like a puff'd and reckless libertine,
> Himself the primrose path of dalliance treads,
> And recks not his own rede. (I. iii. 46-51)

Laertes, no doubt embarrassed by Ophelia's precise exposure of his hypocrisy, offers a flustered reply, "O fear me not," and quickly departs. These lines are extremely important because they reveal Ophelia to be capable of insight and judgment so that her later madness can be understood as the result of the excruciating remorse that comes from self-betrayal.

When Polonius gives Ophelia the same cynical advice as had Laertes, Ophelia at first resists: "My lord, he hath importun'd me with love in honorable fashion." And when Polonius refuses to believe her, she adds succinctly that Hamlet had offered her "almost all the holy vows of heaven." That Hamlet and Ophelia truly loved each other is confirmed later when Gertrude, scattering flowers on Ophelia's grave, remarks that "I hop'd thou shouldst have been my Hamlet's wife." Polonius rejects Ophelia's assertion about Hamlet's sincerity with his abrupt "Do not believe his vows," and so when Ophelia capitulates to her father's ignorant and selfish wishes, "I shall obey, my lord," she has turned against her own best judgment and violated her own integrity. In this important respect, she can be contrasted with Desdemona and Cordelia who stand up to their fathers and maintain their own independence.

It is doubtful that Laertes loved his meddling father as truly as Hamlet loved his father, despite Hamlet's unconscious ambivalence. Yet when Laertes returns from France to attend Polonius's funeral, in contrast to Hamlet, Laertes's unequivocal, yet morally obtuse, commitment to seek revenge. "Give me my father," he rages with his impossible request, and when the Queen tries to calm him down, he proclaims,

> *That drop of blood that's calm proclaims me bastard,*
> *Cries cuckold to my father, brands the harlot*
> *Even here, between the chaste unsmirched brows*
> *Of my true mother.* (IV. i. 118-121)

Hysterical though they are, the excessive sexual innuendo of these words is immensely revealing. Somewhere in the depths of Laertes's thought resides a fantasy of his father being cuckolded and his mother being dishonored, and on this fantasy level Laertes duplicates the actual circumstances under which Hamlet suffers. Laertes, however, radically differs from Hamlet in his lack of moral sensibility: he is not torn, as is Hamlet, between a code of revenge and, on the other hand, both an instinct for empathy and its concomitant morality of reconciliation and forgiveness. The Shakespearean paradox at work here is that morality and neuroticism seem to go together and are manifest in a partly repressed sense of guilt. Their general confusion distinguishes Hamlet from Claudius, who can clearly and rationally identify his guilt, as we see in the scene where he is trying to pray. If historical events are driven by mostly invisible psychological forces, ingrained human morality inevitably contending against one's Darwinian nature to compete and survive, then a successful storyteller will have to include and take into account what is not apparent on the battlefield or in political council, what happens in the mind.

In stark contrast to Hamlet, Claudius has no suicidal inclinations as the result of an unnamed and unconscious sense of guilt that in Hamlet's case is based in part on his identification with Claudius. Claudius, unlike Hamlet, knows exactly what crime he has committed; he has reenacted Cain's primal murder of a brother: "O my offense is rank, it smells to heaven! / It hath the primal eldest curse upon't; / A brother's murther." Claudius's entire meditation while trying to pray is a model of rationality and lucidity. His analysis of his situation is correct at every point, including his conclusion that there can be no forgiveness for his crime since he eschews restitution and is unwilling to give up either the throne or Gertrude which accrued to him as a result of his crime: "Forgive me my foul murther? / That cannot be, since I am still possess'd of / Those effects for which I did the murther, / My crown, my own ambition, and my queen." Claudius is equally lucid in imagining that there can be no equivocating in the eyes of heaven: "There is no shuffling, there the action lies / In his true nature." And Claudius's insightfulness is also precise in his judgment and analysis of Hamlet's character as when he says to Laertes of Hamlet that he, being "Most generous, and free from all contriving, / Will not peruse the foils; so that with ease, / Or with a little shuffling, you may choose a sword unbated." Deliberate villainy, not tormented confusion, characterizes Claudius; he has none of Hamlet's groping uncertainty: "Say, why is this, wherefore, what should we do?"

Claudius's unrepentant rationality is not neurotic in the sense that the cause of his guilt and its symptoms are commensurate with one another. Claudius's conscious angst must be distinguished from Hamlet's confusion and melancholy and his "antic disposition," the defense of acting mad in order not to become mad. Hamlet's madness is aware of itself as such and thus retains its connection to sanity unlike Ophelia. When Ophelia enters the scene in a state described as "distracted," the songs she sings reveal the unconscious content of her mind:

> *How should I your true love know*
> *From another one?*
> *By his cockle hat and staff,*
> *And his sandal shoon.* (IV. i. 23-26)

Ophelia is thinking of the doubt instilled in her by her father about the trustworthiness of Hamlet as a suitor and lover, whether he can be considered a "true love," and these doubts are grounded in images of phallic sexual innuendo, the pun in "cockle hat," the "staff" and the "shoon." In the next stanza of the poem, what emerges is Ophelia's confused identification of Hamlet as lover with her father as the figure of the "true love" which passes over into a recollection of the dead Polonius:

> *He is dead and gone, lady,*
> *He is dead and gone;*
> *At his head a grass-green turf;*
> *At his heels a stone.* (IV. i. 29-32)

When Ophelia interjects what seems to be a cryptic remark between song stanzas, "They say the owl was baker's daughter," the canny Claudius immediately interprets it to be a "Conceit upon her father."

In the next stanza Ophelia tells of an amorous encounter that either refers to her actual relationship with Hamlet or else describes her own fantasy of what might have taken place had she continued to be wooed by Hamlet:

> *Then up he rose, and donn'd his clo'es,*
> *And dupp'd the chamber door;*
> *Let in the maid, that out a maid*
> *Never departed more.* (IV. i. 53-56)

These words express the fear of sexual violation instilled in her by her father, and they make the cynical assumption, as does the following stanza, that men in general cannot be trusted, so that the very idea of sex becomes vulgarized and besmirched as the final stanza's dirty pun connotes:

> *Young men will do't as they come to't;*
> *By Cock they are to blame.*
> *Quoth she, before you tumbled me,*
> *You promis'd me to wed.* (IV. i. 61-64)

It is impossible to tell if Hamlet and Ophelia actually had sex together or whether the fantasy, corrupted by fear, has poisoned and maddened Ophelia's mind. What we unmistakably see is how fear and disgust, promoted by guilt, cause people to think in stereotypes, as Hamlet does also when he says things like "Frailty, thy name is woman." Such thinking leads to further cynicism and further polluted imaginings; it is the cause of Ophelia's suicidal madness and Hamlet's misogyny, his hostility toward both Ophelia and his mother. Will Horatio as historian take such motivation, based on guilt and repression, into account in his chronicle of Denmark?

VIII More Madness

Recognizing one's own (partial) craziness is an aspect of sanity, and such acknowledgment is what Hamlet achieves at the end of the play. When the duel, contrived by Claudius, is about to begin, Hamlet with good will and with the sweetness of nature that characterized his idealism before the death of his father and remarriage of his mother, appeals to Laertes: "Give me your pardon, sir. I've done you wrong; / But pardon't, as you are a gentleman." No contrivance or ulterior motive underlies this appeal to Laertes despite all the betrayals Hamlet has suffered and the connivances he has witnessed. Hamlet is genuinely contrite in having killed Polonius even though Polonius had been hidden behind the arras when Hamlet killed him and could easily have been mistaken for Claudius. But Hamlet goes still further in his address to Laertes and makes a heartfelt confession in which Hamlet, far beyond any passion for vengeance in the name of honor, makes an effort to understand himself by acknowledging what he cannot understand, in the hope that enmity between himself and Laertes can be assuaged:

> This presence knows, and you must needs have heard,
> How I am punish'd with a dire distraction.
> What I have done,
> That might your nature, honor, and exception
> Roughly awake, I here proclaim was madness.
> Was't Hamlet wronged Laertes? Never Hamlet.
> If Hamlet from himself be ta'en away,
> And when he's not himself does wrong Laertes,
> Then Hamlet does it not; Hamlet denies it.
> Who does it then? His madness. If't be so
> Hamlet is of the faction that is wrong'd;
> His madness is poor Hamlet's enemy. (V. ii. 232-243)

Although this plea to Laertes can be regarded as having an element of rationalization, there is no benefit that Hamlet seeks from being excused or excusing himself. His intent is to find a way back into a state of gentlemanly friendship with Laertes only for the sake of friendship. Hamlet wants nothing from Laertes but his pardon, and Horatio's farewell to him, "Good night, sweet prince," is most apt in its selection of the word "sweet" as his concluding description of Hamlet.

Oedipus cannot control his fate, but nevertheless he assumes responsibility for his crimes and punishes himself; so, too, Hamlet distances himself from his own madness as being beyond deliberate choosing, yet he acknowledges and accepts the punishment brought upon him by this madness. In this respect, Hamlet is right in arguing that one's nature can be one's own worst enemy. In recognizing this, in acknowledging what fate has laid upon him, Hamlet asserts his identity, despite his fated madness, in terms of what he is capable of deliberately choosing, his offer of reconciliation to Laertes.

Hamlet goes still further in making this offer in defining the realm of freedom available to each human being, despite his or her given psychology, whether we see a person's character as written in the stars or caused by the gods or, for the modern reader, as determined by Darwinian evolution and by one's genetic makeup:

> Let my disclaiming of a purpos'd evil
> Free me so far in your most generous thoughts,
> That I have shot my arrow o'er my house
> And hurt my brother. (V. ii. 245-248)

The paradox here, as in Sophocles, is that we must acknowledge our own unconscious drives, our own madness, as operating within and upon us, even while we do not identify ourselves in the highest sense with these drives or compulsions. The freedom to choose one's own identity requires some kind of acceptance of that part of us that we would disown so that one's identity includes this act of disowning at the same time that it makes a choice that is within one's deliberate control. To be fully realized, this free choice, since we are social creatures, also must be acknowledged by others, just as Hamlet needs Laertes to choose generosity over hostility by accepting Hamlet's request to be pardoned. If this reciprocity with both self and others can be achieved, then the brother-murder that initiates the cycle of greed, ambition, and vengeance can be replaced by a new alignment of brothers, defined in an extended sense: Hamlet and Laertes at peace with one another.

Before this reconciliation can be achieved, however, Hamlet must suffer one more betrayal. Laertes responds to Hamlet's appeal for pardon and mutual acceptance with utter hypocrisy when he says, "I do receive your offer'd love like love, / And will not wrong it," and Hamlet innocently believes him in the name of the concept of brotherhood: "I embrace it freely, / And will this brother's wager frankly play." But not until Laertes realizes that he is about to die does he undergo a radical transformation and reject his treachery. He pronounces judgment on Claudius in the name of justice, "He is justly serv'd," and now, with no practical gain to be had, he is truly prepared to accept Hamlet's offer of brotherly reconciliation: "Exchange forgiveness with me, noble Hamlet: / Mine and my father's death come not upon thee, / Nor thine on me." This statement is the mirror image of Hamlet's earlier disowning of his own mad aspect and affirming only what he does as a result of will and deliberate purpose. And now, as if in the name of the mysterious providence he had cited earlier— "there is special providence in the fall of a sparrow"—Hamlet consecrates this mutual exchange of forgiveness with what seems like supernatural authority: "Heaven make thee free of it." Intellectual awareness of death is not difficult to come by, though, strangely enough, this very awareness can have the effect of denial. Not until death is truly imminent, however, can its reality be fully apprehended, and then this potent and unequivocal apprehension can have a transfiguring effect—as it does on Laertes whose finest moment, like that of Cawdor in *Macbeth,* is his last.

IX To Tell the Story

Hamlet's final wish to tell his own story, "O, I could tell you," assumes that his story contains some special significance as he asserted at the beginning of the play: "For I have that within which passes show." Though it is doubtful that Hamlet knows precisely what that inner something is, he nevertheless wants Horatio to attempt to give it articulation: "Report me and my cause aright / To the unsatisfied." But what that "cause" might be is as elusive as the essence that Hamlet asserts is deeper than any appearance or seeming. In leaving the story to be told to Horatio, Hamlet's words, in the face of the imminence of his death, "But let it be," have their own immense reverberation and significance. Hamlet's earlier claim that he has been born, as if Denmark's savior, "to set it right" has been replaced by a willingness to accept whatever it is that providence determines. Even the fundamental existential decision of whether one chooses to live or die, "to be or not to be," is relinquished and given over to the "heaven" in whose name Hamlet now speaks.

The first instinct of Horatio—the one person who has remained loyal to Hamlet—is to die with Hamlet, but Hamlet snatches the cup of poison from Horatio and repeats his request:

> *O good Horatio, what a wounded name*
> *(Things standing thus unknown) shall live behind me.*
> *If thou didst ever hold me in thy heart,*
> *Absent thee from felicity awhile,*
> *And in this harsh world draw thy breath in pain,*
> *To tell my story.* (V. ii. 347-352)

Hamlet's philosophy at this point is that even though death is to be regarded as "felicity," nobility requires that one endure one's appointed suffering as this "harsh world" requires it. (This is the virtue of what is "nobler in the mind" that Hamlet evoked earlier in the play. In the name of the great bond of friendship, then, Hamlet asks that Horatio partake of this suffering of "the slings and arrows of outrageous fortune" and draw his breath "in pain" so that his story will get told.) This is the remaining choice that Hamlet is free to make. Suffering and its testimony seem to be the ultimate necessities and the ultimate values that constitute Hamlet's highest volitional concern.

That Fortinbras should have Hamlet's "dying voice" is painfully ironic and disturbing, since there is nothing about Fortinbras that represents what is best in Hamlet—his capacity for empathy and good will. Hamlet's final words, "The rest is silence," are as ambiguous and mysterious as the meaning of Hamlet's life, his identity of what goes deeper than what "seems." Is there peace and rest after death? What is the rest of the story of Denmark after Fortinbras takes control? Horatio chooses to believe that Hamlet finally will find peace in death and prays that "flights of angels sing thee to thy rest." But the moment those words are out of his mouth, the military world of Fortinbras intrudes: "Why does the drum come hither?" asks Horatio.

Horatio attempts to fulfill Hamlet's wish to have his story told:

> *And let me speak to th' yet unknowing world*
> *How these things came about. So shall you hear*
> *Of carnal, bloody, and unnatural acts,*
> *Of accidental judgments, casual slaughters,*
> *Of deaths put on by cunning and forc'd cause,*
> *And in this upshot, purposes mistook*
> *Fall'n on th' inventors' heads. All this can I*
> *Truly deliver.* (V. ii. 382-389)

But it is excruciatingly clear that even the competent Horatio is able only to narrate the plot of Hamlet's story; Horatio's rendering turns into melodrama in which events seem more important than their causes. Despite Horatio's undoubtable love for Hamlet and his demonstrated understanding that history when understood can reveal cycles and patterns, the essence of Hamlet as sufferer, the "heart of his mystery," will go untold. Fortinbras immediately perceives that he has a political opportunity and proclaims, "I have some rights of memory in this kingdom, / Which now to claim my vantage doth invite me," and it is obvious that the immediate fate of Denmark is to fall into the hands of a military opportunist and dictator.

Fortinbras' ceremonial words over Hamlet's body suit his own imperialistic purposes and express his own military values; they are virtually irrelevant to what we have seen of Hamlet's suffering:

> *Let four captains*
> *Bear Hamlet like a soldier to the stage;*
> *For he was likely, had he been put on,*
> *To have prov'd most royal. And for his passage*
> *The soldier's music and the rites of war*
> *Speak loudly for him.* (V. ii. 398-404)

These words have nothing to do with the Hamlet whose melancholy, confusion, and search for nobility and purpose we have witnessed throughout the play. Surely, the identity of "soldier" is not the one the unbiased onlooker would assign to Hamlet. The "silence" that Hamlet both anticipates and evokes is immediately obscured and lost in the noise of the firing of guns that end the play as the result of Fortinbras' order, "Go bid the soldiers shoot."

Fortinbras' commandment is neither that of Hamlet's father for Hamlet to avenge his murder, nor the commandment of a God who says "Thou shalt not kill," or "overcome evil with good." And it is not given to Horatio, the would-be historian, who is so caught up in the political moment to be appalled by Fortinbras or to despair in what the future holds for Denmark. Only Shakespeare can do that—Shakespeare who lives both wholly within the play and wholly outside of it.

CHAPTER THREE

MEASURE FOR MEASURE:
WHAT WILL ISABELLA DECIDE?

I Guises of Divinity

The character of the Duke in *Measure for Measure* is perhaps more wide-ly open to divergent interpretations than any other of Shakespeare's cre-ations. On the one hand, he can be considered godlike in his control of the outcome of the play—a happy outcome seen as forgiving and benevolent—or he can be seen as a self-indulgent manipulator savoring his own power. Unlike Hamlet whose motivation invites speculation but who is basically a good person for whom we feel sympathy, and unlike Iago whose motiva-tion also is complex and uncertain but who is basically malignant and fi-nally repulsive, the Duke is someone whom it is equally possible to admire or detest.

It is impossible to read Shakespeare's plays and fix upon a consistent concept of God that runs through them. Generally speaking, any concept of God depends on the view of a particular character and also may vary according to the situation and circumstance of that particular character. When things go well, God may be seen as benevolent, and when things go badly, God or the gods are likely to be seen as malevolent. So in *King Lear*, for example, when Edgar and Edmund are seeking to reconcile and Edgar says "Let's exchange charity," Edgar sees a kind of grace in that moment and exclaims, "The gods are just"; but, quite to the contrary as a view of dei-ty, the blinded Gloucester cries out, "As flies to wanton boys, are we to th' gods: / They kill us for their sport."

There are vast differences between the plays in their representation of any relationship between a divine creator and the nature he creates. In *King Lear* nature is basically uncaring in its indifference; in *Macbeth* nature seems to exercise a moral power that brings about the punishment of those who violate the integrity of its divine order. *King Lear* ends with only the conso-lation of Lear being relieved of pain as expressed by Kent when he says, "He hates him / That would upon the rack of this tough world / Stretch him out longer." There is no hint of any presence of divinity in such a culminating moment. Quite differently, *Macbeth* ends with the cleansing of evil from the realm and with the restoration of "the grace of Grace" as the young king Malcolm ascends the throne. We see two completely divergent theologies implicit in these tragedies in the toll they take on human lives and on suffering undergone: one with a gloomy conclusion and one with hopeful prospects for the future. Though *Macbeth* does not conclude with any marriages, it does in fact end happily as Malcolm awards his nobles with new titles and order is restored in Scotland. At the very end of *King Lear*, however, Albany asks Kent and Edgar to rule together, "Friends of my soul, you twain / Rule in this realm," but Kent declines and Edgar can think only of the grief he feels: "The weight of this sad time we must obey; / Speak what we feel, not what we ought to say."

The judgment we as audience make of the Duke, whether or not he has godlike qualities, depends entirely on how we evaluate the effects of his manipulations and his plotting. Plotting, of course, carries with it two possible connotations: it is good that an author has a plot for his play, but it is bad when one character in the play plots to harm another character. The Duke, in effect, is the author of the very play that contains him, and we are invited to judge him in his double role as author and as plotter-conniver. He has qualities similar to that aspect of Hamlet who arranges to have the mousetrap play put on in order to catch the "conscience of the king," and, on a comic level, (*Measure for Measure* is a comedy in that we know things will turn out well) he is like Peter Quince and Bottom who stage their version of the play *Pyramus and Thisbe*.

These play-within-a-play episodes bear a close relationship to the storytelling passages that are examined in this book—the theme of characters choosing to tell their stories or wanting to have their stories told. Story-telling is a form of control in a world in which one is not in control of one's life since one is not a god but a mortal human being. The Duke, however, seems to be an exception, since he is unique in being in control of the world from which he is both detached and within which he operates. It may be, however, that this is not an entirely accurate description of the Duke's powers, since we do not know at the play's end whether or not Isabella will accept his proposal of marriage, an outcome seemingly not within the Duke's control.

That Shakespeare wants us to consider the Duke, either seriously or ironically, as a godlike figure is first suggested by his being paired with Angelo, significantly named, as his stand-in when the Duke supposedly leaves the city and takes on the disguise of a friar to observe what happens when Angelo is given power to rule in Vienna. In this sense, Angelo can be viewed as the diabolical aspect of the Duke himself, just as in the Book of

Job, God and the Accuser are seen together, almost as partners, in deciding what temptations and trials Job will be given to undergo. As a pair, the Duke and Angelo may be seen as representing the twin aspects of divine justice—mercy and judgment—both of which are assigned to Angelo when the Duke supposedly departs for Poland: "Mortality and mercy in Vienna / Live in thy tongue and heart," says the Duke.

In giving Angelo this assignment, the Duke, in effect, puts him on trial when he charges him "to enforce or qualify the laws / As your soul seems good." The Duke's decision to turn over authority to Angelo appears at the moment to be sufficiently straightforward and without any ulterior motivation on the Duke's part, but when the Duke says that "I love the people, / And do not like to stage me to their eyes," one well might wonder whether there is a touch of denial in the Duke's disavowal of subjective motivation. This suspicion, I believe, deepens when the Duke goes on even more extravagantly to claim that "I do not relish well / Their loud applause and Aves vehement." As the Duke becomes more and more deeply involved in the elaborate manipulations and tricks of deception to be followed by revelations which constitute his plotting and his plots, we have increasing reason to doubt the accuracy, if not the sincerity, of the Duke's early assertion of his modesty in describing his motivation.

The Duke reveals a lot more about himself, not all of it intentional, in the scene where he explains his plans to Friar Thomas to spy on what will transpire in Vienna during his supposed absence. He tells the Friar that "none better knows than you / How I have ever lov'd the life remov'd," yet the Duke's plan, though it appears like removal, is exactly the opposite of removal: it is involvement in everyone's most intimate affairs, even to the point of his making a proposal of marriage to Isabella. This is not to say that there is only hypocrisy and nothing genuine about the Duke's concern for the increasing licentious behavior in the city where through governmental leniency under his rule "liberty plucks justice by the nose." I hear sincerity in the Duke's voice when he says that "'twas my fault to give people scope," and he cannot be dismissed as a representative of moral consciousness by seeing him only with irony or as a parodic figure. Shakespeare's presentation of him is tantalizingly complex and keeps him open to conjecture and speculation.

The Duke's insight into Angelo's psychology is penetrating and accurate: he "scarce confesses / That his blood flows, or that his appetite / Is more to bread than stone." The Duke well realizes that Angelo has repressed the sensual aspect of his nature, the element of "appetite" that Angelo shares with all other human beings, a repression that will allow Angelo to set such extreme and absolute standards for human control of desire and thus give greater weight to justice over mercy in judging others. But the phrase, "scarce confesses," is extremely subtle; it does not mean that Angelo has no self-awareness at all, that his repression is total and complete. Rather, it suggests that Angelo is at least capable of knowing himself or, even further, that Angelo at some level of consciousness has deliberately chosen not to acknowledge "appetite" in himself; if this is so, Angelo is a pretender about whom the Duke can say, "Hence shall we see, / If power change purpose, what our seemers be." The Duke, then, is able to foretell what will happen later in the play and that events will confirm Angelo to be a "seemer;" the Duke knows how giving Angelo power will provide the temptation in which Angelo will violate his own professed idealism in demanding purity in human behavior. The theme of seeming in its various forms—self-deception through repression, deceiving others, and disguises—is hereby established as a central concern of the play and its fundamental psychological insight.

II *Seeming as a Form of Repression*

Although to be most effective, repression must take place on an unconscious level—seeming as a form of self-deception—as most of this play will demonstrate, yet repression also can be seen at the very border of self-awareness as in Lucio's amusing description in Act I, Scene II, of "the sanctimonious pirate, that went to sea with the Ten Commandments, but scraped one of them out of the table." We do not know, of course, in this little comic parable, exactly how aware the pirate is of the absurdity or utility of removing "Thou shalt not steal," from the realm of moral consciousness as an ethical imperative. Subsequently, as the play unfolds, there will be multiple examples of characters repressing awareness of their instinctual natures, particularly Angelo, Isabella, and the Duke.

Our initial impression of Isabella occurs in Act I, Scene IV when we see her outside the nunnery asking the nun, Francisca, about the rules and regulations of life inside the nunnery: "And have you nuns no further privileges?" Isabella inquires, to which Francisca, incorrectly assuming that Isabella would prefer more "privileges," responds, "Are not these large enough?" Isabella's instant rejoinder no doubt surprises Francisca, as it must also the playgoer, in its self-denying claim: "I speak not of desiring more, / But rather wishing a more strict restraint / Upon the sisterhood." Clearly, there are impulses and urgent desires within Isabella which she cannot identify, that she feels compelled to keep under control with the help of the authority of the Church. That these impulses have a sexual aspect is made apparent by the nun's remark, "When you have vow'd, you must not speak with men / But in the presence of the prioress." A moment later the morally loose Lucio enters the scene and greets Isabella with "Hail, virgin, if you be," an ironic remark that sees more deeply into the heart of Isabella than Claudio has the wit to realize.

Shakespeare's depiction of the unconscious content of Isabella's mind takes place both on the level of innuendo and then more overtly. For example, Isabella—when first appealing to Angelo to hear her suit in behalf of her brother, Claudio, who is sentenced to have his head chopped off for the sin of fornication—proclaims her high moral standard about sexual constraint: "There is a vice that most I do abhor / And most desire should meet the blow of justice." But the use of the word "abhor" is surely a Freudian slip in disclosing Isabella's puritanical obsession with sexual indulgence, and, quite revealingly, Shakespeare places this word on Isabella's lips on two more occasions. Again in conversation with Angelo, Isabella, still in her most high-minded mode of address—a high-mindedness that she projects upon her brother—asserts:

> I'll to my brother:
> Though he hath fallen by prompture of the blood,
> He hath in him such a mind of honour,
> That, had he twenty heads to tender down
> On twenty blood blocks, he'd yield them up,
> Before his sister should her body stoop
> To such abhorr'd pollution. (II. iv. 178-182)

And once more out comes the obsessive word in the phrase, "abhorr'd pollution." It is like Macbeth's slip of the tongue when, in contemplating killing King Duncan, he exclaims, "My thought, whose murder is but yet fantastical," in which the word "murder" whose overt meaning here is "implement" (Macbeth at this point has only imagined the killing) reveals his innermost motivation. Our awareness of the implications of the word "abhor," obsessively repeated, is heightened further by the fact that the executioner is named Abhorson. Remarkable in that he enjoys his profession, his very name links together the ideas of sexuality and violence.

The third occasion in which the loaded word, "abhor," occurs is when Isabella is telling Claudio what Angelo is willing to do in exchange for Isabella's yielding her body to him. She says, "This night's the time / That I should do what I abhor to name," as she names here what she claims she cannot name. This is exactly how repression works: by revealing itself through displacement or indirection as is made explicit by the Queen in *Hamlet* when she expounds: "Murder, though it hath no tongue, / Will speak with most miraculous organ." If the reader has any doubt about Shakespeare's deliberate use of this device of having words proclaim their hidden inner meanings, let the reader also note a similar scene in which Emilia says to Iago that Othello has vilified Desdemona by calling her a whore, "Iago, my lord hath so bewhor'd her," to which Desdemona, unable even to speak the word, replies, "Am I that name, Iago?" Although she does not realize it, Iago mocks her when he asks, "What name, fair lady?" but Desdemona simply cannot bring herself to speak the word, and so she elliptically replies, "Such as she says my lord did say I was," still avoiding the offending word.

The most egregious and consequential of Isabella's verbal slips, of which she is unconscious, appears right after Angelo becomes aware of his sexual response to Isabella's person. Angelo says in an aside, "She speaks, and 'tis / Such sense that my sense breeds with it." Isabella asks him to continue listening to her appeal on behalf of her brother, "Gentle my lord, turn back." The already tempted Angelo tells her, "Come again tomorrow," and Isabella's seemingly inadvertent reply, "Hark how I'll bribe you," astonishes Angelo as he interprets the word "bribe" in its sexual connotation: "How! bribe me?" he exclaims as the passion behind his temptation continues to rise. So, too, does Angelo respond to the unintended double meaning inherent in Isabella's use of the word "pleasure" when Isabella enters Angelo's house and formally says to him, "I am come to know your pleasure." Once again, Angelo is fully aware of the possible sexual meaning of the word "pleasure," and so he responds, "That you might know it, would much better please me, / Than to demand what 'tis."

Repressed sexual emotion, though hinted at, long buried within Isabella, bursts forth in Act III, Scene I, where Isabella answers Claudio's question, "Is there no remedy?" in the negative, "None, but such remedy, as to save a head / To cleave a heart in twain." In other words, the "remedy" of Isabella's having sex with Angelo in exchange for Claudio's life is unacceptable. Yet Isabella senses that Claudio is not entirely willing to rule out such a remedy, and she replies with an urgency that we have not seen in her before, an urgency entirely unlike her reticence when earlier Lucio had to urge Isabella to entreat Angelo with more vehemence: "Give it not o'er so: to him again, entreat him; / Kneel down before him, hang upon his gown; / You are too cold." But now Isabella rises to eloquence in admonishing Claudio:

O, I do fear thee, Claudio; and I quake,
Lest thou a feverous life shouldst entertain,
And six or seven winters more respect
Than a perpetual honor. Dar'st thou die?
The sense of death is most in apprehension,
And the poor beetle, that we tread upon,
In corporal sufferance finds a pang as great
As when a giant dies. (III. i. 73-80)

(There is a deep contradiction in what these words imply—the exhortation to empathy for all living things, even a beetle—that is expressed here, and the cruel fact that this speech is most immediately intended to instruct Claudio to accept immanent death. Claudio's first reaction is extreme, hysterically so, when he cries out, "If I must die, / I will encounter darkness as a bride, / And hug it in mine arms," sexualizing death in his representation of death as a bride. Isabella's approving response gives tacit acceptance to such a representation, and her invocation of her dead father at this moment further extends the circle of libidinal connotations: "There spake my brother: there's my father's grave / Did utter forth a voice." The idealized father is associated by a grim logic with honor, honor with death, and death with marriage.)

Claudio, however, cannot sustain his momentary commitment to embrace death as honor and begins to backtrack in his estimation of sexual indulgence : "Sure it is no sin; / Or of the deadly seven it is the least." He is like the pirate who would revise the Commandments to suit his wishes. But then the dread of death sweeps over him: "Death is a fearful thing"; no longer will he be persuaded by Isabella's counter argument, "And shamed life a hateful." Claudio gives full expression to his terror at the imagining of death, not as a bride, but as decay:

Ay, but to die, and go we know not where;
To lie in cold obstruction and to rot;
This sensible warm motion to become
A kneaded clod; and the delighted spirit
To bathe in fiery floods, or to reside
In thrilling region of thick-ribbed ice;
To be imprison'd in the viewless winds,
And blown with restless violence about
The pendant world; or to be worst than worst
Of those that lawless and incertain thought

> *Imagine howling: 'tis too horrible!*
> *The weariest and most loathed worldly life*
> *That age, ache, penury and imprisonment*
> *Can lay on nature is a paradise*
> *To what we fear of death.* (III. i. 116-130)

Claudio further imagines death as possible punishment for unnamed sins, which in context here may well be sexual desire and manifest sexual behavior. Isabella's response is one of despair, "Alas! Alas!" Claudio, however, no longer can control his outburst of dismay and fear as he pleads with Isabella to do whatever is necessary, including having sex with Angelo, if such a sacrifice on her part will save him:

> *Sweet sister, let me live.*
> *What sin you do to save a brother's life,*
> *Nature dispenses with the deed so far*
> *That it becomes a virtue.* (III. i. 132-135)

Isabella's reaction is astounding in its vociferous excess of disgust. A moment ago she was able to feel sympathy for a "poor beetle" if stepped upon, but now, seemingly without pity but with a passion that rises up within her from some unknown and heretofore concealed depth, she excoriates her brother in her exclamation,

> *O you beast!*
> *O faithless coward! O dishonest wretch!*
> *Wilt thou be made a man out of my vice?*
> *Is it not a kind of incest, to take life*
> *From thine own sister's shame?* (III. i. 136-139)

Isabella's burst of fury seems to be the correlative of a lifetime of energy expended in controlling her own forbidden desires. Her remarkably revealing accusation that Claudio would be committing a "kind of incest" only makes psychological sense if in Isabella's mind Claudio becomes a substitute for Angelo in having sex with Isabella. And still worse, since Isabella has just identified Claudio with her father, "there my father's grave / Did utter forth a voice," the primal sin that Isabella evokes becomes a double incest. This doubling of a younger and a senior male across the generations is much like what occurs in the mind of Ophelia in her madness when the figures of her lover, Hamlet, and her father, Polonius, merge from one stanza to the next in the song she sings:

How should I your true love know [lover]
From another one?
By his cockle hat and staff,
And his sandle shoon . . .

He is dead and gone, lady, [father]
He is dead and gone;
At his head a grass-green turf;
At his head a stone. (IV. i. 23-32)

(The dark and terrible substance of Isabella's thought continues to pour out as she now brings forth a further fear of sexual violation, that her mother might have betrayed her father in producing a son such as Claudio: "Heaven shield my mother play'd my father fair; / For such a warped slip of wilderness / Ne'er issued from his blood." Isabella's conclusion, in this state of extreme and irrational suspicion and anger, is that not only will she do nothing to rescue Claudio from death, but she herself will wish for his death: "I'll pray a thousand prayers for thy death, / No word to save thee." And still in the language of sexual corruption, "Mercy to thee would prove itself a bawd: / 'Tis best thou diest quickly." The Duke has overheard this fervid conversation between Isabella and Claudio, and he seeks to prepare Claudio to accept what seems to be his inevitable fate: "Prepare yourself to death. Do not satisfy your resolution with hopes that are fallible." Somehow these words calm Claudio, and he recants his plea, with characteristic extravagance, to his sister to save his life by her having sex with Angelo: "Let me ask my sister pardon. I am so out of love with life that I will sue to be rid of it."

Perhaps it is Isabella's identification of Claudio—and, by association, her father—with Angelo that will explain Isabella's later plea to the Duke, with its stretch of legal logic, to spare Angelo's life. Mariana implores Isabella to join her in trying to persuade the Duke to spare the exposed Angelo's life, "Isabel, / Sweet Isabella, do yet but kneel by me," which Isabella does. Isabella offers the Duke two not entirely convincing reasons why Angelo should be spared:

I partly think
A due sincerity govern'd his deeds,
Till he did look on me; since it is so,
Let him not die. (V. i. 146-149)

After Isabella's earlier profession that justice requires that fornication be severely punished even with death, and after her outburst with her brother, calling him a "beast," Isabella's sympathy for Angelo's lusting after her is, to say the least, astonishing. Can it be that here she herself is identifying with Angelo as she had earlier identified Claudio with him in what then would constitute a moment of narcissistic self-love? Or shall we simply consider this empathy for Angelo a new and admirable stage in Isabella's moral growth and development?

Isabella then becomes more technical in coming up with a legalistic rationalization for seeing Angelo's intended crimes in an extenuating light:

> My brother had but justice
> In that he did the thing for which he died:
> For Angelo,
> His act did not o'ertake his bad intent,
> And must be buried but as an intent
> That perished by the way. Thoughts are no subjects;
> Intents but merely thoughts. (V. i. 449-455)

We can barely recognize the former Isabella in this state of mind and in the pedantic dryness of her reasoning. We cannot help but speculate whether there is something in Isabella's seeming transformation, which includes her empathy for Angelo, that might give us a clue as to whether or not Isabella will accept the Duke's proposal of marriage which is shortly to follow. Will there be something about the Duke—perhaps no more than his sexual interest in her—that will cause Isabella to identify him too with Angelo? With steady and unmistakable intent, Shakespeare sends our minds into a vertigo of wondering.

But let's consider one more factor: the bonding between two women, Isabella and Mariana, which is much like the bonding between Desdemona and Emilia at the end of *Othello*. Although it is possible to read Mariana's motivation to be wedded to Angelo as based on the general social and financial dependency of women on men in the society of the time, Shakespeare is deliberate in having the Duke tell Mariana that she will inherit Angelo's wealth: "For his possessions, / Although by confiscation they are ours, / We do instate and widow you withal, / To buy you a better husband." So it is clear that Mariana's motivation is not materialistic when she replies to the Duke, "O my dear lord! / I crave no other, nor no better man." Although our credulity is stretched, she does appear to love him; her explanatory statement to Isabella acknowledges, with some measure of hope, the complexity and ambivalence of human sexual love:

> *They say best men are moulded out of faults,*
> *And, for the most, become much more the better*
> *For being a little bad: so may my husband.* (V. i. 437-439)

The distinction between neurotic or perverted love and so-called normal love here is broken down. Human love is human love, take it as it comes, in all its guises and disguises, and, I believe, the sharing of the reality of human ambivalence and contradiction constitutes the touching bond between these two women. On this basis, and with this realization beyond the permutations of seeming, it is no longer necessary for Isabella to retreat into a nunnery to escape the challenges of desire and sexual love. So, yes, she is now ready and will accept the Duke's hand in marriage.

III Angelo & the Denial of Self-Denial

Angelo's repression of his own nature, with its bestial component, is much like Isabella's, though perhaps not as intricately complex, and the sexual aspect of his being breaks though the veneer of his moral seeming more abruptly and more definitively. Although the Duke may see through Angelo's self-image as a man of justice, using his new power as a corrective to the Duke's leniency and emphasis of mercy over judgment and punishment, Angelo does not possess such self-awareness. We first see him as the Duke offers him the "commission" to rule in his stead, to which Angelo responds with what appears to be genuine modesty: "Now, good my lord, / Let there be some more test made of my metal, / Before so noble and so great a figure / Be stamp'd upon it." Whether this is hypocrisy or not, or unconscious self-knowledge about the need truly to be tested, we do not know at this point. But it soon becomes apparent that Angelo's self-confidence that he is equipped to rule in the Duke's absence is what he believes when he assumes an assertive tone in addressing Escalus, his fellow executor, at the beginning of Act II: "We must not make a scarecrow of the law, / Setting it up to fear the birds of prey." There is no question but that this statement implies a criticism of the Duke's previous lenient style of ruling and of Angelo's own sense of how the law ought to be more strictly administered.

Angelo's belief that the law must be rigidly applied is related to his confidence that human beings are capable of acting according to the dictates of will, rather than the inclinations of desire, and are thus to be held entirely responsible for their behavioral choices: "'Tis one thing to be tempted, Escalus, / And another thing to fall." The pride that Angelo takes in his own assumed capacity for self mastery and control is shown in the boast he makes: "When I, that censure him, [referring here to Claudio] do so offend, / Let mine own judgment pattern out my death." Angelo cannot conceive of the possibility that he himself might give in to sexual temptation, but when he does and is exposed for doing so, he will be good to his word and request that he be punished by death, thus exhibiting a characteristic consistency at the rational level that is exactly opposite to the irrationality of his lustful behavior. Armed thus with confident self-righteousness, Angelo gives the command, "See that Claudio / Be executed by nine tomorrow morning." Escalus's oracular response, however, to Angelo's unequivocal willingness to judge and punish, "Well, heaven forgive him, and forgive us all! / Some rise by sin, and some by virtue fall," foreshadows the ending of the play with its acquittals and acceptances in the spirit of mercy. Escalus's "forgive us all!" sounds a note that we hear throughout Shakespeare's plays—as if spoken by Shakespeare himself—as when the doctor in *Macbeth* says "God, God, forgive us all," or when King Lear says to Cordelia, "Pray you now, forget and forgive."

To his astonishment, Angelo will discover that he is not his own master, that his will cannot control his desires, that he is unable to rule the realm of his own body, that he is not like Cordelia who is aptly described as "queen / Over her passion." Angelo's discovery of his own unrestrainable concupiscence will not take place until after he and Isabella have a highly intellectual debate about their philosophy of how the law is to be applied in human affairs. At first Isabella takes the position that the law against sex before marriage—a law that her brother, Claudio, has broken—is just even though it is severe, "O just, but severe law," and on this basis she passively accepts her brother's punishment of death: "I had a brother, then," she says with icy objectivity. But then, after Lucio's urging, "Give't not o'er so; to him again, entreat him; / Kneel down before him, hang upon his gown; / You are too cold," Isabella's thinking expands to include the concept of mercy to balance against judgment, so she adds, "you might pardon him, / And neither heaven nor man grieve at the mercy." But Angelo remains adamant, "I will not do't," to which Isabella quickly and wittily responds, "But can you, if you would?" Angelo's rejoinder reveals both the sophistry of his reasoning and his inordinate emphasis on the sovereign power of will: "Look, what I will not, that I cannot do," as if his will were something other than his own, an authority to which he must submit. This is not true, nor is it true, as Angelo goes on to argue, that "It is the law, not I, that condemns your brother." Law does not exist apart from human interpretation and application, apart from the possibility of pardon and mercy that is based on the awareness of human fallibility. To assert that the law exists as a thing in itself is to eschew personal responsibility in applying it in actual situations which may well have extenuating factors.

As the debate between them continues, Isabella becomes more and more impassioned, and as she does, her reasoning—contrary to the overly simple idea that reason and emotion are mutually exclusive opposites—becomes more and more persuasive as it addresses the quintessential issue of the play—the abuse of authority and power:

> . . . but man, proud man,
> Dress'd in a little brief authority,
> Most ignorant of what he's most assured,
> His glassy essence, like an angry ape,
> Plays such fantastic tricks before high heaven
> As makes the angels weep. (II. ii. 117-122)

Although this speech perfectly describes Angelo and even suggests that his appropriate response should be to "weep" like the angels after which he is named, he is not yet ready to so respond. Isabella's follow-up is equally probing and powerful, "Go to your bosom; / Knock there, and ask your heart what it doth know / That's like my brother's fault," which Angelo indeed does, but in the most ironic sense which reverses what Isabella had hoped would be the effect of asking Angelo to perceive and acknowledge what is in his heart. The "fantastic trick" that is in his heart, to Angelo's appalled discovery, is his lust for Isabella: "She speaks, and 'tis / Such sense that my sense breeds with it." Rather than producing empathy for Claudio, whom he condemned to death, in discovering in himself sexual desire just like Claudio's, Angelo is now inclined to act out of desire himself, though with total selfishness. The revelation that he is both prone to and capable of acting out of a lustful "sense" comes with stunning suddenness to Angelo, and it will determine his subsequent behavior, his descent into corrupt plotting and conniving machinations.

Angelo's mind opens to a new awareness of human complexity and its inherent possibility of perversion, to what surely must be seen as the diabolic. Now, newly open to himself, he asks, "Can it be / That modesty may more betray our sense / Than woman's lightness?" This is an excruciatingly honest question that touches on the attractiveness of the forbidden in human relationships, perhaps even relating to Isabella's speculation about incest. And in asking this question, Angelo now is in doubt about his very identity: "What dost thou, or what art thou, Angelo? / Dost thou desire her for those things / That make her good?" And if this is so, does such desire testify to the presence of some infernal aspect inherent within the very nature of human love: "What! do I love her?" Angelo inquires as his mind stretches to an extremity of wonder and uncertainty heretofore undreamed of by his reasoning intellect. Can love be the domain of the devil is what Angelo now wishes to know: "O cunning enemy," Angelo says in defining the devil, "that to catch a saint, / With saints does bait thy hook." Angelo's conclusion, then, in his encounter with Isabella, leaves him with a totally transformed vision of himself and who he is: "this virtuous maid / Subdues me quite," and from here on until another reversal takes place at the play's conclusion, Angelo, like a fallen angel, will indeed behave as his supposed opposite, the devil, the master of deception and disguise, of "false seeming," and he confesses in soliloquy, "Blood, thou art blood: / Let's write good angel on the devil's horn."

Angelo will continue his intellectual debate with Isabella, savoring it like a kind of foreplay, even as he offers to spare Claudio in exchange for Isabella's having sex with him:

> *I shall pose you quickly,*
> *Which you had rather, that the most just law*
> *Now took your brother's life; or, to redeem him,*
> *Give up your body to such sweet uncleanness*
> *As she that he hath stain'd?* (II. iv. 52-56)

Isabella refuses him, "Better it were a brother died at once, / Than that a sister, by redeeming him, / Should die forever," but Angelo is still enjoying the devil's pleasure of philosophizing, the pleasure of manipulating words, of "seeming," and, pleased with his own wit, he replies: "Were it not you then as cruel as the sentence / That you have slander'd so?" Isabella holds to her position, "I have no tongue but one," and at that moment Angelo—does he even know what he is saying or whether he believes his own tongue?—replies, "Plainly conceive, I love you." Angelo has by now destroyed the possibility of plain speech or plain understanding and communication, and Isabella points out the contradiction between what he has done and what he says, "My brother did love Juliet; and you tell me that he shall die for't." Angelo's retort is: "He shall not, Isabel, if you give me love." Love? What can that word possibly mean in this context? Isabella dismisses

Angelo's proclamation with the ringing word, "Seeming, seeming," a word that has by now become a fully developed motif in the play. "I will proclaim thee, Angelo," says Isabella, and with the demise of the word "love" in their discourse, Angelo now speaks only of "appetite" as he acknowledges: "I have begun; / And now I give my sensual race the rein. / Fit thy consent to my sharp appetite," as if this decision were really a choice, rather than a compulsion.

Angelo's attempt to coerce Isabella into having sex with him, his diabolical "seeming," is bad enough even though we can comprehend it as the result of "appetite," but Angelo's additional betrayal, his reneging on the deal he has made to trade a reprieve for Claudio for sex—an Iago-like maneuver—seems cruel almost beyond imagination. Against his word, Angelo had gratuitously given instruction that "Claudio be executed by four of the clock." His earlier remark at the dawning of self-realization, "She speaks, and 'tis / Such sense that my sense breeds with it," has proven to be prophetic as we have seen corruption breed further corruption, evil breed more evil. Angelo has come to the point where it seems that there is no turning back; he is like Macbeth when, with deluded logic, Macbeth says, "I am in blood / Stepp'd in so far, that, should I wade no more, / Returning were as tedious as go o'er."

Unlike Macbeth who never repents, Angelo, when confronted with the fact of his crimes, seems wholeheartedly to express genuine contrition as he addresses the Duke as if the Duke, "like power divine," were indeed God's representative:

> *O dread my lord!*
> *I should be guiltier than my guiltiness*
> *To think I can be indiscernible,*
> *When I perceive your Grace, like power divine,*
> *Hath look'd upon my passes. Then, good prince,*
> *No longer session hold upon my shame*
> *But let my trial be mine own confession:*
> *Immediate sentence then and sequent death*
> *Is all the grace I beg.* (V. i. 367-375)

Angelo's self-judgment is as extreme and absolute as his crime. He is no more capable of mercy toward himself than he was toward Claudio, and though there is a kind of virtue in Angelo's clarity and tidy consistency as he goes on to speak of "my penitent heart / That I crave death more willingly than mercy, / 'Tis my deserving, and I do entreat it," yet the awareness of human fallibility and the concomitant capacity for empathy is grievously lacking here. Is this something the Duke, after exorcising his own inclination to have Angelo executed, ascends to comprehend so that he actually now believes that Angelo is capable of love and that he and Mariana can find happiness in marriage? The Duke's invocation to them, "Joy to you, Mariana! love her, Angelo" surely is a further challenge to ordinary credibility, yet can its possibility be ruled out by us or by the attending Isabella?

IV Liberty & Restraint

The capacity for self-transcendence, represented by the possibility of marital love between Mariana and Angelo, is the opposite of the deterministic effects of power to corrupt. Thus, to believe that power necessarily corrupts, as this play emphatically shows, is implicitly to assume that there is something about the instinctual makeup of human beings that is inherently immoral or evil, as is also suggested here. The tacit assumption within this concept of power being a corrupting force is that the only constraint that prevents us from behaving selfishly for personal satisfaction or aggrandizement is some external (or internalized) set of laws or ethical concepts that can counteract our hidden wishes. The commandments of society, either rationally understood or interiorized as a sense of guilt, perform this needed function of controlling or modifying our behavior. For Shakespeare the mark of the moral person is that he or she willingly and deliberately chooses a life of self-overcoming in which one's highest human identity is achieved through the mastery of one's passions and desires and the acceptance, usually through forgiveness, of the offenses committed by others. Pleasure is to be pursued and liberty and freedom are to be cherished, but only within limits. The danger of having power is that power itself becomes a form of temptation as it allows one to exceed those limits which continually must be affirmed by an effort of personal choice to achieve restraint and thus compassion for the needs and vulnerabilities of others.

This theme of liberty versus restraint is introduced early in the play when Lucio questions Claudio as to why he is being led to prison: "Why, how now Claudio! whence comes this restraint?" asks Lucio, to which Claudio replies:

> *From too much liberty, Lucio, liberty.*
> *As surfeit is the father of much fast,*
> *So every scope by the immoderate use*

Turns to restraint. Our natures do pursue—
Like rats that raving down their proper bane—
A thirsty evil, and when we drink we die. (I. ii. 134-139)

Claudio compares human nature to that of rats, and he regards immoderation as a form of poisonous self-destruction. Lucio's reply, "I had as lief have the foppery [meaning folly or frivolity] of freedom as the morality of imprisonment." Both of them acknowledge the need for restraint and the containment of excessive or immoderate behavior. The Duke expatiates further on this same theme as he describes the comparable necessity of raising children with parental discipline:

> *Now, as fond fathers,*
> *Having bound up the threat'ning twigs of birch,*
> *Only to stick it into their children's sight*
> *For terror, not to use, in time the rod*
> *Becomes more mock'd than fear'd; so our decrees,*
> *Dead to infliction, to themselves are dead,*
> *And liberty plucks justice by the nose;*
> *The baby beats the nurse, and quite athwart*
> *Goes all decorum.* (I. iii. 23-31)

[margin handwriting: image of prison]

The image that Shakespeare most uses in this play to describe the condition of social and socialized humankind is that of a prison, sometimes with its obvious connotation of punishment, but sometimes, paradoxically, with the suggestion that the mind is free to make what it will of its own confining circumstances. Prison in *Measure for Measure* is thus both a physical fact for Claudio and a state of mind, as when he fearfully imagines death as a condition in which one is "imprisoned in the viewless winds, / And blown with restless violence round about / The pendant world." In contrast with the tormented Claudio, Shakespeare, with marvelous comic irony, shows us the convicted criminal, Barnardine, as fully at peace within prison. Provost, when asked by the Duke if Barnardine is "penitent," describes him as "A man that apprehends death no more dreadfully but as a drunken sleep; careless, reckless, and fearless of what's past, present, or to come." The Duke construes such an attitude to be a form of thoughtlessness and says, "He wants advice," but Provost continues with the paradoxical observation that "He will hear none. He hath evermore had the liberty of the prison: give him leave to escape hence, he would not." Prison for Barnardine (like the cloister as imagined by Isabella) is not a place of limitation but of freedom through enforced or self-enforced discipline. It is exactly the opposite of what Denmark is for Hamlet, who claims "Denmark's a prison," and, later, "I could be bounded in a nutshell, and count myself a king of infinite space, were it not that I have bad dreams." One's sense of space, as Shakespeare shows, is dependent on one's psychology and attitude toward one's circumstances.

Examples of prison as a place that cannot confine the affirming mind abound in Shakespeare's plays, such as when the captured Lear says to his daughter, Cordelia, "Come, let's away to prison. We too alone will sing like birds i' th' cage." Father and daughter are able to sing rather than bemoan their condition simply because they are together and can take upon themselves what Lear calls "the mystery of things." Or, in *The Tempest*, when Ferdinand, in love with Prospero's daughter, Miranda, and momentarily made immobile by the admonishing Prospero's magic, describes his bodily confinement:

> Might I but through my prison once a day
> Behold this maid: all corners else o' the earth
> Let liberty make use of; space enough
> Have I in such a prison. (I. iv. 487-490)

Although Barnardine may be thought of ironically as the freest character in this play, the model for sexual desire within necessary constraints, the feeling of liberty as achieved within limits, may be seen as partially embodied at the play's conclusion in the marriages as arranged by the Duke. Shakespeare's depiction of these marriages, however, may equally be viewed as even more ironic than his depiction of Barnardine at peace in prison, and, if so, these apparent resolutions tell us much about the Duke who arranges them. In the next section I will further examine the manipulating and controlling figure of the disguised Duke who, finally, we might speculate, reveals something more about himself than he consciously intends.

V Will Isabella Choose to Marry the Duke?

As I claimed at the beginning of this chapter, the Duke in *Measure for Measure* is an enigmatic figure whom it is difficult or maybe impossible to fix in one's considered estimation. Surely this is the bard's intent. Isabella's choice whether or not to marry the Duke will depend on what she has seen in him by the conclusion of the play. Shakespeare's plays often deliberately leave questions open and issues at least partly unresolved for the realistic

open
questions

reason that human beings are too complex to be fully fathomed. For example, we do not know whether Prospero's offer of forgiveness to his brother Antonio will be accepted with grace or even whether Antonio will begin plotting again against Prospero when they return to Milan. We do not know whether Caliban will accompany Prospero back to Milan, even though Prospero has acknowledged him as "mine," or remain on the island in continued enmity with Ariel. At the very end of *Twelfth Night* the cruelly abused (in the pretext of a practical joke) Malvolio, just released from a dark prison, exclaims in his final words, "I'll be reveng'd on the whole pack of you." The Countess Olivia gives credence to Malvolio's assertion that he has been treated unjustly: "He hath been most notoriously abus'd," and Duke Orsino gives instructions to his servants, "Pursue him, and entreat him to a peace." Although the play ends with two marriages, and is a comedy in that respect, the audience does not know how Malvolio will receive the Duke's entreaty or what revenge he might indeed seek to enact on the whole court. Many other examples readily come to mind: Will Iago confess under torture? Will Donalbain remain loyal to his brother? Will Horatio come to realize that Fortinbras has turned Denmark into a fascist police state and seek to overthrow him in memory of Hamlet?

will
Isabella
marry the
Duke?

    The main question that is left unresolved at the end of *Measure for Measure* is whether Isabella—whom we last see kneeling before the Duke in supplication for the life of Angelo—will accept the Duke's proposal of marriage, and that, of course, depends on her impression of the Duke. The first uncertainty attendant on that question is based on the fact that the Duke is surely at least a generation older than Isabella. Nevertheless, one might speculate that Isabella's idealization of her dead father suggests that she would be inclined to accept the Duke's offer to make "What's mine is yours, and what is yours is mine." The play, nevertheless, concludes with her in silence. As in the other plays discussed in this book, Shakespeare depicts his characters as surprising us with stunning changes in their behavior or outlook. The Duke is a perfect and extreme example of this in his sudden display of sexual interest, of which we have had no hint throughout the play; rather, in disguise as a Friar and referring to himself as Duke, he asserts to the insulting Lucio that "I never heard the absent Duke much detected for women; he was not inclined that way." The only emotion the Duke readily acknowledges during the entire play involves his political and social identity, as when, still in disguise as a Friar, he professes to Isabella "the love I have in doing good." The Duke seems interested only in managing the love lives of others until virtually the last moment of the play.

    The Duke is most in his element when arranging marriages and displaying the largess of his power to pardon and forgive. He enjoys himself most when exercising this power to bring about transformations in the lives of those within his control. If we include the Duke's own possible marriage, there are four marriages that he decrees and arranges. With ostentatious public display, he orders Angelo to marry Mariana, whom he, Angelo, earlier had abandoned when her dowry was lost. "Go take her hence, and marry her instantly," commands the Duke. Right after giving this order, however, the Duke sentences Angelo to death, "An Angelo for Claudio, death for death," on grounds that the Duke well knows are not factual since he is fully aware that Claudio is still alive. His proclamation is theatrical. What the Duke pretends to enact, with contrived deliberation, is all a fiction: "We do condemn thee to the very block / Where Claudio stoop'd to death." Mariana, however, not knowing that this is pretense, suffers from true distress, and she urgently pleads with the Duke, "I hope you will not mock me with a husband." The Duke, playing his lead role of ruler in power with full swagger, takes her words as an opportunity to display his wit with his mocking line about mockery: "It is your husband mock'd you with a husband."

(The Duke continues with the pretense that Claudio is dead and that Angelo must therefore be punished with a commensurate death until the very moment that Claudio is unveiled and revealed to be alive, and, at that exact moment, the Duke—pretending that the "Unmuffled" figure only resembles Isabella's brother, Claudio—pardons Claudio, both for "his sake" and for Isabella's "lovely sake." In the following breathless instant, the Duke then proposes to Isabella, "Give me your hand and say you will be mine," but either he gives her no time to answer or, taken by surprise, she is not ready with a reply. A second after his proposal, he reverses his condemnation of Angelo and, verbally adroit as usual, forgives him: "Well, Angelo, your evil quits you well: / Look that you love your wife; her worth worth yours." The only explanation the Duke offers for reversing his punishment of Angelo is that "I find an apt remission in myself," as if the Duke has just discovered in himself—and maybe he has—in addition to his love for Isabella, a still higher compassion within himself for offering pardon. All this happens so stunningly fast that the audience barely can take it all in, though perhaps one might say that the audience's astonishment at the Duke's behavior matches his own astonishment about what in that instant he learns himself.)

Arguing that "Like doth quit like, and Measure still for Measure," the Duke seemed to have based his moral judgment that Angelo should be executed on the ancient law of talion, a "death for a death," which he incorrectly rationalizes by citing the passage from The Gospel According to St. Matthew 7:2, the whole of which reads:

> *Judge not that ye be not judged. For with what judgment*
> *ye judge, ye shall be judged: and with what measure ye*
> *mete, it shall be measured to you again.* (1)

In making this argument, however, the Duke—is it unknowingly?—seems to be ignoring the first sentence in the St. Matthew passage, the sentence that reads, "Judge not that ye be not judged," and is acting only on the section of the biblical passage that follows, which is not really advice at all but ironic warning *not* to judge. Let us assume that the Duke does realize the implications of the entire biblical passage, its injunction against passing judgment; would that realization then explain why he forgives Angelo and perhaps had intended to forgive him throughout all the theatrics of feigning that Angelo be punished and executed? If this conjecture is correct, it would put the Duke in a more favorable (or more Christian) light, and perhaps that would mitigate or even remove the criticism we (and Isabella?) are likely to have of the Duke in causing the suffering of Isabella, Claudio, Mariana, and even Angelo for the purpose of finding a remedy for the fear of death, which is exactly what the Duke had tried to do for Claudio in his great speech midway through the play that begins, "Be absolute for death; either death or life / Shall thereby be the sweeter."

The motif of finding a "remedy" for injustice—or justice too strictly defined—in the face of the mournful awareness of death's power to undo the potential sweetness of life, is introduced early in the play in an exchange between Escalus and the Justice. Escalus bemoans Claudio's seemingly inescapable fate, "It grieves me the death of Claudio: but there's no remedy." The Justice replies, "Lord Angelo is severe," to which Escalus, ruling out the possibility of "mercy" or "pardon," reiterates, "there is no remedy." Shortly after this scene, Isabella asks Angelo about her brother, "must he needs die?" and Angelo succinctly responds, "Maiden, no remedy." Later, when Claudio asks Isabella what she can do to save him, "Is there no remedy?" her response is, "None, but such remedy, as to save a head / To cleave a heart in twain." One might interpret the conclusion of this play with its emphasis on mercy, pardon, and forgiveness as making the point that there is indeed a remedy in the morality of mercy: "Judge not that ye be not judged," but one would have to add on a darker note that it is not the morality of tolerance alone that makes possible the marriages at the conclusion of the play, but the brute fact that the Duke's power triumphs over

Angelo's power. A pessimist might well conclude that only power can defeat the abuse of power.

The Duke's exoneration of Claudio takes place almost in passing. He is "pardon'd" because, as Isabella's brother, he would, in a sense, also be the Duke's brother, should Isabella marry him. This claim of surrogate brotherhood is hardly persuasive as the basis for a legal decision, but it suffices for the Duke, one assumes on emotional grounds. The case of Lucio, however, is quite different, and it reveals an egoistic aspect of the Duke that needs to be taken into account in our, or Isabella's, estimate of him. Lucio, talking to the Duke when disguised as a Friar, has made insulting remarks about him, including accusations of stealing, lechery, and drunkenness; yet these criticisms are proffered in a somewhat positive context, though the Duke fails to perceive this. Lucio is the expositor of the humane position that people's natural inclinations need to be tolerated: lechery is a vice that "is impossible to extirp it quite, Friar, till eating and drinking be put down." And although Lucio goes on to say that the absent Duke "had some feeling for the sport" (of lechery), Lucio adds with approval that the Duke "knew the service, and that instructed him to mercy," and he is flatteringly accurate about the Duke's penchant for ruling with mercy. But when Lucio claims that the Duke "would be drunk too," the Duke testily replies, "You do him wrong, surely," and goes on to accuse Lucio of "malice," a questionable accusation. Lucio's response to this charge, however, seems forthright, "Sir, I know him, and I love him," but this will not satisfy the Duke who, always ready with an aphoristic phrase, wants unequivocal praise: "Love talks with better knowledge, and knowledge with dearer love."

In the final moments of the play, after proposing to Isabella and forgiving Angelo, the Duke turns to Lucio with overt anger as "one I cannot pardon." Why? Not because Lucio has attempted to commit murder as had Angelo, but because he has insulted the Duke. The Duke's response to Lucio does not even qualify as a "measure for measure" reckoning. With obvious oversensitivity, the Duke exaggerates Lucio's criticisms of him: "You, sirrah, that knew me for a fool, a coward, / One all of luxury, an ass, a madman," to which Lucio lightly replies, "'Faith, my lord, I spoke it but according to the trick," by which he means that he merely was following the fashion of insulting people behind their backs, surely a universal practice. Still half joshing and cajoling, cannily acknowledging the fact that someone in power can have his way whether fairly or not, Lucio adds: "If you will hang me for it, you may; but I had rather it please you I might be whipped." The Duke's response is excessive in its vehemence: "Whipp'd first, sir, and hanged after, / Proclaim it, provost, round about the city." This is another grand, theatrical gesture made by the Duke as public display, and, indeed, taken at face value, it reveals a sadistic aspect of his character. The Duke goes on to identify Lucio's crime, which is much like that of Claudio—fornicating with a woman and getting her with child: "I have heard him swear himself there's one / Whom he begot with child—let her appear, / And he shall marry her."

(There is an important distinction, however, between Claudio's sleeping with Juliet, whom he loved, and Lucio's sleeping with a "whore," but the Duke does not follow this with a distinction of his own as for whom marriage is suitable, nor does he claim that he is concerned with the welfare of the illegitimate child.)Rather, the Duke, in this vengeful mood, repeats his order: "the nuptial finish'd, / Let him be whipp'd and hang'd." But perhaps the Duke's intent here is only more theatrical display. No longer in a comic mode, Lucio's agonized response, "I beseech your highness, do not marry me to a whore," defers abjectly to the Duke's power. Although the Duke perseveres in the punishment of enforced matrimony he has allotted to Lucio, "Upon mine honor, thou shalt marry her," he suddenly and surprisingly (at least to those who behold the scene, including the now silent Isabella) pardons Lucio and rescinds the penalty of death: "Thy slanders I forgive; and therewithal / Remit thy other forfeits." It might well be that this is an outcome the Duke had in mind all along. Lucio, however, is not much relieved by this particular reprieve, and his reply expresses his dismay: "Marrying a punk [whore], my lord, is pressing to death, whipping and hanging." This attitude is not consistent with Lucio's earlier philosophy of tolerance; consistency, however, has not been much in evidence throughout this play. The Duke is not merely play-acting when he grimly responds, still showing the wound of injured pride, "Slandering a prince deserves it."

The Duke's brief but final words to Claudio, "She, Claudio, that you wrong'd, look you restore," are appropriate and apt in affirming marriage as a positive outcome in his case. And the Duke's final words to Angelo in which he touchingly and urgently repeats his injunction to Angelo to "love" Mariana, "Joy to you, Mariana! love her, Angelo," fall within the celebratory spirit of marriage, despite the skepticism the audience might have about the prospects of this marriage, given what we have seen of Angelo. Is this hopefulness on the part of the Duke in supporting this marriage an expression of the Duke's innate idealism, or is it merely the manifestation of a pragmatic and materialistic view of the benefits of legal matrimony? It might well appear to Isabella that the Duke's marrying Lucio to a whore does not speak favorably of any concept of marriage as a holy state of intimacy and love. Although *Measure for Measure* will (likely?) end with four marriages, as does *A Midsummer Night's Dream*, it lacks the earlier play's celebratory optimism which looks forward to producing healthy children and successful parenting. Despite all the lovers' vicissitudes in *A Midsummer Night's Dream*, the singing and the dancing at the end anticipate the procreation and nurturing of healthy children.

Unlike Prospero in *The Tempest*, the Duke does not relinquish his power at the play's end, and, also unlike Prospero, he has used his power to achieve dubious resolutions and dubious marriages. Although the play concludes with multiple forgivings and thanksgivings, the Duke, who makes no personal sacrifices during the play, is less like a god whose injunction is not to judge than the Hebrew Yahweh who tempts and puts on trial his human representatives, like Adam, or Abraham, or Moses, or Job. The play leaves us with profound uncertainty as to how we regard the god-like Duke, as when Yahweh—with a great rhetorical flourish which reveals nothing but which nevertheless betokens his unanswerable power—says to Moses, "I shall grant grace to whom I grant grace, and have compassion for whom I have compassion." (Exodus 33:19) (2) The estimate that we the audience will make of the Duke is highly speculative and depends on our interpretation of the play, but the estimate that Isabella will have to make of the Duke when she again finds her voice will impact on a momentous choice posed within the play itself. Will Isabella, who at first is drawn to the authority of the Church, find the authority of the Duke to be attractive and assuring? Is it likely that Isabella's extenuating response to Angelo—whom she might regard as the dark alter self of the Duke since they both have made sexual overtures toward her—suggest some deep-down proclivity to accept the Duke's advances? Does Isabella, who is quite eloquent herself, find the Duke's eloquence and articulate facility romantically, as well as intellectually, engaging even though he is uncharacteristically succinct, even blunt, in proposing marriage to her? Is she sufficiently in a pardoning mood herself to forgive the Duke for what might well be regarded as the gratuitous suffering he has caused her in order to test Angelo and make the point that power corrupts, that people are not always what they seem to be, that often they misjudge themselves and are therefore not equipped to judge each other? The Duke had soliloquized when earlier he heard Isabella approaching in order to

> . . . *come to know*
> *If yet her brother's pardon be come hither;*
> *But I will keep her ignorant of her good,*
> *To make her heavenly comforts of despair,*
> *When it is least expected.* (IV. iii. 115-119)

Should the Duke, after marriage, some domestic morning at breakfast, get around to explaining his motivation for the role he has played in her life to Isabella, would she approve the means, as well as the ends, of his good intentions? Or would she be dismayed by his presumption in having so manipulated her? So, given what we know about Isabella and about the Duke, can we predict whether she will accept his marriage proposal? Shakespeare challenges whatever presumption we might have to fathom the heart of the mystery of how, and out of what depth, human beings make their most significant choices.

CHAPTER FOUR

OTHELLO: INCREDULITY & THE POSSIBLE

I Incredible Reality

Othello is a play grounded on the theme of incredulity. It is virtually impossible for Othello to believe in the existence of evil for its own sake as depicted in the figure of Iago, and no one in the play, including Iago's sophisticated and skeptical wife, Emilia, believes that Iago is truly what he is: the Satanic embodiment of evil. When Emilia comes close to suspecting that some "eternal villain, / Some busy and insinuating rogue, / Some cogging, cozening slave, to get some office / Hath not devis'd this slander," Iago replies, ironically relishing how close she comes to identifying him: "Fie! there is no such man. It is impossible." Iago knows that he is exactly such a person (or demon), but that Emilia will not find his denial credible because she considers that the idea of a human being acting as the devil incarnate is "impossible." Iago further relishes his obfuscation on the word "man" saying that "there is no such man," since Iago does indeed think of himself as the devil, not as a man. This is how Iago has seen and characterized himself from the beginning of the play when he says to Roderigo, "I am not what I am," (his parody of Yahweh's statement to Moses, "I am that I am," when Moses asks Yahweh what to tell Pharaoh to assert his authority. Yahweh says to Moses: "Tell him [Pharaoh] I am sent you.") With his "I am not," Iago casts himself in the role as liar and negator, for a lie is a negation of what *is*. As Iago well knows, the devil is the father of lies and the master of disguises, and his best strategy is to persuade those he would manipulate and tempt that he does not exist.

Just as Iago is incredible for his evil, too extreme to seem possible, so, too, is Desdemona equally incredible for her goodness. The tragic conclusion of the play, Othello's murdering of Desdemona, is the result, finally, of Othello's inability to believe in her goodness, as much as it is his failure to believe in Iago's malignancy. Either realization, of extreme goodness or extreme evil, could have saved him. As Emilia comes close to comprehending Iago's Satanic nature, so, too, Othello, even when distraught and tempted by Iago's version of Desdemona as unfaithful and perfidious, has sufficient understanding of Desdemona's virtue, if only he could choose to commit himself to the reality of that understanding:

> *'Tis not to make me jealous*
> *To say my wife is fair, feeds well, loves company,*
> *Is free of speech, sings, plays, and dances well.*
> *Where virtue is, these are more virtuous.* (III. iii. 183-186)

Othello is worldly enough to realize that Desdemona's falling in love with him was not within the realm of social expectation in Venetian society. He is older than she, of another race, another culture, another class. The challenge to Othello's identity is that he must believe and trust in love that is exceptional; he must give credence to Desdemona's angelic nature. Under the influence of Iago, this is exactly what Othello fails to do. In judging Othello, however, we must remind ourselves over and over that no one in the play sees Iago as anything other than "honest." Only under the extreme circumstances of being manipulated by Iago is Othello reduced to such degrading and deluded jealousy.

The pervasive emotion of this play is jealousy, an extreme form in Othello's case. We see jealousy in its many guises of distorted credulity in other characters besides Othello, such as Brabantio and Iago. No writer has ever probed its dark recesses as deeply as Shakespeare. It must be recognized that jealousy is not an aberrant or freakish state of mind; rather, it is universal and is to be found in all human societies and always related both to lying and to self-deception. Only the extreme—ironically in this most ironic play—when jealously turns murderous and defeats its evolutionary purpose of assuring that a male's offspring are indeed his own, is it unusual. Jealously in its ubiquitous aspect must be understood as an adaptive behavior, stressful and risky, but serving a purpose, since males who are not sexually protective of their mates will not get their genes into the gene pool. This is a basic evolutionary premise and one of its fundamental manifestations, as articulated by David Buss in *The Evolution of Desire* (1), is that "Cuckolded men are universal objects of derision." Othello's own Darwinian wisdom is explicit when he envisions himself as just such an eternal type, the cuckold:

> *But, alas!, to make me*
> *A fixed figure for the time of scorn*
> *To point his slow unmoving finger at!*
> *Yet I could bear that too. Well! very well!*
> *But there, where I have garner'd up my heart,*
> *Where I must live or bear no life;*
> *The fountain from the which my current runs*
> *Or else dries up . . .* (IV. ii. 52-59)

As cuckold, so the deluded Othello further speculates, no children of his own will succeed him, he will "bear no life," and the fountain of his love for Desdemona, the natural concomitant of his sexuality, will prove fruitless. The "fountain" of his potential fecundity, so he dreads, will dry up, and he will be barren. He will fail in the first and most Darwinian of all the biblical commandments to be "fruitful and multiply." (2)

Othello is not alone in failing to believe in Desdemona for what truly she is; so, too, her father, Brabantio, cannot understand her virtue. He perceives her as a betrayer of his fatherly love or as having been deluded by what he assumes is Othello's black magic. The idea of Desdemona's falling in love with Othello or finding him sexually attractive belongs also for Brabantio in the category of the "impossible." He sees her new allegiance to Othello as a "treason of the blood," and bluntly says to him, his former friend, that "such a thing as thou—to fear not to delight." Roderigo is still another character persuaded by the stereotype that Iago puts forth that would see Desdemona as susceptible to changeability and lust as any other woman who married an older man: "She must change for youth. When she is sated with his body, she will find the error of her choice." And even Emilia assumes that any woman would betray her husband if the advantage were great enough: "who would not make her husband a cuckold to make him a monarch? I would venture purgatory for't." That Desdemona does not fall into the category of such temptable worldly behavior, commonly understood, is truly remarkable, yes, even incredible.

II Marriages & Divorces

The main structural device by means of which Shakespeare organizes the plot of this play is to be found in the establishment of a pattern of marriages or commitments and divorces or the breaking of previous commitments. To recognize this, one must take the idea of marriage and divorce in a symbolic or emotional sense, not merely in a literal sense, and keep in mind that commitment is a form of credulity in the possibility of truth and faithfulness. For example, Desdemona's marriage to Othello is regarded by her father Brabantio as a betrayal, with all the sexual innuendo that betrayal implies. "O, she deceives me / Past thought," cries Brabantio, as if Desdemona's primary commitment were to her father and should continue to be so. Desdemona understands clearly that it is not unusual for a father and his daughter's husband to be natural rivals, and she makes this point to Brabantio in trying to explain to him why her primary loyalty must now be to her husband, Othello:

> *But here's my husband;*
> *And so much duty as my mother show'd*
> *To you, preferring you before her father,*
> *So much I challenge that I may profess*
> *Due to the Moor my lord.* (I. iii. 185-189)

Unlike Ophelia, who does not have the strength to assert her own independence and remains obedient to her father, Polonius, thus betraying Hamlet who truly loves her and has pledged himself to her, Desdemona is both courageous and forthright in making a mature marital choice based on love. It will prove to be cruelly ironic that Brabantio's words to Othello, "Look to her, Moor, if thou hast eyes to see: / She has deceived her father, and may thee," false though they are, will come to be believed by Othello when Desdemona's innocence is no longer credible to him.

Othello marries Desdemona, both literally and emotionally in the sense that they reciprocally love one another. Othello testifies before the Duke that "She lov'd me for the dangers I had pass'd. / And I lov'd her that she did pity them." (The word "pity," as Othello uses it, means to empathize or identify with.) And Desdemona's testimony, likewise, emphasizes the depth of her love for Othello when she says that "I saw Othello's visage in his mind, / And to his honors and his valiant parts / Did I my soul and fortunes consecrate." In this play about true and false seeing, Desdemona asserts that she sees beneath Othello's appearance into the quality of his "mind." Desdemona's love for Othello is of both soul and body as is clear when she acknowledges "the palate of my appetite" in requesting to be given permission to go to war with Othello so that she is not bereft "of the rites for which I love him." Their love is balanced and complete, both of the body and the mind, before Iago subverts it.

Iago will bring about the separation and, in effect, the divorce of Othello and Desdemona, and in a shocking scene, Iago will completely replace Desdemona in Othello's heart with himself. Shakespeare dramatizes this shift in commitment by depicting what, symbolically, is a marriage ceremony between Othello and Iago in which the passion of love is replaced by the passion of "wide revenge," a passion that has been spawned by Othello's jealousy. Othello kneels and makes this pledge: "Now by yond marble heaven, / In due reverence of a sacred vow / I here engage my words." The sacred vow of marriage, made in the eyes of heaven, is hereby superseded by an antithetical "vow" of an unseeing and uncaring "marble heaven." Never missing an opportunity, Iago kneels down beside Othello and improvises from the vow Othello has just made the further implications of a marital commitment based on Iago's swearing "to obey":

> *Iago doth give up*
> *The execution of his wit, hands, heart,*
> *To wrong'd Othello's service! Let him command,*
> *And to obey shall be in me remorse,*
> *What bloody work soever.* (III. iii. 465-469)

The word "execution" is either a Freudian slip or a touch of Iago's delight in irony, but the vow binding Othello and Iago is consecrated in a pledge of "blood," which for Othello has now usurped the meaning of his marital love.

"I greet thy love," says Othello, and he goes on to replace the marital hope of bringing forth new life with his request to Iago about how to kill Desdemona, that you "furnish me with some swift means of death." Iago's reply, "I am your own for ever," which ends the scene, completes the black parody of marriage, as Iago's ironic remark echoes the traditional marriage ceremony, "I now pronounce you man and wife." The dying Othello will attempt to remarry Desdemona, to restore her earlier credibility; but before that desperate and belated attempt occurs, Emilia, in effect, will divorce Iago and symbolically marry Desdemona.

After Othello strangles Desdemona, Emilia comes upon the scene and asks, "O! who has done this deed?" Desdemona replies: "Nobody. I myself. Farewell! / Commend me to my kind lord. O farewell!" This is a baffling moment as incredible as any in the entire play. There are several ways, all uncertain, that it might be interpreted. "Nobody," in some clairvoyant sense possessed by Desdemona in her dying moment, might quite accurately refer to Iago in his "I am not" aspect. "I myself," might refer to Desdemona's own minor culpability, for which she now assumes excessive responsibility, in having evaded Othello's questioning her about the whereabouts of the handkerchief when she said "it is not lost," and then in replying to Othello's "Fetch't, let me see't," with uncharacteristic evasiveness: "Why, so I can sir, but I will not now." Even Desdemona can be tainted by Iago's insinuating spirit of prevarication. But unlike Othello's false indictment of Desdemona, she will not allow herself to be more deeply tainted by blaming or becoming defensively hostile to Othello, and so she tells Emilia: "I find I had suborn'd the witness, / And he's indicted falsely." In this spirit of refusing to judge Othello, Desdemona speaks her final words, "Commend me to my kind lord." On a literal level it is, of course, not true that Othello has proven to be "kind," but Desdemona continues to see him with her mind's eye, as ideally as she did when earlier she declared: "I saw Othello's visage in his mind." In doing so, Desdemona maintains her own virtuous identity which subsumes her own incredulity in the face of Othello's moral culpability.

Othello, for an instant, thinking that he can use Desdemona's words to exculpate himself, says to Emilia, "You heard her say herself it was not I," to which Emilia dryly and skeptically replies, "She said so. I must needs report a truth." And from this point until her death, the word "truth" becomes Emilia's mantra and obsession. The word "truth" stings Othello into withdrawing his false claim that he did not kill Desdemona, and, still blaming her, he cannot yet truly condemn himself: "She's like a liar gone to burning hell. / 'Twas I that killed her." Emilia, however, judges Desdemona accurately as "the more angel she," and continues to assert "O she was heavenly true," as the word "true" echoes throughout the room. "Thy husband knew it all," retorts Othello, and with Emilia's incredulous, "My husband!" the divorce between Iago and Emilia moves toward completion.

Her incredulity is sustained through four reiterations of her astonished, "My husband!" culminating in Emilia's devastating realization in her accusation of Iago: "You told a lie, an odious damned lie." For Emilia, all morality and meaning now hangs between the poles of truth and lying. She is further appalled to acknowledge that earlier she had suspected that Iago was a liar. "I thought so then," Emilia says, acknowledging that previously repressed truth. But such repression or denial, at some level, occurs in all the characters in this play in their believing (or wishing) that Iago is "honest." No one wants to believe in the existence of the devil. When Iago commands Emilia, "get you home," Emilia disobeys, yet with a final acknowledgment of the gravity of her now broken marriage bond, "'Tis proper I obey him, but not now. / Perchance Iago, I will ne'er go home." These are immensely moving lines, and they conclude the separation between Iago and Emilia whose consummating wish now is to be placed beside Desdemona on her wedding bed. Emilia's culminating choice is thus to be wedded both to Desdemona and to the ultimate value of telling the truth on which belief must be based. Just before Othello strangled Desdemona she had sung the lugubrious willow song, and at the moment of her own death, Emilia reprises the same song, "Willow, willow, willow," which had expressed Desdemona's grief in facing an incomprehensible death as the result of losing her husband through jealous violence. Worldly Emilia, skeptical about marital relationships, now emulates the idealism and divinity of her mistress Desdemona and achieves "bliss" in death by becoming an apostle of the truth: "So come my soul to bliss as I speak true. / So speaking as I think, I die, I die." The split between what is true and what is falsely spoken, Iago's mode of manipulation, is healed in the unlikely figure of Emilia.

III Iago's Motivations

There are several ways to interpret what motives drive Iago's behavior, and they all have some degree of plausibility without excluding the validity of the others. All of them, I want to suggest, must be considered partially true, and the reader must hold them all in mind simultaneously in ongoing speculation. In general, one might say that Iago is offended by any faith or belief he cannot share. Only disbelief, ironically, seems credible to him. On the most immediate level, however, Iago can be seen in sibling rivalry with Cassio, rivalry that flames into jealousy toward Cassio (whom Iago will later plot to kill) and in resentment toward Othello, who is placed in the role of surrogate father to Iago when Othello selects Cassio as his lieutenant over Iago. Such ordinary jealousy is common enough, and it introduces jealousy as the emotion that will pervade the play and find its extreme in the tormented Othello. Iago's explanation to Roderigo of his own motivation to revenge himself on Othello is that although his "mediators" preferred him, Othello unreasonably and unfairly chose Cassio although Cassio "never set a squadron in the field." Iago complains about Othello's favoritism and professional military prejudice when he says, "'Tis the curse of service. / Preferment goes by letter and affection, / And not by old gradation," by which Iago means seniority and duration of service. There is no reason at this point in the play for either Roderigo or the audience to doubt Iago's explanation which, on the surface, seems plausible. Everyone is familiar with such social prejudice and unfair discrimination.

Iago's self-revelation, however, is more problematic when he bases his claim for honesty in confessing to Roderigo that "I follow him [Othello] to serve my turn upon him." In other words, to acknowledge selfishness—so Iago assumes and Roderigo accepts the assumption—is not only proof of one's veracity, but also, more remarkably, a sign of one's singular merit. Iago develops this line of thought in extolling the type of people who, loving themselves:

> Keep yet their hearts attending on themselves,
> And throwing but shows of service on their lords,
> Do well thrive by 'em, and when they have lin'd their coats
> Do themselves homage. Those fellows have some soul,
> And such a one do I profess myself. (I. i. 51-55)

Although the motive of competitive jealousy is credible, Iago's praise of serving one's own interest might well have given Roderigo pause to worry whether Iago is applying the same principle in manipulating him. And it should have been even more worrisome to Roderigo when Iago reverses the concept of "soul," which usually implies some form of virtue in caring for others, to mean exactly the opposite: fellows with soul, according to Iago, are those who act only in their own behalf. Ordinary competitive jealousy may indeed be animating Iago's behavior and speech, but a more alert Roderigo (a Roderigo less blinded by lust for Desdemona) might well have been aware that Iago is talking tautological nonsense when he says: "It is as sure as you are Roderigo, / Were I the Moor, I would not be Iago." Already we see that Iago's identity (or non-identity as his above statement implies) contains something more complex than ordinary jealousy. Roderigo is only the first of the characters who are successfully deceived by Iago.

Beyond Iago's sibling-like jealousy toward Cassio, Iago's contempt and hostility toward Othello is apparent in his opening description of Othello as someone who, "loving his own pride and purposes, / Evades them with a bombast circumstance / Horribly stuff'd with epithets of war." Iago's description will prove to have some truth to it; and the efficacy of Iago's power to manipulate others, we will come to see, resides in Iago's capacity to understand both the strengths and the weaknesses of other people. The devil, incarnate as Iago, turns out to be a perspicacious psychologist. Very quickly it will become apparent that Iago's antipathy toward Othello is motivated by more than resentment for having been passed over in favor of Cassio. Iago's hatred seems inextricably bound up with Iago's depiction of Othello's sexuality in animal terms, as when he calls to Brabantio, "an old black ram / Is tupping your white ewe," and then again, "your daughter and the Moor are now making the beast with two backs." Iago's wish to revenge himself on Othello, even before a plan has been formulated, thus has an explicit sexual content: he wants to see Othello cuckolded; he wants to see his belief in human infidelity confirmed. He says to Roderigo: "I hate the Moor. My cause is hearted: thine hath no less reason. Let us be conjunctive in our revenge against him. If thou can'st cuckold him, thou dost thyself a pleasure, me a sport." Iago's plot to have Roderigo commit adultery with Desdemona and thereby cuckold Othello may well be a projection of Iago's own repressed wish to have sex with Desdemona. The plot itself is basically a fantasy since Iago knows that Desdemona would never dally with the pathetic Roderigo, and, as we shall see, Iago's plotting is often based on his own extreme fantasies and his disbelief in any human capacity for selflessness or altruism.

The soliloquy that follows the scene where Iago coaches Roderigo on how to woo Desdemona reveals such an overheated sexual fantasy. Iago reiterates his hatred of Othello, but goes on to say:

> *I hate the Moor,*
> *And it is thought abroad that 'twixt my sheets*
> *He's done my office. I know not if 't be true,*
> *But I, for mere suspicion in that kind,*
> *Will do as if for surety.* (I. iii. 385-389)

Iago's perverse ability to fantasize seriously and, at the same time, to know that he is fantasizing, places him again in the realm of "I am not what I am," the realm of negative being. His obsession with sexuality, however, is clear enough, and, like a voyeur, he seems even to enjoy in his perfervid imagination watching himself being cuckolded. Othello is a figure of authority, older than Iago by a generation, a surrogate father who has rejected his son and slept, so Iago chooses to suspect, with his wife, and, in turn, Iago wants "To get his place," by bringing down the powerful totem (as sexual animal) father. And thus a plot is concocted to destroy Othello by undermining his sexual dominance, both in reality and in fantasy—a fantasy which expands from Iago's projected imagining of his sleeping with Desdemona and Othello's sleeping with Emilia. Iago's fantasy extends to an even more extreme form in which, in effect, he has sex with himself and creates—"I have't! it is engendered"—his own reality, which he aptly describes as a "monstrous birth." The image of what is "monstrous" will be repeated and developed throughout the play.

Iago's Oedipal overthrow of Othello, which includes the fantasy of sleeping with his young wife, Desdemona, has still another dimension (as in the reverse Oedipus complex) in which Iago identifies with a fanta-sized Desdemona and competes with the actual Desdemona for the love of Othello. In this formulation, Iago then feels doubly betrayed by Othello when Othello marries Desdemona, and Iago's jealousy thereby is further exacerbated. This multiple Oedipal aspect of Iago's complex of fantasies is revealed by Shakespeare when Iago recounts to Othello a supposed experi-ence with Cassio:

> *I lay with Cassio lately;*
> *And, being troubled with a raging tooth,*
> *I could not sleep.*
> *There are a kind of men so loose of soul*
> *That in their sleep will mutter their affairs.*
> *One of this kind is Cassio.*
> *In sleep I heard him say, "Sweet Desdemona,*
> *Let us be wary, let us hide our loves!"*
> *And then, sir, would he gripe and wring my hand,*

Cry out "Sweet creature!" and then kiss me hard,
As if he pluck'd up kisses by the roots
That grew upon my lips; then laid his leg
Over my thigh, and sigh'd and kiss'd; and then
Cried, "cursed fate, that gave thee to the Moor."(III. iii. 413-426)

Iago has surely invented this episode with Cassio, and thus what is expressed therein reveals nothing about Cassio, but much about Iago. In this scene, Iago, in a state of agitated desire, expressed symbolically by his "raging tooth," casts himself as Desdemona who willingly commits adultery, according thus to Iago's own wish, since this is really Iago's dream. With an even more subtle dream displacement, Iago also identifies with Cassio, who has replaced Othello, and not only has sex with Desdemona, but also with himself, just as previously his own mind "engendered" a monster entirely of his own making. Othello's response to Iago's recounting of Cassio's supposed dream is a horrified, "O monstrous! monstrous!" which recalls Iago's description of his "monstrous birth." To Iago's phony objection, "Nay, this was but a dream," Othello replies, "But this denoted a foregone conclusion." Othello is correct in detecting some deep causation here, but the causation as assumed by Othello is misplaced, for the "foregone conclusion" derives not from any reality about the inevitable consequences of human lust (from which Desdemona is an "incredible" exception) but from the hellish region of Iago's fantasies and negating spirit.

A further possibility (again in the realm of necessary speculation) is that Iago's obsession with lustful sexuality, his inability to imagine love which he can only see as lust, derives from Iago's sexual incompetence. Although in two early soliloquies Iago had assumed that he had been cuckolded by Othello and that he would take that "mere suspicion" as a certainty, and that, repeating this same thought, he claims that he did "suspect the lusty Moor / Hath leap'd into my seat," it is later revealed, in a conversation with Emilia, that this is more than "mere suspicion." Emilia boldly asserts to Iago that "Some such squire he was / That turn'd your wit the seamy side without, / And made you to suspect me with the Moor." It is surely possible that someone with such sexual insecurity, whose fantasies of being cuckolded are so unlikely and so far-fetched, is deficient in sexual capacity and probably impotent. We need to keep in mind as well that Iago had remarked "For I fear Cassio with my nightcap too," though it is also possible that Iago, enjoying his own evil machinations, says this with a comic flourish.

The result of Iago's incapacity could well be a hatred of women, which he continuously exhibits, since women are the primary cause of his humiliation. Desdemona shows stunning insight when, after listening to Iago recite his misogynist poem early in Act II, she exclaims "O most lame and impotent conclusion!" And, true to his degraded view of women, Iago's penultimate words to his wife, Emilia, are to call her a "Villainous whore!" In Iago's eyes, all women are promiscuous, creatures driven by lust whose claims of innocence cannot be found credible. When Othello tells Iago that he intends to kill Desdemona with poison, Iago revealingly suggests an alternative: "Do it not with poison. Strangle her in her bed, even the bed she hath contaminated." Clearly, strangulation is more sexually suggestive than poisoning, as if it were the extension of an embrace, the demonic consummation of sexual passion. Again, there is something voyeuristic in Iago's suggestion as if Othello's killing of Desdemona would enact Iago's perverse projection of himself as her murderous lover.

Finally, despite the possibility of his having human motives and unconscious drives, we must also consider the possibility that Iago truly is the devil, who, therefore, cannot be understood in terms of even the most complex patterns of human behavior and unconscious drives and impulses. As devil, either he improvises or creates his own motivation as he goes along, as suggested by Coleridge's "motiveless malignancy" or else he destroys only for the sake of destruction or negates only for the sake of negation, which carries him beyond even the most vicious forms of sadism. Iago does not have in mind any personal ambition or gain: he ceases to think about being promoted and, although he enjoys manipulating money, he does not show any real interest in becoming wealthy. He makes no attempt to seduce Desdemona, but only projects such a wish onto Roderigo as "sport." He is, rather, best explained by Emilia's analysis of jealous souls: "They are not jealous for the cause, but jealous for they are jealous. 'Tis a monster / Begot upon itself, born on itself." This depiction of "jealous souls" as creating their own motivation coincides with Iago's imagery of self-engendering. Iago thus may represent some cosmic principal of the potentiality for destructiveness in the very structure of the universe, a destructiveness that takes the form of jealousy when it comes to human affairs and negativity for its own sake. Although the play is ostensibly about Othello's jealousy, on a metaphysical level of abstraction it is about the unbounded capacity for jealously as symbolized by Iago, a jealously so vast that it staggers everyone's imagination, including incredulous playgoers.

Iago not only sees himself as the devil, but he even delights in seeing himself as such, the delight reinforcing his own concept of the diabolic.

While improvising the "net" that he believes "will ensnare them all," Iago exults, "By the mass, 'tis morning: / Pleasure and action make the hours seem short." At the play's end, when Othello fully realizes Iago's villainy, incredible though it still seems, Othello declares: "I look down towards his feet, but that's a fable. / If that thou be'st a devil, I cannot kill thee." Iago, with smirking irony which nevertheless confirms Othello's speculation, replies, "I bleed, sir, but not killed." What Iago is saying is that since he is indeed a devil it is true that Othello cannot kill him. Iago's final line, "From this time forth I never will speak word" is fitting in that all Iago's lying should end in a kind of inchoate silence as if he will now vanish back into the void from whence he came, leaving us with uncertain knowledge, "What you know, you know," in a final state of tremulous disbelief. Whatever that knowledge might be remains undisclosed, and any explanations we might have to elucidate Iago's being or his behavior must remain, so Shakespeare will have it, in the realm of our enlarged and apprehensive speculation.

IV The Genesis of Lying

In his introduction to Richard Dawkins' *The Selfish Gene*, which propounds the basic tenets of modern Darwinism, Robert Trivers offers the following insight into the nature of deception:

> *If* [as Dawkins argues] *deceit is fundamental to animal communication, then there must be strong selection to spot deception and this ought, in turn, to select for a degree of self-deception, rendering some facts and motives unconscious so as not to betray— by the public signs of self-knowledge—the deception being practiced.* (3)

The implications of this insight in respect to the relationship between men and women is enormous. Given the fact, as Dawkins says, "that the sex cells or 'gametes' of males are much smaller and more numerous than the gametes of females," it inevitably follows that the optimal strategy of males in getting their genes into the gene pool is to mate with as many females as possible. Males of all species do this by persuading females of their own fitness or status and by false advertising or deception whenever necessary. Females, in response, inevitably evolve the ability to detect such deception for the good of their own genetic offspring; then, of course, males have to get better at lying and females better at detecting lying, and thus an ongoing battle of the sexes forevermore characterizes one significant aspect of the relationship between men and women.

The complexity of mendacity, as articulated by Dawkins and Trivers, is grim in its social implications in that male deception of females is made more effective by the male's lying to himself in order to appear sincere and thus be more persuasive. Thus, if a man convinces himself that he is indeed in love with a woman, he is more likely to convince her as well in the articulation of his vows that he will be faithful to her and a good providing father for her children. The repression of doubts and reservations into the unconscious mind creates a split in the psyche in which one part of the self is hidden from the other. Such a split helps define a central aspect of Freudian thought and its depiction of the mind as an arena of conflict. Troubling as this is, self-deception can be even more harmful when serving aggressive and hostile emotions in addition to amorous ones, as is the case with Othello.

Although jealousy within limits, natural as it is, can serve to keep a couple attentive to each other, when those limits are exceeded and broken by misjudgment which leads to further self-deception and lying, jealousy can destroy the very relationship that it is designed by evolution to preserve. Iago then, in the Darwinian sense, seems to be the force that drives nature to defeat its own purposes. For this reason, we see Iago truly as unnatural; yet, given Shakespeare's paradoxical understanding of human morality and behavior, we must contemplate the unnatural as an aspect of the natural or as intersecting with it and affecting it.

V Divided Othello

Othello is another of Shakespeare's many characters who are represented as having split or divided selves with Iago as the demonic underside within Othello's own makeup. Hamlet, for example, acknowledges that one part of himself is mad, and he tries to disassociate himself from that part as if it were not an aspect of his own real identity. He says to Laertes:

> *If Hamlet from himself be ta'en away,*
> *And when he's not himself does wrong Laertes,*
> *Then Hamlet does it not; Hamlet denies it.*
> *Who does it then? His madness. If 't be so,*
> *Hamlet is of the faction that is wrong'd;*
> *His madness is poor Hamlet's enemy.* (V. ii. 238-243)

Hamlet paradoxically acknowledges (and apologizes for) his madness by disowning it as representative of his chosen self and his consciously and freely proclaimed identity. Hamlet regards himself as the person who chooses not to be a particular aspect of who he is. Like all the heroes in Shakespeare, he is in conflict with himself; and thus, his ultimately chosen identity must be the result partly of self-abnegation and, largely, of self-mastery. Othello, likewise, is composed of antithetical selves, his warrior self, based on a capacity for aggression, and the self that expresses its passions through loving.

From the very beginning Othello identifies himself in two ways: as a soldier servant to the state, "my services which I have done the Signory," and as a lover who thus "consecrates" his heart. As he says unabashedly to Iago, "I love the gentle Desdemona." These are the qualities of Othello's choice of who he wishes to be, and he seems fully capable of realizing both aspects of himself in being true to this chosen identity. Yet the stories that Othello tells to Desdemona that represent his past and his origin are mainly about war and adventure, and they contain a strong element of the fantastic as in his account of the "men whose heads / Do grow beneath their shoulders." We are given a hint of Othello's capacity for superstition and mythic belief. Iago with some accuracy describes Othello's wooing Desdemona as "bragging and telling her fantastic lies." Yet Iago is also right in describing Othello elsewhere as having "a constant, noble, loving nature; / And I dare think he'll prove to Desdemona / A most dear husband." Both depictions are true. For all his self-control, however, when confronted with disruption in the streets, Othello cries out with more self-revelation than he intends as he threatens immediate violence:

> My blood begins my safer guides to rule,
> And passion, having my best judgment collied,
> Assays to lead the way. Zounds! If I stir,
> Or do but lift this arm, the best of you
> Shall sink in my rebuke. (II. iii. 206-210)

Othello knows well what passions tempt him; therefore, it is somewhat surprising that he is so quick to leap to precipitate judgments as he does when he challenges the authorities to "let your sentence / fall upon my life" if his testimony about how he wooed Desdemona proves untrue, and then when he peremptorily discharges Cassio: "Cassio, I love thee; / But never more be officer of mine." Such a judgment is too absolute, and it discounts the mitigating factors of his love for Cassio and Cassio's previous loyal service. In this action we can see anticipated the extremity of Othello's judgment of Desdemona. Othello, it turns out, cannot tolerate ambivalence, delay, or uncertainty; he cannot tolerate his own divided feelings that are nevertheless inherent in his own divided self, so he seeks immediate and complete resolution and relief. Although he claims that he requires proof, it is really the irresolution of doubts that drives him into the murderous passion that at this crucial moment is beyond his control.

The split within Othello also can be regarded as a doubleness between Othello as he chooses himself to be and as he allows the Iago principle that lurks within him to dominate. The Hebrew Bible describes the serpent, the father of lies, as the "most subtle beast of the field that the lord God had made," and it is strongly implied by the biblical text's emphasis that the serpent is God's own creation, an aspect of the God who created him. So, too, is the Satanic aspect of Iago, his hateful "I am not," the negative echo of Othello's identity as a lover. Again and again, Shakespeare has Othello echo Iago and Iago echo Othello, so that at times one can hardly tell their voices apart. "By heaven, he echoes me," says Othello of Iago, "As if there were some monster in his thought / Too hideous to be shown." But the monster, Iago's insinuating words, is now in Othello's thoughts, a monster that does not readily show itself as such. At the play's conclusion, Othello will have to kill this monster, this Satanic rebel against civilized order, this precipitator of chaos within himself. Suicide, paradoxically, will be the only way for Othello to heal the wound that he has become. The final devastating echo of Iago comes when Lodovico and others enter the room where Iago is now held prisoner, and look for the killer of Desdemona: "Where is this rash and unfortunate man?" Othello replies in identifying himself: "That's he that was Othello. Here I am." Othello's "I am" echoes Iago's earlier "I am not"; his present being is denoted now as an Othello who no longer exists. Othello has become the absence of himself, merely a negation.

Particularly excruciating is the fact that Othello really knows enough about himself and Desdemona to remain true to their love for one another despite the Iago within him who is unknown to him as one's unconscious mind is unknown. It is not likely that anyone other than the devil could ensnare Othello and Desdemona in a fatal "net" of jealousy and mistrust, an extreme irony that Othello himself expresses, without realizing the accuracy of his prophetic remark: "Perdition catch my soul / But I do love thee! and when I love thee not, / Chaos is come again." What Othello knows with sufficient certainty is that his love for Desdemona, incredible as it may seem, carries an ultimate meaning; what he does not know in this hypothetical comment of the moment is the full reality that chaos surely will come if he is not true to his professed love for her. And chaos does indeed come again when, almost immediately after killing Desdemona, he says: "Methinks it should be now a huge eclipse / Of sun and moon, and the affrighted globe / Should yawn at alteration."

The failure of self-knowledge, Othello's capacity for denial and self-deception is subtly but surely depicted by Shakespeare in Othello's misinterpretation of the symbolism of the handkerchief, given to him by his mother and therefore precious to him. What Othello represses, or does not realize, is that the handkerchief represents a warning against male infidelity, not against female infidelity, as Othello assumes. In Othello's recounting of his mother's being given the handkerchief by an Egyptian woman, his mother is assured that "while she kept it, / 'Twould make her amiable and subdue my father / Entirely to her love." The danger of infidelity, as it is here expressed, derives from male, not female, unfaithfulness. Othello does not realize that he, not Desdemona, may be the source of violation in their marriage. And indeed Othello is the one who proves to be unfaithful, but not in the way ordinarily imagined in which the male seeks sex with another woman. Rather, in this extraordinary case, Othello betrays Desdemona by "marrying" Iago as we have seen earlier in Act III, Scene II as if marrying the devil were not in itself incredible. In warning Desdemona that his mother "dying gave it me; / And bid me, when my fate would have me wive, / To give it her," Othello completely misses the point that just as the handkerchief was originally meant to keep his father faithful, its meaning and import must now appropriately apply to him. His feverish carelessness causes him to drop it, for it to be found by Emilia, who then gives it to Iago against her own better judgment. When Othello, trying to intimidate Desdemona, claims that "There's magic in the web of it" and that a sibyl "In her prophetic fury sew'd the work," he determines the very fate and future that he was trying desperately to avoid.

In Othello's final speech before he commits suicide, he describes himself as "one not easily jealous," and, strangely, this is both true and false at the same time. Were Iago, with the most dubious and incredible of motivations, not determined to destroy Othello, it is most unlikely that Othello would have descended into murderous jealousy. Surely, Desdemona never would have given him "cause." And yet, there was something in Othello, some strange insecurity, perhaps like Iago's fear of impotence or perhaps some vulnerability inherent in all males because of their universal dread of being cuckolded, that made Othello susceptible to Iago's insinuations and temptations. Only when Othello's self-confidence is damaged does he become aware of his blackness and his age as marital impediments.

At the very end Othello tearfully reviews his past in the full realization of his monstrous misjudgment of Desdemona and her infinite worth, and then, in a kind of trance, as if wishing he might have the final word about himself, he says:

> *Set you down this;*
> *And say besides that in Aleppo once,*
> *Where a malignant and a turban'd Turk*
> *Beat a Venetian and traduc'd the state,*
> *I took by the throat the circumcised dog,*
> *And smote him thus.* (V. ii. 351-356)

Just as Hamlet splits himself into two parts, sane and mad, so, too, Othello splits himself into servant of civilized values and enemy of the state. To be true to his sense of himself as loyal to civilization and its values of love and duty, Othello must destroy the enemy self within him, which he does by committing suicide. He kills himself to rescue his sense of himself and restore his chosen identity. His madly rationalized cause in killing Desdemona so that she will not betray more men is converted into his final cause of defending the state against himself. In describing the Turkish enemy as "circumcised," he also reaffirms his sense of himself as a Christian with the implication of Christianity's belief in the final victory over Satan and death, and beneath that religious meaning lies the implication of Othello's sexual potency restored in his imagination.

VI Cause & Causation

Everyone in this play professes to have a "cause." The theme is first introduced somewhat casually with Brabantio's remark: "Mine's not an idle cause." What Brabantio means by "cause" is that he has sufficient justification in accusing Othello of wooing his daughter with "black magic" and requesting that the authorities return her to him. Soon after, the theme is picked up with Othello's "little shall I grace my cause / In speaking for myself," in which he uses the term much as did Brabantio to express self-justification. When Iago, speaking to Roderigo, says "My cause is hearted: thine hath no less reason," he, too, is talking in the language in which a claim is being made to vindicate one's intent as the basis for choice of one's behavior. Even Desdemona uses the concept of cause in this way when she says to Cassio, referring to Cassio's attempt to be restored into the graces of Othello, with cheering words to assure him of her support; "Therefore

cause

be merry, Cassio; / For thy solicitor shall rather die / Than give thy cause away." Later she will tell Emilia that nothing she ever did can in her mind explain Othello's jealous behavior: "Alas the day," says Desdemona, "I never gave him cause." But when Emilia responds, "But jealous souls will not be answered so. / They are not jealous for the cause, / But jealous for they are jealous," the concept of cause as the legitimate explanation for behavior becomes more dubious and complex. Cause and causation cease to be definitively linked as each character's claim of having a cause is revealed as a form of possessing some element of rationalization, and this disjunction heightens the play's overriding sense of incredulity.

The culmination of this theme comes in Othello's speech just before he goes into Desdemona's bedroom to kill her, which begins: "It is the cause, it is the cause, my soul. Let me not name it to you, you chaste stars! / It is the cause." Othello imagines here that he is simply the medium through which divinity enacts its own cause of punishing sexual infidelity, as if somehow his killing of Desdemona is impersonal and not his own choice. Since Othello, in a state of extreme self-deception, now believes that this is a cause written in the cosmos itself, as represented by the "chaste stars," the cause carries with it the connotation of fate or destiny, thus removing the ordinary sense of Othello as free to make a choice of his own for which he can be held responsible. His comment, "Yet she must die, else she'll betray more men," reveals Othello at his worst as a blinded rationalizer, and this pathetic rationalization cannot conceal the arrogance of Othello's electing to act in the name of cosmic fate when he, unconsciously so it seems, parodies God's "Let there be light," with his, "Put out the light." Yet even at this moment of self-delusion, Othello realizes that this is not "destiny unshunnable, like death" (as he claimed earlier about the inevitability of women cuckolding men) and that he might still be compelled to make a choice later "should I repent me." Heaven's cause then clearly would not preclude Othello's making some choice of his own. Still, the option of future repentance, as Othello well knows, is diminished since he will not be able to restore Desdemona to life. Othello acts according to a cause that creates a pattern of causation in which the possibility of further choice, though not eliminated, is severely limited. Repentance will be the only option remaining to Othello at the play's end; yet repentance, though merely a psychological state, is not an option to be dismissed as worthless or without meaning.

To see how Othello has turned cause into causation and thus diminished his freedom of choice, one can compare his use of the word "cause" to Cordelia's use of the word when she attends Lear as he wakes disoriented at her camp. Lear says to her: "I know you do not love me, for your sisters / Have (as I do remember) done me wrong. / You have some cause, they do not." Cordelia's reply marks a moment of radical, almost miraculous, freedom as her words, "No cause, no cause," as an extreme act of will, break the potential causative connection between the wrong that Lear has indeed done to her and her reaction to that cause. Cordelia's refusal to respond causally, in anger or in judgment, to Lear's earlier injustice to her, gives birth to a whole new possibility in their relationship, the opposite of Othello's closing down of possibility, except for the option of repentance, in his killing of Desdemona. As Othello rightly says: "I know not where is that Promethian heat / That can thy light relume."

There is still more bitter irony to pain the onlooker when we see Othello's inclination toward merciful self-judgment, mercy which he failed to extend to Desdemona, despite the fact that he will tell Lodovico, "nothing extenuate," in recounting his story. When he replies to Lodovico's question, "What shall be said to thee?" Othello replies with an extremely generous self-description: "An honorable murderer, if you will; / For nought did I in hate, but all in honor." An awful lot of extenuation is needed for us to accept such a description of himself.

Is the extenuation sufficient for Othello ultimately to be "saved" in the terms earlier expressed by Cassio: "there be souls must be saved, and there be souls must not be saved." This is God's judgment about which we can only speculate. But it is at this moment in the play that one of its main themes—the theme of being on trial—intersects with Othello's final attempts at self-vindication and repentance. His cause has come to be receiving a fair trial himself.

The play's first trial scene takes place earlier when Othello stands before the Duke and other high officials of the state to defend himself against Brabantio's charge that Othello has used drugs, "mixtures powerful o'er the blood," to bewitch Desdemona into marrying what, he claims, "she fear'd to look on." The Duke replies succinctly, "To vouch this is no proof," and this statement will cast all of Iago's vouching without proof into an ironic light. Othello tells the story of his life and asserts that it is his storytelling that successfully wooed Desdemona. He concludes, "She lov'd me for the dangers I had pass'd. / And I lov'd her that she did pity them. / This only is the witchcraft I have us'd." And then, what will add even further irony later in the play when Othello, in effect, puts Desdemona on trial, he says, "Here comes the lady; let her witness it," since Othello will not allow Desdemona to testify for herself against Iago's insinuations.

When the Duke publicly declaims, "I think this tale would win my daughter too," he becomes a model both for insisting on proof and listening sympathetically, without prejudice. This is a model that Othello will not be able to emulate. Desdemona's following testimony is remarkable for its directness, truthfulness, and accuracy in asserting that "I do perceive here a divided duty" and going on to express how natural it is for a daughter to transfer her primary allegiance from her father to her husband:

> *My life and education both do learn me*
> *How to respect you: you are the lord of duty,*
> *I am hitherto your daughter. But here's my husband;*
> *And so much duty as my mother show'd*
> *To you, preferring you before her father,*
> *So much I challenge that I may profess*
> *Due to the Moor my lord.* (I. iii. 182-138)

(If we remind ourselves of how Ophelia fails to assert herself when told by Polonius to stop seeing Hamlet, even though she knows Hamlet loves her and wishes to marry her; and if we recall that even Cordelia could not find the proper words to assuage the excessive demands of King Lear, her father, when he asks her to express her love for him, we will realize how admirable and remarkable is Desdemona's reply to Brabantio. And when, further, Desdemona explains to the Duke, "I saw Othello's visage in his mind, / And to his honors and his valiant parts / Did I my soul and fortunes consecrate," we see a young woman, fully mature, who is capable of bearing witness and explaining herself with great accuracy and eloquence.)

As we have observed, Othello is overly hasty in judging and sentencing Cassio. It does not occur to him to inquire if there are extenuating circumstances, nor does it occur to him that Cassio's past devotion to him might constitute a factor to be considered judiciously. Othello himself has sufficient knowledge—should he choose to act upon it—to be more objective and more temperate in judging Desdemona. As he says to Iago, "For she had eyes and chose me. No, Iago, / I'll see before I doubt; when I doubt, prove." But Othello will fail to be true to his own sense of what constitutes proof, to the cause of justice, and to his own awareness of the uncertainty of doubt itself.

In bringing Desdemona to trial, Othello will presume to play the roles of prosecuting attorney, witness, judge and sentencer, lord high executioner, and father confessor. Assuming all these roles as properly belonging to oneself is arrogance in the extreme. Yet even before he kills Desdemona, he has a realization that ought to have stopped him: "I will kill thee / And love thee after." Failing once again to make the right choice, the humane choice, Othello's gesture of mercy becomes a parody of mercy, just as Othello has become a parody of a real judge: "I that am cruel am yet merciful. / I would not have thee linger in thy pain." With Emilia's entry into the room, the realization of what he has done immediately begins to dawn on him: "My wife! my wife! what wife? I have no wife," and with Emilia's testimony, it quickly becomes apparent to Othello what a deluded fool he has become. Othello tries but fails to kill Iago, and, for a moment, reverts to his sense of himself as someone who can solve problems through violence: "Behold! I have a weapon. / A better never did itself sustain / Upon a soldier's thigh." But he quickly catches himself in the realization that no weapon can save him now that he has become his own worst enemy. And when he asks, "Who can control his fate?" the onlooker is tempted to say that he could have controlled his fate, that everyone is free to some extent to control his fate, even as Hamlet controls his fate merely by changing his attitude toward it to one of acceptance: "But let it be." And yet, after a moment's meditative pause, can it not also reasonably be said that Othello's fate, what earlier he had called "destiny unshunable," was controlled and determined by Iago. Again and again in Shakespeare, fate and free choice, though mutually exclusive in logic, are, nevertheless, both equally real aspects of human experience. Beyond logic, that is the way events unfold with fate and free choice inextricably bound to one another, so Shakespeare's play strongly intimates.

The theme of all people having causes, and the ease with which they are misconceived and misread, comes to a resolution when Cassio says to Othello, "Dear general, I did never give you cause," to which Othello now gives humble recognition and assent: "I do believe it, and I ask you pardon." Othello then asks Cassio to help in getting some explanation from Iago to learn what caused Iago to instigate his incredible villainy: "demand that demi-devil / Why he hath ensnar'd my soul and body." But that mystery in its full incredulity will never be disclosed. Iago's last words are: "Demand me nothing. What you know, you know: / From this time forth I never will speak word." The deep mystery of evil goes back into the silence out of which it emerged. Iago's use of the words, "nothing" and "never, " represent him as the spirit of negation to the last. That negation and destructiveness seemingly for their own sake do exist in the world, despite our incredulity, is something that perhaps we already knew at some deep level, but, out of fearfulness, it is knowledge that we have repressed. That we are often blind to ourselves and our motivations is all that we know with painful confidence. Whether such limited knowledge will suffice in confronting evil in the future remains uncertain. And the question that we are left with is what effect will Lodovico's telling of Othello's story (who himself had wooed Desdemona with his story) have on those to whom the story subsequently will be related.

VII *The Story Is Told*

Hamlet wants Horatio to live to tell his story: "Absent thee from felicity a while to tell my story," he demands of him. At the end of *King Lear* Edgar commits himself to telling what he has learned with emotional veracity: "The weight of this sad time we must obey; / Speak what we feel, not what we ought to say." Edgar's commitment to speaking truly is much like Emilia's. Prospero vows to tell the story of his life as *The Tempest* rounds to its conclusion. Macbeth's assumption that storytelling is meaningless, "Life's but a tale told by an idiot, full of sound and fury, signifying nothing," is much like Iago's ultimate silence. If life means something and has some value, then storytelling is a worthwhile choice to facilitate continuity, but if life is without meaning, then indeed no story is worth telling. In the comedies, some character will step forth and address the audience, as Puck does in *A Midsummer Night's Dream,* acknowledging and reminding the onlookers that everything they have witnessed is a story with its own challenge to credulity, the challenge of what one makes of fictive representation, or as Touchstone claims: "the truest poetry is the most feigning."

When a story is told, cause and causation (and their mystery) are seemingly locked in, seemingly frozen forever. Things are what they are by being, finally, what they have been. The freedom inherent in causation as a force to be acted on or revised, so it appears, has come to an end, and only the appearance of fixity remains. And yet it must be asked what the story's effect will be on the audience and even the coming generations to whom the story is retold? Will the story remain closed and complete, or will it become the source of new and further causation? Since we cannot "open" Iago's lips to explain himself and his incredible motivation, and since he returns to the inchoate non-storytelling silence out of which he first emerged, will we whose role it is to listen to Lodovico who concludes the play with this accepted charge to speak: "Myself will straight abroad, and to the state / This heavy act with heavy heart relate," be changed by what we hear? Will we, the survivors, be inclined to believe that Iago, like Satan, is merely a myth, a fiction within a play or will we become open to the reality of what Shakespeare's imagination summons forth? And how might that "fiction" help us live our lives? Might we become more empathetic to the fated suffering of our fellow human beings and more cognizant of human potentiality and volition for good or evil?

Or might we choose, as an act of our own willed self-making, to reinvent ourselves—thanks to the illumination offered by Shakespeare's art—in affirming what is precious through the heightened awareness of what we have to lose, as Othello loses the blessings of the love that bound him to Desdemona which, before the breach in their marriage, enabled him to exclaim, "If it were now to die, / 'Twere now to be most happy?"

CHAPTER FIVE

I The Romantic Dilemma

I know of no play so good-naturedly skeptical about romantic love as Shakespeare's lyrically comic masterpiece *A Midsummer Night's Dream*, replete with contending couples and rhymed couplets. Its only competitor, I believe, is Mozart's opera, *Cosi Fan Tutti*, with its symmetry of paired lovers, in which infidelity is also forgiven and discord is resolved in marital commitment. Shakespeare's essential insight is that romantically-smitten lovers do not see their love objects for who they really are, but as projections of their own wishes and desires. Impassioned lovers exist in a world of fantasy or even lunacy; thus Shakespeare presents his love-obsessed characters both literally and symbolically in moonlight, their lunar (lunatic) medium. This phenomenon of projection, recognizable to us as love at first sight (though, more accurately, it is love at second sight), is what Freud describes as transference, in which the patient projects feelings from his/her early childhood onto the doctor:

> *. . . the whole readiness for these feelings is derived from elsewhere, that they were already prepared in the patient, and, upon the opportunity offered by the analytic treatment, are transferred onto the person of the doctor. Transference can appear as a passionate demand for love.* (1)

This transference of feelings marks exactly the same process as the ordinary experience of falling in love, as opportunity presents itself, in which the love object becomes an invention of the doting admirer. Janet Malcolm, in *The Impossible Profession*, succinctly describes the consequences of romantic love:

> *The most precious and inviolate entity—personal relationships—is actually a messy jangle of misapprehensions, at best*

> *an uneasy truce between powerful fantasy systems. . . . The*
> *concept of transference at once destroys faith in personal rela-*
> *tionships and explains why they are tragic: we cannot know*
> *each other.* (2)

What romantic lovers project onto each other are experiences from the past, described by Freud as "already prepared in the patient"; and these experiences derive from our first love objects, our parents, and they form what Jared Diamond (3) calls "the search image," which closely resembles "imprinting" in animals as it determines the identity of future attachments: the newly hatched bird, for example, which takes the first moving object it sees to be its mother. To describe the phenomenon of falling in love—the image of falling suggesting that one is out of control—as love at first sight is, in effect, a profound denial that this love actually is based on an earlier love of a parent, most likely the mother. It would be more accurate, then, to describe romantic desire as love at second sight with first sight having become part of the unconscious mind. Malcolm sees romantic love as fated, since it is driven by unconscious motivation whose origin lies in the deep past, and that fatality is what makes it tragic, along with the disparity between desire and fulfillment as described so grimly by Troilus in *Troilus and Cressida*:

> *This is the monstruosity of love, lady, that the will is infinite,*
> *and the execution confin'd; that the desire is boundless, and*
> *the act a slave to limit.* (III. ii. 85-87)

One certainly can find great literary models, such as the Tristan and Isolde myth, to support Malcolm's view, but Shakespeare's play is a comedy: it ends happily, despite the fact that all the lovers are continually on the brink of mayhem and murder. A substantial reading of the play therefore requires an explanation of what resources of understanding enable the lovers to achieve a positive outcome in which they do not destroy each other, in which they accept the limits of both desire and mortality, and in which their vicissitudes prepare them for marriage.

The play opens with an exchange between Theseus, Duke of Athens, and Hippolyta, Queen of the Amazons, now betrothed to one another, in which Theseus comments first on the changing of the moon, which establishes moonlight as the play's central image. Hippolyta responds with her depiction of the moon as a "silver bow," thus linking the moon to an allusion of Cupid. Theseus anticipates the triumph of "mirth" over "melancholy," evoking the play's primary emotional dichotomy; then, significantly, he goes on to recount the history of their courtship as involving coercion and potential violence: "I wooed thee with my sword," he says, and, further, he acknowledges that I "won thy love doing thee injuries." The danger of love, its potential for destruction—some fundamental antipathy between men and women—is immediately established as the condition of romance that will have to be fully recognized and overcome. Also immediately, a distinction is made between romance and marriage, as Theseus proclaims to Hippolyta that I "will wed thee in another key." How this transition from courtship to marriage, from the instability of romance to the ability to be true to a vow of fidelity, is made and what it involves will constitute the substance of the entire play. The rhythm of the play thus moves us, as spectators, from a vision of potential tragedy to one of marital ceremony and "reveling," from illusion and fantasy to a substantive reality upon which the continuity of a relationship can be founded. This reality of socially sanctioned marriage will in turn place its emphasis on genetic fruitfulness, on having children to whom one can leave an inheritance.

II Children & Inheritance

Before I return to one of the most significant subplots of the play, the relationship between Titania and Oberon, which involves their contention for the proprietorship of "the lovely boy stol'n from an Indian king" and thus deals most directly with the theme of parentage, let me leap ahead to examine the play's penultimate scene before Puck's final address to the audience. The dialogue between Oberon and Titania reveals in its culminating imagery the play's underlining concern with the fate of marriage—the future, as represented by children.

After all their contention, Oberon and Titania have resolved their bitter differences and are now reconciled in the spirit of what Theseus had called "revelry," which Oberon now evokes in an invitation to "Sing, and dance it trippingly." Titania wants this singing to be done properly, artfully (unlike the play performed by the mechanicals), as she says to Oberon, "First perform your song by rote, / To each word a warbling note." Then she links the uses of accomplished art to the sense of blessing, the consecration of love in the spirit of loyalty and commitment: "Hand in hand with fairy grace / Will we sing and bless this place." This is indeed what they do as the stage direction, "Song and dance," makes explicit. Control in creating a work of art is compared to control of amorous emotions in creating the structure of a marriage.

Oberon picks up on the theme of blessing and connects it both to the idea of marriage and to the idea of natural fruitfulness as the result of being in a married state:

> To the best bride-bed will we,
> Which by us shall blessed be;
> And the issue there create
> Ever shall be fortunate. (V. i. 381-384)

By "issue" she means the children that the married state will bring forth. Oberon extends his wish to Titania to include the other couples to be married on this day, in effect making his wish—a wish grounded in nature herself—a universal aspiration: "So shall all the couples three / Ever true in loving be, / And the blots of nature's hand / Shall not in their issue stand." Two values are stressed in these lines: one is the importance of fidelity, truthfulness in making a vow of love, something that does not come easily to any of the lovers in this play. The other value is the belief that, according to the laws of nature, there is a connection between fidelity and good health, particularly the health of one's offspring who, as a result of their parents' truthfulness, will be spared the "blots" of malformation, such as—the next lines tell us—"Never mole, harelip, nor scar, / Nor mark prodigious, such as are / Despised in nativity, / Shall upon their children be." Oberon's speech could not be more lucid and explicit in summing up the values and consequences of what is at stake as romance and courtship pass over into marriage and family with the birth of children. This speech affirms that it has been the fate of children, the outcome in the future, that has been at risk all along even when the lovers have been completely absorbed with their own passions and their need to have passionate love returned and rewarded. In this respect, it is illuminating to compare the nihilistic childlessness of the Macbeths with the imagery of happy fertility with which this play concludes. The ending of the play in the ceremony of marriage produces the spirit of commencement at the "break of day," in which dawn terminates the spell of moonlight that has dominated the lovers' imaginations.

III Parenthood

For many readers, the conflict between Titania and Oberon seems to be a digression from the main thrust and plot of the play, the confused identities and loyalties of the central pairs of would-be lovers: Lysander and Hermia, Demetrius and Helena. Why should the ownership or possession of an adopted Indian boy be so important to them, particularly to Oberon, that he would want to humiliate Titania to get his way about the boy? If we ask this question as a way of exploring Shakespeare's representation of the psychology of parenthood, especially the uncertainty of the father's role, it becomes apparent that the outcome of the conflict between the Fairy King and Queen anticipates the role that any of the other prospective fathers will or will not play in their future marital relationships. Will each prospective father, despite his demonstrated fickleness and proclivity to change love objects, stick around and help care for his future child, or will he break his vows in search of other sexual conquests? Likewise, will any of the mothers-to-be cuckold her husband and, worst of all, trick him into supporting a child that is not genetically his own? In the light of these Darwinian uncertainties, it becomes explicable why Oberon wants to claim the child as his own in some important symbolic sense; he wants to have his parental commitment acknowledged and accepted by Titania. Not until she does this can they achieve a state of marital compatibility and stability.

Puck, speaking to one of the fairies, warns her of Oberon's state of acute jealousy—an emotion that resonates with sexual implications:

> *The King doth keep his revels here tonight.*
> *Take heed the Queen come not within his sight.*
> *For Oberon is passing fell and wrath,*
> *Because that she as her attendant hath*
> *A lovely boy stol'n from an Indian king;*
> *She never had so sweet a changeling,*
> *And jealous Oberon would have the child*
> *Knight of his train, to trace the forest wild.* (II. i. 18-25)

The hidden assumption here is that the child, if not given to Oberon as "knight of his train," would represent sexual infidelity on the part of Titania, so that, emotionally at least, the child would be hers alone and she would not share the parenting of him with Oberon. This can be called cuckold anxiety, the fear of being betrayed through infidelity, a fear that is represented frequently in Shakespeare's plays where jealousy and love go hand in hand.

Titania's attraction for the boy goes beyond the proper limits of parental affection: "But she perforce withholds the loved boy, / Crowns him with flowers, and makes him all her joy." Surely this excessive dotage suggests one of the aspects of an Oedipal entanglement, the mother's love for her son, which is a correlative of the archetypal father's jealousy of his wife, in this case, Oberon's jealousy of Titania. The spell which Oberon later will arrange to have cast on Titania, to make her fall in love with the childish Bottom with a donkey's head, is both a repetition and a parody of Titania's love for the Indian boy. Both of these loves are inappropriate, and they represent a degrading retrogression of what should be an equal and thus healthy relationship between a man and a woman.

When Titania and Oberon meet in the forest, his initial words are "Ill met by moonlight, proud Titania," since they are deep in the realm of moonlight, that is—romantic lunacy, which necessarily involves compulsive jealousy and the transference of one's own fantasies onto a love object. Immediately they confront each other with their past infidelities; Oberon responds to Titania:

> How can'st thou thus, for shame, Titania,
> Glance at my credit with Hyppolyta,
> Knowing I know thy love to Theseus?
> Did'st thou not lead him through the glimmering night
> From Pereginia, whom he ravished,
> And make him with fair Aegles break his faith
> With Ariadne, and Antiopa? (II. i. 74-80)

Titania's reply, "These are the forgeries of jealousy," is accurate in attributing jealousy to Oberon as part of his motivation, yet at the same time her remark also has the effect of a denial in that her accusations against Oberon function as a rationalization for her own infidelities. What is abundantly clear about the relationship between Theseus and Hyppolyta, as well as that of Oberon and Titania, is that they both involve infidelity, humiliation, and coercion. Why should this be so? What is it about romantic love, what is its endemic lunacy, that makes these violations and distortions virtually inescapable as Shakespeare depicts them, invariably linking them to the emotion of jealousy? How can the temptations of attraction and desire be contained by the keeping of "faith," by fidelity to one's vows?

In expressing her anxiety about infidelity, Titania's long harangue against Oberon reveals what is most deeply in her mind: her concern about "progeny" and their being "parents." She depicts nature, the cycling of the seasons, in its "angry" and destructive aspect, producing "rheumatic diseases," and she compares the distorted production of nature in which "the seasons alter" with their own angry contention with each other:

> And this same progeny of evils comes
> From our debate, from our dissension,
> We are their parents and original. (II. i. 115-118)

Not only their marriage is at stake, but also their identity as parents as reflected in the roles that they can agree upon in respect to the Indian boy. Oberon remains adamant, insisting that the boy have a defined role to play in respect to his own role as king or father: "I do but beg a little changeling boy / To be my henchman." In being a "changeling," the boy can become the child, the surrogate son, according to the choice and designation of the parents who adopt him.

Titania continues to refuse Oberon's request and proceeds to recount the boy's history and origin, identifying herself with the boy's pregnant mother who "gossiped by my side" as if the child, described as "my young squire," were her own. The mother's fruitfulness is approvingly and abundantly expressed in Titania's indulgent imagery:

> His mother was a votress of my order,
> And in the spiced Indian air by night
> Full often hath she gossiped by my side,
> And sat with me by Neptune's yellow sands
> Marking th'embarked traders on the flood,
> When we have laughed to see the sails conceive
> And grow big-bellied in the wanton wind;
> Which she, with pretty and with swimming gait
> Following (her womb then rich with my young squire)
> Would imitate. (II. i. 123-132)

Perhaps the depicted ship with its sails that "grow big-bellied in the wanton wind," symbolizes the journey into parenthood, nature fulfilling her proper role. Yet part of the great rhythm of nature also includes death, and the death of the boy's mother becomes a metaphor for Titania's own awareness of mortality and her willing participation in the processes of nature, according to her special status as a fairy:

> But she, being mortal, of that boy did die,
> And for her sake do I rear up her boy;
> And for her sake I will not part with him. (II. i. 135-137)

The awareness of death, as well as potential violence, pervades the play as a reminder of the fragility of human love and human bonding. At this point, Titania's sense of herself is based primarily on her female identification with the boy's mother, rather than on her relationship to Oberon as a husband with whom parenthood should be shared. Oberon renews his plea again, "Give me that boy, and I will go with thee," but Titania is adamant: "Not for thy fairy kingdom." At this juncture, they are like Milton's Adam and Eve, blaming each other for the Fall, about whom the Miltonic narrator says: "And of their vain contest there seemed no end."

Oberon's response to this rejection by Titania is extreme, the mad result of jealousy and the concomitant loss of his sense of dignity and self-worth. *a control over her* His wish for revenge, in the spirit of talion, a humiliation for a humiliation, reveals precisely what he takes to be his own injury. He says to the just departed Titania: "Thou shalt not from this grove / Till I torment thee for this injury." Here is another example in the play of couples falling into hate as rapidly and readily as they had fallen into love. (As Hermia says to Helena: "The more I hate the more he follows me," and Helena replies: "The more I love the more he hateth me.") Love and hatred are almost indistinguishable from each other, and, as we come to see, only an act of will, a vow, can keep them apart by each lover's choosing to affirm the independent identity of the beloved person.

Oberon's plan for revenge, ironically, is to cause Titania to fall in love, and he instructs Puck to fetch for him the herb which is located where the "bolt of Cupid fell: / It fell upon a little western flower." Cupid is described as "all armed," his "fiery shaft" will be the cause of "love's wound," and that wound, that injury, will cause the person, smitten with love, to "madly dote." In effect, the malady of love is literally a form of insanity, the inability to distinguish the real from the illusory, waking from dreaming, one person from another. The afflicted lover is plunged into a world of total subjectivity and solipsism. Again, quite literally, one cannot truly "see" what is before one's very eyes—another of the image themes, that of false seeing, that Shakespeare weaves throughout the play.

The first person (or creature) that one sees after the juice of the herb, derived from Cupid's arrow, has been dropped in her or his eyes while sleeping will, upon waking, instantly become one's love object. This phenomenon, known to us now as "imprinting," the phenomenon of a newly born animal taking as its mother the first moving object it sees is described by Ernst Mayr as having "much in common with human learning." (4) Imprinting constitutes a profound metaphor for choicelessness, whose diametric opposite is the making and faithfully keeping of a vow:

Having this juice
I'll watch Titania when she is asleep,
And drop the liquor of it in her eyes:
The next thing then she, waking, looks upon—

Be it on lion, bear, or wolf, or bull,
Or meddling monkey, or on busy ape—
She shall pursue it with the soul of love.
And ere I take this charm from off her sight
(As I can take it with another herb)
I'll make her render up her page to me. (II. i. 176-185)

"Waking," here, ironically means waking into an illusion, into a dream. Waking and dreaming are thus reversed and confused, just as the word "soul" is also ironically used here to refer to one's lower animal self, not to one's reason or one's spirituality. The extensive list of animals that Titania might fall in love with suggests further the complete randomness of falling in love, as well as its physical or psychological imperative. In other words, to be driven by psychological forces of which one is not aware—at the level of unconscious motivation—is tantamount both to madness and to the degradation of "sight" into hallucination. Oberon's motive for seeking such vengeance for what he takes to be rejection never comes within the scope of his scrutiny, for it, too, remains unconscious. The compulsive power and intent of his desire is, however, unmistakable; he wants some share in the parenting of the boy: "I'll make her render up her page to me," Oberon grimly asserts.

IV Titania's Waking

As suggested above, Bottom, as an object of Titania's amorous affection, is a comically parodic version of the Indian boy. Just as Titania had crowned the boy with flowers, so, too, is Bottom associated with flowers in Titania's mind, who upon waking, asks "What angel wakes me from my flowery bed?" and, shortly after, adds: "while thou on pressed flowers do sleep." Once again, we are shown waking as a changed state not into reality, but into fantasy. The underlying theme of this fantasy, as Bottom instinctively understands, is adultery and cuckoldry as universal aspects of human amorous desire. Bottom's song, to which Titania has awakened, thinking him to be an angel, expresses an animal or evolutionary basis (Shakespeare's intuitive understanding of the Darwinian principle of "sexual selection") for deception and infidelity: "The finch, the sparrow, and the lark, / The plainsong cuckoo grey, / Whose note full many a man doth mark / And dares not answer nay." Bottom comprehends that the cuckoo bird, representing cuckoldry, symbolizes a behavioral and psychological truth that cannot be denied: "Who would give the bird the lie, though he cry 'cuckoo' never so?"

Titania, under Oberon's spell, misconceives her passion for Bottom not as the breaking of faith but as genuine love, and she is ready to swear to this grievously mistaken belief, "to swear, I love thee." The content of her unconscious mind has become overt, yet her apparent willingness to make such an oath constitutes a betrayal of language, as well as a marital betrayal, since swearing should testify to truthfulness. Bottom may be of limited intelligence, but he is not deluded when he contradicts Titania's statement about being in love with the simple but accurate observation that "reason and love keep little company together these days." Titania, however, is so blinded by her lunatic infatuation that she does not even realize that Bottom has contradicted her in distinguishing reason from love and describes him, to our comic amusement, with extravagant foolishness: "thou art as wise as thou art beautiful." Nevertheless, the dark underside of her passion immediately shows itself as she warns Bottom, threatening coercion: "Out of this wood do not desire to go: / Thou shalt remain here, whether thou wilt or no." Her threat is not unlike the sword of Theseus.

The ludicrous aspect of the relationship between Titania and the transformed Bottom is developed further on in the play when we see the fairies attending Bottom in Titania's bower, though the fact that Oberon is observing this scene is itself suggestive of the potential for dangerous reprisal. Sexual desire for Bottom is represented on a regressively low, even infantile, level, as an itch to be scratched. "Scratch my head," he pleads, and as a wish for food, "bring me the honey-bag," he requests; and then "I have a great desire to a bottle of hay." These wishes of basic appetite are immediately followed, not by the desire for genital fulfillment, but for sleep. "I have an exposition of sleep come upon me," he says to Titania who is denied sexual consummation and, still doting, is further depicted in her humiliation of which she remains unaware as she falls asleep next to Bottom. In contrast to Titania, whose amorous lunacy shows her degradation, Bottom's transformation into an ass marks no real change from his previous identity; his outer image remains concordant with his inner identity, though there is something about his open good nature that prevents him from being truly humiliated as is Titania, and makes him a figure who is poignant as well as comic.

When Puck enters the scene, Oberon steps forward to address him, and we learn that something essential has already taken place—Titania had earlier agreed to give Oberon the "changeling child" at his repeated request. And now, as the result of "pity" for Titania's humiliation of which he, Oberon, so he confesses, is the cause, he decides to restore Titania to her sanity. "And now I have the boy," says Oberon, "I will undo / This hateful imperfection of her eyes." This choice on Oberon's part is of extreme importance since it constitutes Oberon's recognition of some aspect of his own character that is hating and hateful. Having exorcised his own "fierce vexation," derived from his own vulnerability, Oberon is now ready to express the positive aspect of his love for Titania: "Now, my Titania, wake you, my sweet Queen." With his self-identity as father triumphantly asserted, Oberon is able once again to see himself as part of a marital relationship. And just as Oberon has enjoyed a new awakening as a result of self-recognition, so, too, does Titania awaken from degraded emotions and desires: "My Oberon, what visions have I seen! / Methought I was enamored of an ass."

Bottom also will have his awakening as Puck foretells, "Now when thou wak'st, with thine own fool's eyes peep," but before we are shown Bottom's vision with consummate comic yet tender irony, Oberon responds directly and unequivocally to Titania's revelation of her amorous foolishness by pledging himself to Titania as if he were renewing his marital vows:

> Sound, music! Come, my Queen, take hands with me,
> And rock the ground whereon these sleepers be.
> (They dance.)
> Now thou and I are new in amity,
> And will tomorrow midnight solemnly
> Dance in Duke Theseus' house triumphantly,
> And bless it to all fair prosperity. (IV. i. 83-88)

It must be emphasized that this reconciliation into new "amity" (the word on which the play ends) between Oberon and Titania was absolutely contingent on their resolving their parental roles in relation to the Indian boy, their surrogate child. And the blessing that will follow this reconciliation is "prosperity," just as it was promised earlier by Titania that Oberon would bless Theseus' wedding bed with "joy and prosperity." Prosperity in these usages not only means happiness, but also carries with it the unmistakable suggestion of bearing healthy children.

Oberon continues in this great speech of reconciliation, this model of "amity" leading to "prosperity," which is meant to apply to all lovers: "There shall the pairs of faithful lovers be / Wedded, with Theseus, all in jollity." Self-awareness and reconciliation, though essential, are not by themselves sufficient for marital success as the culmination of love as the qualifying word "faithful" strongly implies. We, the audience, will continue to be reminded that the essential distinction between romantic desire and marital love is that desire is not within one's control, while faithful love is the result of making a vow, a willful and willing conscious choice, which Titania, having undergone the catharsis of madness (Oberon's spell), is now capable of articulating.)

V Bottom's Waking

The effect of Titania's and Oberon's enlarged self-awareness has the concrete and practical result of enabling them to reestablish their relationship and assume responsibility for their adopted child, the Indian boy. Bottom's waking and the attempted recounting of his dream does not have such a readily apparent effect since it does not change his relationship to any particular person, but, rather, it has a bearing on the play itself (as well as the play within the play) as Bottom claims that he will "sing it in the latter end of the play." I cannot resist quoting it in full:

> *I have had a most rare vision. I have had a dream, past the wit of man to say what dream it was. Man is but an ass if he go about to expound this dream. Methought I was—there is no man can tell what. Methought I was—and methought I had—but man is a patched fool if he will offer to say what methought I had. The eye of man hath not heard, the ear of man hath not seen, man's hand is not able to taste, his tongue to conceive, nor his heart to report what my dream was! I will get Peter Quince to write a ballad of this dream; it shall be called 'Bottom's Dream,' because it hath no bottom; and I will sing it at the latter end of the play, before the Duke. Peradventure, to make it more gracious, I shall sing it at her death.* (IV. i. 200-211)

Although Bottom is aware that he has had a "rare vision," it is remarkable that he cannot remember or recount any of the dream's substance or imagery. His dalliance in the bower with Titania has vanished from his mind, totally repressed upon his waking. And no doubt for good psychological reasons: the dream has enacted a forbidden fantasy with adulterous, perhaps even incestuous implications, since it is suggestive of a child's impossible (asinine) Oedipal desires for his mother, seen in her exalted form as a "queen." What remains of Bottom's dream is an abstraction of its sensuality in a confused evocation of all the organs of sense: eye, ear, hand, tongue, heart. If sexuality for a child is not essentially genital, but "polymorphous perverse" as Freud

no- he remembers but it is so amazing (to have been loved by the fairy queen) it can not dares not put it into words

claimed—which is to say that the entire body functions in a highly sensual way—then Bottom's fantasy, which cannot be repeated in adult actuality, only can be reexperienced as something lost beyond recovery. When Bottom exclaims that "Man is but an ass if he go about to expound this dream," he continues in the mixed mode of both denial and confession, since in rejecting the temptation to expound an interpretation of his dream he is saying that he will not do what an ass would do and therefore he himself is not an ass. His would-be logic leads him to a false conclusion.

The deep paradox of Bottom's being who he is not, and thus a metaphor for the power of the imagination, which derives from "airy nothing," is made even more explicit when Bottom proclaims about his dream that "it shall be called 'Bottom's Dream,' because it hath no bottom." But the dream does indeed have a bottom, the dreamer himself who cannot fathom the bottom of his own dream, his own self-identity, and who therefore both exists and does not exist in the very same way that the fabrications of art do not exist in a literal way yet do exist in their own mode as representations. Thus Bottom instinctively knows that his dream, rendered as art in Peter Quince's ballad, is appropriate to be sung at the theatrical production in which Bottom will play a part. Bottom's fiction will become part of the real world by virtue of the Duke's attendance at the play in which the death of Thisbe is enacted. An even deeper level of implication, however, supports the awareness that art always has some ultimate relationship in actuality to death itself because it provides additional worlds in which an individual, bound within his/her single life, may dwell.

The implications evoked by the fact that Bottom's ecstatic speech is a corruption of a well-known passage from 1 Corinthians 2:9-10, "The eye of man hath not seene, and the eare hath not heard, neither have entered into the heart of man, the things which God hath prepared for them that love him" are virtually inexhaustible. First, Bottom's confusion and lack of verbal adroitness are just plain funny. Foolish as he appears to us, we cannot help but empathize with Bottom's attempt to render his vision in spiritual terms—terms, which the biblical passage alluded to, describe as the yearning for love in the very heart of man "which God had prepared for them that love him." Bottom's yearning for visionary meaning constitutes his vulnerability, as no doubt it does for everyone, and his limitations render him as sympathetic in our eyes, even to the point of his enabling us as audience to achieve some kind of grace which is akin to the spirit of laughter and comedy. Thus Bottom's final hope for his song, based on his dream, is "to make it the more gracious." We cannot forget, however, that at the bottom of all this lies his sensual "itch" and his fantasy of both sexual stimulation and sexual relief (though not adult orgasm) in the presence of a forbidden and idealized figure, a fairy queen.

It is instructive to compare Bottom with Caliban, Shakespeare's other low-down dreamer, to see how they resemble each other and how they differ. Bottom is basically harmless; we see him in his fictive role, which he delights in playing, as a ferocious lion, but worries about the effect of the lion's roaring on the ladies in the audience: "a lion among ladies is a most dreadful thing." Caliban, on the other hand, is truly dangerous and would, if he could, rape Miranda and murder Prospero. Yet what the two of them have in common is a love of music and the pleasure they take in dreaming. Seemingly out of character for an enchanted moment, Caliban says:

> . . . *the isle is full of noises,*
> *Sounds, and sweet airs, that give delight, and hurt not.*
> *Sometimes a thousand twangling instruments*
> *Will hum about mine ears; and sometimes voices,*
> *That, if I then had wak'd after long sleep,*
> *Will make me sleep again: and then, in dreaming,*
> *The clouds methought would open and show riches*
> *Ready to drop upon me; that, when I wak'd,*
> *I cried to dream again.* (III. iii. 146-154)

Shakespeare's point is that the higher capacities of the visionary imagination, the human aptitude for art, particularly for music, are grounded in the basic senses themselves, and are different from the sources of morality, which—though based on the native human capacity for empathy (as Darwin so powerfully understood) and the advantage conferred by the evolved ability to cooperate—nevertheless demand deliberate choice and will. The making of a vow and faithfully keeping it does not have exactly the same origin as does sensual pleasure. The capacity to choose, not just to feel and desire, emerges in the form of the will's freedom, and this capacity comes as the culmination of a series of developmental stages, all of which are portrayed in one form or another in *A Midsummer Night's Dream*.

VI *The Stages of Growth*

The idea that life unfolds in stages is congenial to Shakespeare's imagination as we know from Jacques' famous speech in *As You Like It*, in which he compares the world to a stage and asserts that "one man in his time plays many parts, / His acts being seven ages." There is no systematic presentation of such ages in *A Midsummer Night's Dream* which finds its focus in the phases of sexual identity, but such stages can be discerned within the play, numbering more than Jacques' seven.

- The stage of infantile sexuality is represented by Bottom's wish to have the "itch" of his ears scratched, and by his preoccupation with eating and sleeping.
- The stage of prepubescent attachment is represented by Hermia's reminiscence about her friendship with Helena: "And in the wood, where often you and I / Upon faint primrose beds were wont to lie. / Emptying our bosoms of their council sweet."
- The stage of male bravado in seeking female acceptance is represented by the competition between Lysander and Demetrius as when Lysander makes the case for his own worthiness as a suitor for Hermia: "I am, my lord, as well-derived as he, / As well-possessed: my love is more than his, / My fortunes every way as fairly ranked."
- The stage of a young person trying to win independence from parental supervision and authority is represented by Hermia's distressed thoughts about her father: "I would my father looked but with my eyes."
- The stage of testing the reality of one's feelings in the course of the process of wooing and courting, discovering oneself, we see in the wavering and changing of attachments of the four central would-be lovers: Hermia, Helena, Lysander, and Demetrius.
- The stage of marital stress and the need for reconciliation is seen in the conflict between Oberon and Titania.
- The stage of defining one's role and responsibility as a parent is made apparent in Oberon's and Titania's contention over the Indian boy.
- The stage of "amity" that comes as the culmination of emerging from the vicissitudes of all the earlier phases is depicted in the marriages that ceremoniously conclude the play.
- The possible fate of marriage in its manifestation of self-serving parenthood is darkly suggested in the play by the figure of Egeus, whose authority, happily, will be replaced by that of the enlightened Theseus.

In his speech about the seven ages of man, Jacques concludes bitterly with the following description of the final stage of old age: "Last scene of all, / That ends this strange, eventful history, / Is second childishness and mere oblivion, / Sans teeth, sans eyes, sans taste teeth, sans everything." This gloomy representation of old age, however, is contradicted within *As You Like It* in the remarkable portrait Shakespeare gives us of Corin, an old shepherd, who in dialogue with the supercilious clown, Touchstone, makes the following statement in defining his values and his deep sense of who he is:

> *Sir, I am a true laborer. I earn that I eat, get that I wear;*
> *I owe no man hate, envy no man's happiness; glad of other*
> *men's good, content with my harm; and the greatest of my*
> *pride is to see my ewes graze and my lambs suck.* (III. ii. 69-73)

Nowhere in all of Shakespeare do we find a character more in harmony with himself and his own condition. We see him as a model for what Hamlet would call "ripeness," and what we might take to be the triumph of the parental imagination whose essence is caretaking and nurturing. Between Jacques' depiction of old age as "second childishness" and Corin's mellow maturity, we can see the great alternative of failure or success in the journey of life from romantic wooing, to marriage, to parenthood in the choices one makes in the face of necessity as defined by what is fixed in human psychology or current social conditions.

In *A Midsummer Night's Dream* the figure who represents old age is Egeus, Hermia's father, and he is an ugly sight, selfish and possessive, cruel and vindictive, the opposite of Corin. Egeus is a reminder throughout the play of how marriage and childbearing can end in hatefulness, rather than in nurturing. He evokes Athenian law to threaten his daughter with death or her being sent to a convent if she does not marry the man he, her father, chooses, and at first Theseus supports his right to make such a decision: "Either to die the death, or to abjure / For ever the society of men." It is of great symbolic significance that Egeus's line ultimately would prove barren if he were to get his own way. The awareness of such an outcome casts its shadow over the entire play and makes the audience realize what is at stake as the lovers navigate their uncertain way toward marriage.

The fate of the lovers remains in balance, depending on whether or not Egeus prevails in realizing his selfish wishes according to the laws of Athens as at first upheld by Theseus. There is no more significant decision, therefore, made in this play than when Theseus changes his mind and withdraws his support from Egeus. Theseus does so after Demetrius pledges himself to Hermia: "And will for evermore be true to it." Perhaps there is some connection between Demetrius's oath, with which Theseus identifies, and his reversal in which he informs Egeus, "Egeus, I will overbear your will; / For in the temple, by and by, with us / These couples shall eternally be knit," but basically this is a leap that, given Theseus's earlier obduracy, we could not readily have anticipated. Theseus's changed attitude, expressed also in his concurrent decision that "hunting shall be set aside," (since hunting carries with it strong associations with violence and death), exhibits one of those mysterious moments of radical freedom, made manifest in an act of will, that this book has attempted to identify and elucidate. In such a moment we witness, to our surprise or even our astonishment, a character suddenly transcend himself and become other and more than what he or she has been. In effect, what the transformed Theseus achieves in this moment is the rejection of Egeus's failed parental imagination, and, still more radically, Theseus abnegates the false and perverted law that had embodied selfish possessiveness. Within the terms of this play, Theseus has reinvented society and civilization and has thus made room for the possibility of love freely chosen and the commitment to sanctify that love. This enlargement of possibility, emphasized by Theseus's deliberate selection of the word "eternally," is its own kind of awakening, and, indeed, it will be followed by two further episodes of awakening, one where Bottom tries to articulate his "rare vision," discussed above, and one involving the four lovers, which will be fully discussed below in Section VII.

At the basis of all storytelling, as this play abundantly shows, resides the world of dreams and unconscious motivation, upon which is built the fabricating power of human imagination. The waking mind, conscious of its capacity to dream, becomes, finally, the actual audience's awareness of the play itself, just as the lovers, along with Theseus and Hippolyta, are audience to the play within the play. Theseus and Hippolyta, in particular, exhibit their awareness of themselves as watchers of the play. Puck's final address to the audience will acknowledge this mirroring awareness that they all are watching the characters within the play and have, in this extended way, agreed to the making of a compact which involves the acknowledgment of and the retelling of their dreams—an idea that the late Shakespeare, through Prospero, will express in universal form: "We are such stuff as dreams are made on."

VII The Lovers

Shakespeare's depiction of his characters, when most driven and irrational, shows them as if they were performing in their own dreams. They are indeed "such stuff as dreams are made on," as is love itself. Two predominant psychological factors characterize Demetrius, Lysander, Hermia, and Helena as compulsive lovers: one, they are virtually interchangeable, and two, their emotions and attitudes toward each other are excruciatingly ambivalent. They continue to change places as love objects in each other's eyes, as when Helena, referring to Cupid, declares that "so the boy Love is perjured everywhere; / For, ere Demetrius looked on Hermia's eyne, / He hailed down oaths that he was only mine." Their emotions range from declarations of devotion, such as Lysander's, "Helen, I love thee, by my life, I do," to fulminations of hatred, such as Lysander to Helena (whom he formerly loved), "'tis no jest / That I do hate thee and love Helena." Expressions of hatred extend to threats of physical violence and even to rape, as when Demetrius says to the now doting Helena, "Or if thou follow me, do not believe / But I shall do thee mischief in the wood." Shakespeare presents the sexes, at some fundamental level, as being at war with each other (as well as men being at war with men and women with women) as Cupid's bow and arrows and Theseus's sword powerfully suggest. Their peacemaking cannot be accomplished without prior recognition both of their fickleness and their proclivity toward infidelity—in sum, of their embattled condition. Lysander's remark, "The course of true love never did run smooth," is right on the mark, but at this point early in the play, there is no explanation for why this must be a general truth about human psychology.

The hint of an explanation for the cause of love's inescapable vicissitudes emerges when Lysander claims that "Love looks not with the eyes, but with the mind, / And therefore is winged Cupid painted blind." His important insight comes to this: if one's eyes were not blinded by some hidden preconception, to look with the eyes would be to see who actually is there and to love that person for what he or she actually is. Such love would be based on objective reality. But to love someone for how he or she appears in the mind is to love that person subjectively. The beloved person would have to correspond in some reductive way to an internal image that already exists at a deep level of the dreaming mind. In this sense, what appears as love at first sight is, in reality, as I have argued, love at second sight. A primary image, "the search image," based on an infantile experience of nurturance and love received from a parental figure, becomes idealized, as in the figure of a fairy queen feeding the infantile Bottom, and fatalistically determines the object of one's love irrespective of that person's actual character and identity. The random aspect of romantic love, therefore, its basis on chance and fortuity, is presented by Shakespeare as a stage of growth which one must undergo and go through, hopefully to be superseded by a willful act of choice and the concomitant making of a vow. Only in this way is marriage able to achieve a stability that romantic love cannot emulate.

It is much easier, however, to make a vow than to stick to it, and so through much of their wavering courtships, the lovers make extravagant vows, which they are not able to keep, since they cannot yet truly distinguish waking from dreaming, reality from illusion, rationality from rationalization. An impassioned and confused Lysander, for example, switching his love allegiance to Helena, and thus betraying his former love, proclaims:

> *Content with Hermia? No, I do repent*
> *The tedious minutes I with her have spent.*
> *Not Hermia, but Helena I love.*
> *Who will not change a raven for a dove?*
> *The will of man is by his reason swayed,*
> *And reason says you are the worthier maid.* (II. ii. 118-123)

In the very guise and name of reason, Lysander shows himself to be most unreasonable. Reason here has become its opposite, rationalization, and is in full denial of its own self-contradiction.

(After Oberon squeezes the love juice on the eyes of sleeping Demetrius, he awakens and immediately begins to pledge himself to Helen in the mode of making a comparison; instantly he turns into a doting poet, drunk on his own words: "O, Helen, goddess, nymph, perfect, divine! / To what, my love, shall I compare thine eyne?" Again, it is significant that the lover has idealized his beloved as a goddess (like a fairy queen), and thus his image of her, which he projects unrealistically upon her, can only have derived from some unconscious depth—the depth of dreams.

All this pledging and vow-making comes into intensified focus as Lysander and Demetrius, now both in love with Helen, compete for her approval: Lysander says: "Helen, I love thee, by my life I do: / I swear by that which I will lose for thee / To prove him false that says I love thee not." And Demetrius replies: "I say I love thee more than he can do." Their contention rises to the level of imminent violence as they draw their swords, so Lysander cries: "If thou say so, withdraw, and prove it too," and Demetrius: "Quick, come," just as Hermia enters to intervene. The sword-wielding here reminds us again of the play's opening when Theseus told Hippolyta, "I wooed thee with my sword," and we see as universal the image of the phallic sword, love in its double aspect of both desire and violence.

The contention between the two men spreads to the two women, previously seen as true friends, virtually as lovers, who now also perceive themselves as competitors. Helena disparages Hermia in complaining, "She was a vixen when she went to school, / And though she be but little, she is fierce." What is revealed here is not only Helena's present anger, but some resentment from deep in their childhood past that had been repressed and which now emerges as the result of amorous jealousy. All this emotion, as revealed in all four lovers, is driven by forces that the lovers simply do not comprehend; they are behaving like automatons, as if they themselves were merely figures in a dream, what Puck later calls "shadows."

The scene (Act IV, Scene I) in which the four lovers awake from sleep shows them as being uncertain as to whether they are waking or dreaming, as if the two states are indeed barely separable. Demetrius says, "Are you sure / That we are awake? It seems to me / That yet we sleep, we dream." In order to distinguish dreaming from sleeping, they make the effort to recollect events which they then assume actually occurred: "The Duke was here," says Demetrius, and Hermia responds, "Yea, and my father," and Helena adds further, "And Hippolyta," so that Demetrius is able to conclude: "Why, then we are awake." But this waking carries with it a new and extended dimension since it includes waking as being aware of itself, which it only can do by distinguishing itself from dreaming. Yet, in doing so, waking must include not only the awareness of dreaming as such, but also the content of dreaming, which Bottom had failed to do. This then is the very moment in which Shakespeare uncovers the basic concept of psychoanalysis: the mind includes unconscious wishes and thoughts that affect one's waking behavior. This tremendous discovery (given such great emphasis by Freud) takes place at this very instant when Demetrius invites his companions to "recount our dreams." Their awareness of themselves as dreamers, and of dreams containing the imperative to be recounted and interpreted, begins their transformation from one-dimensional figures into two-dimensional human beings. Now, conscious of their own unconscious selves, they are ready, by virtue of this new potential for self-mastery that derives from self-knowledge, to make marriage vows that are not based merely on fantasies and delusions.

Finally, while watching the play within the play, as performed by Bottom and his companions, the lovers become fully aware of the moonlight madness of romance which determined their earlier restricted identities. The story of Pyramus and Thisbe, based on unfortunate timing and misperceptions, would be a tragedy, like *Romeo and Juliet*, were it not for the maladroitness of the performers. Shakespeare surely is suggesting how close comedy and tragedy are to one another, how easily the characters in *A Midsummer Night's Dream* could have killed each other out of jealousy and competitiveness. What the lovers witness in the performance of the play is a version of their own foolishness which now can be acknowledged for what it is even if the lovers must adopt some aesthetic distance in order to gain this recognition. Lysander, in commenting on Quince's prologue, says with self-satisfied irony, "He hath rid his prologue like a rough colt; he knows not the stop. A good moral, my lord; it is not enough to speak, but to speak true." Indeed, this is a good moral after all the false professing of which the lovers have been guilty. In the image of the actor Quince, unable to control the metaphorical horse on which his speech rides, Lysander acknowledges what the play has demonstrated—the need for self-control, the need for fidelity and truthfulness in order to prevent mayhem. Art must reveal the truth contained by its own metaphorical fictionalizing until, as Quince continues, "truth make all things plain."

A bemused Theseus asks, "I wonder if the lion be to speak?" to which Demetrius replies, "No wonder, my lord; one lion may, when many asses do." Demetrius, Bottom and the other lovers, have all been asses and spoken their asinine declarations of love. One is left to imagine whether or not, or how fully, Demetrius is aware of the irony of his own words. Demetrius's subsequent comment in response to Snout's presentation of himself as the wall, "It is the wittiest partition that ever I heard discourse, my lord," suggests that, yes, Demetrius is now fully aware of the dimension of irony, the doubleness of perspective, of which he had not been capable when caught up in the passions of a lover. One might think of this as the culmination of his awakenings, the potential possessed by all lovers, to see, paradoxically and comically, that their sanity is based on their awareness that when filled with desire they are moonstruck and crazy.

VIII Puck & Theseus

George Bernard Shaw's masterpiece, *Man and Superman* (5), concludes with an original and inspired (by Shakespeare?) stage direction, which reads, as the final curtain comes down: "Universal laughter." Puck, I believe, embodies the spirit of such laughter—laughter that only can be enjoyed when one achieves a detached perspective from the passion or the situation in which one is entrapped by circumstance, as when—to use an extreme example—King Lear, imprisoned with Cordelia, claims that they "will laugh / At gilded butterflies." Puck is such a spectator: from his detached perspective, he can take a bemused and tolerant overview of the farce of human wooing, yet he can also involve himself, if he so chooses, as a participant in exacerbating human folly for the sake of creating laughter. In this respect, he is like an author, Shakespeare himself, devising the plot of the story to be told. Puck defines himself early in the play as follows: "I am that merry wanderer of the night. / I jest to Oberon and make him smile." The perspective of laughter, which this play abundantly supplies despite its underlying seriousness, is what love most needs to relieve the agonies and compulsions of desire, to provide some breathing space for self-awareness.

Puck's spirit of laughter is closely related to the imagination as described and defined by Theseus. After all, it is the role and purpose of art to entertain and to delight. And in the sense, as Theseus says, that "The lunatic, the lover, and the poet / Are of imagination all compact," the poet composes laughter out of his other identities as lunatic and lover and answers the question that Theseus will pose: "How shall we find the concord of this discord?" Theseus's discourse on the imagination culminates in the deep question of what the artist (or the lover) can make of "airy nothing," a question parallel to how concord can be made of discord.

> The poet's eye in a fine frenzy rolling,
> Doth glance from heaven to earth, from earth to heaven;
> And as imagination bodies forth
> The forms of things unknown, the poet's pen
> Turns them to shapes, and gives to airy nothing
> A local habitation and a name. (V. i. 12-17)

Clearly, this "fine frenzy" is a form of pleasure, a kind of sublime laughter that is the quintessence of storytelling, the mind's freedom over the constrictions of one's individual psychology and the compulsions of blind desire.

By the end of the play when everyone is attending a would-be artistic production, the link between laughter and the capacity for irony should become doubly apparent, for the only time we see the lovers laughing is when, while attending Peter Quince's production, the lovers are bemused by absurdities virtually identical to their own. Freedom of the mind, comic tolerance, a Puckian spirit, now become apparent in the lovers. This expansion of imaginative perception, already articulated theoretically by Theseus, is now embodied in what we witness as still another expansion of Theseus' character. To review briefly: at the play's beginning, Theseus acknowledges that he has changed his style of wooing from coercion, "I wooed thee with my sword," to something more gentle and considerate "in another key." Then we see Theseus upholding the strict and cruel Athenian law in behalf of Egeus's selfish wishes, but, as discussed above, Theseus, in behalf of the lovers, radically reverses himself and reinvents the law so that the wishes of the lovers can be realized. Finally, at the play's conclusion, we become aware of still another development in Theseus's character: a newly expanded capacity for empathy.

Just before the play within the play is about to begin, Hippolyta, anticipating an incompetent performance, says to Theseus, "I love not to see wretchedness o'ercharged, / And duty in his service perishing," to which Theseus replies, "Why, gentle sweet, you shall see no such thing." But Hippolyta persists, citing the warning of Philostrate, the master of revels, about the performance "And it is nothing, nothing in the world, / Unless you can find sport in their intents," and, echoing Philostrate's repetition of the word "nothing" (itself an echo of Theseus' depiction of the imagination as giving shape to "airy nothing") Hippolyta makes her rejoinder, repeating her skepticism about the performance to take place: "He says they can do nothing in this kind." And then Theseus makes a remarkable and profound statement, surpassing anything he has said before in its humanity: "The kinder we, to give them thanks for nothing." At this moment, a concept enters the world of the play that goes beyond desire as a motivating factor in human relationships; here, we are introduced to the gentler concept of kindness—a capacity well within human control, more the result of choice than the fortuity of falling in love. What was only Theseus's theoretical description a moment ago of figments produced by "the poet's pen" as the creation of the imagination out of "airy nothing," now becomes an act of sympathy of one character for another within the larger structure of the play.

Amazingly, Theseus goes further still: "Our sport shall be to take what they mistake; / And what poor duty cannot do, noble respect / Takes it in might, not merit." What Theseus is professing here is the principle that everyone, no matter how low or foolish, by virtue of his or her innate humanity, is deserving of "noble respect." This sentiment closely resembles Hamlet's admonishment to Polonius as to how he should treat the visiting players. Polonius says, "My lord, I will use them according to their just desert," to which Hamlet adamantly replies: "God's bodkin, man, much better! Use every man after his desert, and who shall 'scape whipping? Use them after your own honor and dignity: the less they deserve, the more merit is in your bounty." With this concept of tolerance and respect for innate human dignity in mind, Theseus now redefines the proper use of language and speech to emphasize not "eloquence," as the primary virtue, but "Love, therefore, and tongue-tied simplicity / In least speak most." In effect, love has been redefined from being based on infatuation to being based on honesty and empathy.

IX Puck & His Audience

The play within the play ends as tradition and the myth require, with the deaths of Pyramus and Thisbe, to which Theseus and Demetrius respond with comic aplomb: Theseus says that "Moonshine and Lion are left to bury the dead," and Demetrius adds, "Ay, and Wall, too." The reality and seriousness of death remain in the minds of the audience, but the spectators are given a respite, a hiatus, from the grip of that reality. Bottom, the stage direction tells us, is seen "starting up" in a parody of resurrection which the spirit of laughter brings forth. For the moment, all the characters, as well as the play's audience, live within the realm of merriment that laughter has made possible. The risen Bottom—as the play and the play within the play completely merge—asks Theseus, "Will it please you to see the epilogue, or to hear a Bergomask dance?" Theseus prefers the music and the dancing to the prospect of an epilogue, "But come, your Bergomask; let your epilogue alone." Although there will not be an epilogue given by Bottom or any of the other mechanicals, there soon will be a final address to the audience that comes, so it seems, of Puck's own authorization, despite Theseus's reluctance.

The company of players returns to fill the stage, "two of them dance," and they all depart, leaving Theseus to deliver what feels like a soliloquy, in which he acknowledges that soon it will be time to dream again, "'tis almost fairy time," again invoking his awareness of the barely visible line that separates waking from sleeping. Though the performance of *Pyramus and Thisbe* has not evoked tragic emotions in the audience, it has not failed to entertain, as Theseus asserts: "This palpable-gross play hath well beguiled / The heavy gait of night." Theseus leaves the stage, anticipating "new jollity," and is then replaced by Puck who augments Theseus's comic perspective—as well as his own earlier representation of himself as the spirit of merriment—with a surprisingly modulated vision of his own that differs from his earlier view in that he now articulates the awareness of reality in its darker aspects. The awareness of sorrow and death must be acknowledged, yet held in suspension, if laughter is to flourish in a transitory moment of triumph over "dust."

Puck now enters "carrying a broom," which is heavily symbolic of the role he is given to perform. He claims that he has been "sent," but it is not certain by whom, perhaps by Oberon, as a representative of "fairy" imaginings. Theseus's comic observation that "Moonshine and Lion are left to bury the dead," is echoed and countered by Puck's somber reminder that there are real lions and wolves in the world, and that the moon shines not only on the follies of lovers but also on the actual dangers of the natural world. Puck offers up a catalog of real troubles and sorrows: the "heavy ploughman," weary with the burden of the day's labor; the "screech-owl" whose scream seems to correspond to the "wretch" who has in mind his own "shroud," the image of a churchyard filled with "graves." If the fairies are indeed to introduce the spirit of "frolic" into the world of the lovers, Puck must hold in abeyance and yet not deny the awareness of what Macbeth calls "dusty death" and "sweep the dust behind the door." Although it is true that the concealed dust, representing mortality, cannot be entirely expunged from thought, its suspension from disturbing attention is what enables Puck and the fairies to offer their blessing into "this hallowed house," the house of civilized values, protected from the forest world of real lions, real wolves, real violence.

Oberon returns and continues Puck's allusion to "the hallowed house" by extending the sense of blessing through the spirit of song and dance, commanding the fairies to "Sing, and dance it trippingly." Titania, having now achieved marital harmony with Oberon, adds, "Hand in hand with fairy grace / Will we sing and bless this place." Oberon continues to expound the idea that the fairies will bring blessing to the "house," which has now become a symbol for the residence of married and parental love, but, just as Puck had reminded the play's audience of the reality of sorrow and death, so, too, does Oberon now warn the audience of the dangers of marriage and having children. Oberon makes an explicit connection between marital fidelity, "So shall all the couples three / Ever true in loving be," with having children that are not blighted by nature: "And the blots of nature's hand / Shall not in their issue stand." This, it must be repeated, is the essential optimism of the play, its comic hopefulness, that true blessing derives from love, not in its aspect of desire, but in its capacity for fidelity and trust—virtues that are fabricated by the moral imagination out of "airy nothing," like the very vision of the fairies whom the audience has witnessed on the stage. With this belief in blessing fully articulated, Oberon now assumes that we are all ready to move from the moonlit world of amorous projections to the world of waking daylight: "Trip away, make no stay; / Meet me all by break of day."

The stage is now empty again as Puck steps forth to address the audience in attendance at the play, taking it upon himself to compose an epilogue to complete the breaking down of the distinction between the actual audience and the play they have witnessed, just as within Shakespeare's play the distinction is broken down between the mechanicals who perform *Pyramus and Thisbe* and the characters within the play, all the lovers, who attend

Peter Quince's production. In doing so, [Puck must first acknowledge that everyone who has appeared on stage is a "shadow" in the sense that shadows are to real objects as dreams are to real events. This crucial definition is made explicitly in Hamlet's exchange with Rosencrantz and Guildenstern as they try to plumb Hamlet's motivation, assuming it must be ambition. Hamlet says: "O God, I could be bounded in a nutshell, and count myself a king of infinite space, were it not that I have bad dreams." Guildenstern replies: "Which dreams, indeed, are ambition, for the very substance of the ambitious is merely the shadow of a dream." To which Hamlet succinctly responds: "A dream itself is but a shadow."

It is not that dreams and shadows do not exist or have no reality and therefore can be dismissed from serious thought, but that they have a particular (and important) relation to reality. When Puck begins his epilogue by speculating, "If we shadows have offended," he is talking about a possibly real offense taken by real people, the audience, in real time and place, depending on what they make of Shakespeare's play or, in the larger sense, what they take to be the role of imagination in human life. Puck therefore proposes to the audience, "Think but this, and all is mended: / That you have but slumbered here / While these visions did appear." What Puck proposes is that the audience regard the play not in the dismissive sense of rejecting it as illusion, merely as entertainment; rather, that they accept the play as making manifest the reality of dreams and their causative power.

Puck's next lines, "And this weak and idle theme, / No more yielding but a dream," are somewhat tongue-in-cheek because we have seen how love—the overriding theme of the play—has not yielded to objective reality anymore than have dreams been separated from waking behavior. Puck wishes to assert the truthfulness of poetic and dramatic art, just as he has asserted the reality of dreaming, in the spirit of Touchstone's paradoxical claim in *As You Like It* that "the truest poetry is the most feigning." It is in this sense that Puck wishes to be regarded as "an honest Puck," free of the double curse that attended the fall of Adam and Eve at the beginning of human history, the curse of lying and the hostility inherent within the passion of lust. This is what Puck means when he asserts that he wishes to "'scape the serpent's tongue," an image that refers not only to the audience's possible hissing disapproval, but also to the biblical serpent traditionally regarded as the forked-tongued father of lies, and, still further, to the serpent as a symbol of sexual predation. Hermia had earlier described just such a serpent on waking from her traumatic dream: "Methought a serpent ate my heart away." The serpent of sexual desire, willing to exploit another human being for one's own gratification, constitutes an anxiety that suffuses the entire play.

If Puck cannot make "amends" to the audience because he fails to persuade them to accept dreamlike artistic representation as an aspect of reality in its largest dimension, then they, the audience, would be right to "Puck a liar call." Fantasy and dreaming and artistic representation must be placed within the service of reality, or they become lies. The limitations of tempted human nature, to which the play must give true testimony, are represented in their overcoming by the equally human capacity to make a vow to a single person and faithfully to uphold it. Puck's final gesture to the audience, therefore, is one of reconciliation—the last of the many reconciliations depicted in the play—in which he reaches out his hand in friendship in the wish for acceptance and approval which the audience will offer—if they choose to do so—in the form of applause in the celebratory spirit of laughter as they join Puck to "restore amends." And thus the audience can participate in sanctifying the tenuously hopeful story of the multiple marriages that has just been told.

CHAPTER SIX

BETRAYAL & NOTHINGNESS:
THE BOOK OF JOB & KING LEAR

I The Problem of Suffering

When Job, in his undeserved suffering, loses his faith in the justice of God and feels betrayed by Him, Job curses the fact of his human existence and wishes not merely to die, but never to have been born. In his despair, Job's way of trying to control the future is by denying time itself. He tries to negate himself even from his own history:

> *God damn the day I was born*
> *and the night that forced me from the womb.*
> *On that day—let there be darkness;*
> *let it never have been created;*
> *Let it sink back into the void.* (1)

God's initial act of creation—"Let there be light"—is replaced in Job's mind with the nothingness of original darkness. From then on, throughout the book, nothingness remains an alternative to existence itself since the universe seems to be devoid of moral meaning and of justice. It is not until the poem's conclusion that the intertwined themes of nothingness and justice finally are resolved in Job's attitude toward the apparent randomness and indifference of nature. Job, confirmed in his knowledge that Bildad is wrong in his assertion that "God never betrays the innocent," nevertheless accepts his return to dust.

So, too, is the theme of nothingness central to Shakespeare's *King Lear* and here, as well, the indifference of the gods and of nature are inextricably bound to the question of justice. When Lear asks Cordelia to proclaim publicly her love for him so that, illogically, he can give her an equal share of his inheritance that is larger than what he gives his other two daughters, "What can you say to draw / A third more opulent than your sisters," the embarrassed Cordelia responds: "Nothing, my Lord." Lear questions, "Nothing?" and Cordelia repeats the ominous words, "Nothing," to which Lear's reply will echo throughout the play: "Nothing will come of nothing." Spiritually, however, everything of meaning and of value in this play eventually will emerge out of nothing because Lear will be reduced to nothing before he is reborn out of the empty figure he had become when he gave away his kingdom and banished the one daughter and the true friend, Kent, who sincerely love him.

(In the Book of Job the motif of nothingness, conceived as the human opposition to God's creation of human life, is made manifest in the imagery of dust, and Job's changing attitude in the way he views himself as dust most fully reveals his spiritual transformation. After Job's sons and daughters have been killed by a desert wind, but before Job's friends appear on the scene to comfort him, Job still holds onto his faith in God. Job's faith is expressed in a gesture of acceptance in which he lies down "with his face in the dust." In effect, Job affirms that he was essentially nothing before God breathed life into the dust in order to create him and that he will return to the condition of non-being as a consequence of the inevitable rhythm of nature. And so Job, still without bitterness, is able to say: "Naked came I from my mother's womb, and naked I will return there. The Lord gave, and the Lord has taken; may the name of the Lord be blessed." Even after Job's wife loses faith and, with extreme bitterness, urges Job to "Curse God, and die," Job remains grateful and true to the God who has created him, and he replies to his wife: "We have accepted good fortune from God; surely we can accept bad fortune too." When Job's friends arrive to comfort him, they see how terribly he has changed, and they "cried out and tore their clothing, and sprinkled dust on their heads." There seems to be something about their gesture—as if in beholding them as dust Job now truly sees himself also as dust—that breaks Job's mood of sublime acceptance of God's inscrutable will and causes Job to abandon his faith, curse his own existence, and challenge God.)

Job's sense of himself as dust is a close variant of envisioning himself as being essentially naked; his attitude, as represented by these two words "dust" and "naked" includes feelings that range from self-contempt to complete vulnerability. Lear's vision here is identical to Hamlet's when, in his disillusionment (which results, like Lear's, from suffering the betrayal of loved ones) Hamlet characterizes mankind as a "quintessence of dust." For both Job and Lear, man in his nakedness and human life seen as dust are versions of nothingness that appear to be beyond redemption and that cannot be accepted in any way by the reflections of consciousness. It appears brutally paradoxical that the only ways to contend with nothingness, so understood, are to escape consciousness through madness, in which the mind avoids the concept of the future, of ongoing time, or, suicidally, to seek the nothingness of death and become the very nothingness that one abhors.

Lear's denial of the future can be seen in the interrelated images of space and time when Lear, with the map of his kingdom before him, determines to appropriate his lands according to his manipulation of his daughters' professions of love as if in controlling their speech, their language, he can control their feelings as well. When Lear proclaims: "Know we have divided / In three our kingdom; and 'tis our fast intent / To shake all cares and business from our age, / Conferring them on younger strengths while we / Unburthen'd crawl toward death," he is, in fact, fantasizing a condition of power so great, and therefore free of care, that it does not require further worldly power to sustain it. Imagining a human state without burdens is, in effect, a fundamental denial of the human condition; it is an illusion into which the aged Lear plunges as he faces his impending death. In the most terrible darkness of their psyches, all parents feel that they have been betrayed by their children when their children become separate and unique individuals for in doing so, they leave their parents uncloned and thus mortal, not to be replicated into eternity. Lear's prototypical wish to control his children psychologically is the same as his wish to determine the future, and both are manifestations of his unconscious refusal to accept his mortality, the ultimate condition of returning to dust.

Lear's presumptive will to control the lives of his children is made further explicit when he says: "We have this hour a constant will to publish / Our daughters' several dowers, that future strife / May be prevented now." The irony of this statement is immense, since the effect of Lear's attempt to determine the future according to his conscious will (though it may well correspond to an unconscious desire to destroy a future without him by rendering it back into chaos) is to precipitate strife between the daughters and their husbands. Out of the despair that comes from discovering that the consequence of abnegating worldly power is not a blissful state beyond care and without burdens—a despair that leads inevitably to madness as a defense against the impotent nothingness that he has brought upon himself—Lear will come to learn the equally powerful, but kinder, paradox of fertile nothingness.

After the fool has recited a nonsense poem, Kent comments, "This is nothing, fool," and the bantering fool, turning toward Lear, rejoins with "Then 'tis like the breath of an unfee'd lawyer. You gave me nothing for 't.— Can you make no use of nothing, uncle?" But Lear has not yet begun to discover, within the depths of his own darkness, this astonishing paradox of fertile nothingness, and repeating his earlier remark to Cordelia, he dumbly responds to the fool's pointed question: "Why, no, boy, nothing can be made out of nothing." The fool continues to taunt Lear's conscience with elliptically penetrating remarks:

I had rather be any kind o' thing than a fool;
and yet I would not be thee, uncle. Thou hast
pared thy wit o' both sides, and left nothing in the
middle . . . Now thou art an O without a figure.
I am better than thou are now.
I am a fool, thou art nothing. (I. iv. 189-98)

Lear will begin to understand his own nothingness when, naked himself, he is able to empathize with other people's losses and deprivations, and he will then measure whatever is good in life against that nothingness. During the storm in Act III, Lear instructs Kent and the fool to enter a hovel before he does; in his mind, they become emblems of human nakedness in the face of nature's indifferent cruelty, and in the following speech, Lear reaches outside the hollow "O" of his own figure:

Poor naked wretches, whereso'er you are,
That bide the pelting of this pitiless storm,
How shall your houseless heads and unfed sides,
Your loop'd and window'd raggedness, defend you
From seasons such as these? O! I have ta'en
Too little care of this. Take physic, pomp;
Expose thyself to feel what wretches feel,
That thou mayst shake the superflux to them,
And show the heavens more just. (III. iv. 28-36)

For Lear "superflux" is the antithesis of nothing. In physical terms superflux is any commodity, like food or clothing, that protects mankind from its nakedness as a creature of bodily vulnerability; in moral terms superflux means human compassion, what Darwin called "sympathy" which he considered to be the evolutionary basis for morality. (2) In Lear's world, where the cruelty and indifference of nature are synonymous with the absence of a merciful or a just god, only human caring and generosity have the power to counteract existential nothingness, to fill the empty space of absent divinity, and, thus, to "show the heavens more just." Divinity, paradoxically, is made manifest only through the humanity of compassion.

Having been betrayed by his daughters, Lear's vision of his own past failure to care sufficiently for the suffering of others, the "wretches" of nature, elevates the capacity for empathy and compassion to a divine status. Lear's speech implies that if we would care for each other, that in itself would be a sufficient sign of heavenly justice on earth. The absence of God is virtually synonymous with the deliberate cruelty of human beings to one another so that there is no moral force to counteract the thoughtless indifference of nature. Lear's sense of having been betrayed by his daughters epitomizes betrayal as the inescapable law of family intimacy, just as Job's sense of having been betrayed by his inscrutable God is inseparable from his experience of being misunderstood and thus emotionally deserted by his friends:

> All my friends have forgotten me;
>   my neighbors have thrown me away.
> My relatives look through me
>   as though I didn't exist.
> My servants refuse to hear me;
>   they shun me like a leper.

For Job, as for Lear, the appeal to an absent God is made as an appeal for pity and empathy between human beings. Lear looks into his own heart to find this resource, and Job directly asks his condemning comforters: "Have pity on me, my friends, / For God's fist has struck me." Betrayal becomes a morbid expectation in Lear, and when the destitute Edgar emerges with the fool from the hovel into the storm, the now half-mad Lear assumes that Edgar, too, must have been betrayed by daughters to have come to such a state; Lear exclaims: "What! have his daughters brought him to this pass? Could'st thou save nothing?" Lear sees Edgar as reduced to "nothing," just as he has been, and, envisioning himself as the representation of the fundamental human condition of having been betrayed, Lear strips himself of his clothing: "Unaccommodated man is no more but such a poor, bare forked animal as thou art. Off, off, you lendings!" "Unaccommodated man" is Lear's version of nothingness in the absence of the "superflux" of human kindness—a kindness that even here on the desolate heath is growing as a new capacity in Lear as the result of his increased understanding of nothingness.

In the overt structure of the play, Gloucester is ostensibly represented as a figure parallel to Lear because he, too, is a father betrayed by a child. Both fathers are treated by their rejected offspring with extreme cruelty beyond any measure of deserving. Goneril is correct in saying bitterly to Regan that "He always loved our sister [Cordelia] most." Gloucester's preference for Edgar over Edmund, whom he crudely humiliates in the first scene by joking about his illicit conception, is based on Edgar's legitimacy. These rivalries between brothers or between sisters are variants of the Cain and

Abel story which in *Hamlet* results in one brother's murdering another and which Shakespeare calls the "primal eldest crime." But if Gloucester is Lear's parallel as father, Edmund is Edgar's alter-image as son. The converse of Lear as the abandoner and the betrayer of his daughter is the betrayal of Edgar by both his brother and his father. Thus we, the audience, will witness Edgar, in his own deliberate way, undergo a regenerative process of moral understanding that first requires a descent into nothingness remarkably similar to Lear's.

Having been forced to flee his home and his father's intemperate and injudicious wrath, Edgar elects to disguise himself as a beggar:

> *To take the basest and most poorest shape*
> *That ever penury, in contempt of man,*
> *Brought near to beast. My face I'll grim with filth,*
> *Blanket my loins, elf all my hair in knots,*
> *And with presented nakedness outface*
> *The winds and persecutions of the sky.* (II. iii. 7-12)

With uncanny exactness, Edgar's words and conjured images anticipate Lear's subsequent rejoinder to Goneril when she tells Lear to reduce the number of his followers, and Lear replies, "O reason not the need. Our basest beggars / Are in the poorest things superfluous," and when Lear strips himself naked on the heath to face the storm as "unaccommodated man," Edgar concludes his speech with the ringing words, "Edgar I nothing am," and thus he is profoundly linked with Lear's descent into nothingness. Although Edgar means that he has lost his identity as Edgar, Gloucester's son and inheritor, his words equally imply that his true identity now resides in his banished and betrayed condition. This vision of nothingness is precisely the one that Lear will come to acknowledge and embrace. What Lear will learn is that to be nothing, to be naked, to be stripped of all superfluity, all necessities, is to know what man cannot live without. "The art of our necessities is strange," Lear later says to Kent, "That can make vile things seem precious."

Edgar is betrayed by both his brother, deliberately, and by his father, unknowingly; Lear is betrayed by two of his daughters, and, as he comes deeply to understand, by himself as well. Likewise, Job is also twice betrayed: by God who dallies with him in consort with Satan, and by his friends who are willing to renounce Job out of their need to cling to their consoling philosophy that the world is morally comprehensible. Mysteriously, these two betrayals are inextricably linked to each other, and it seems as if Job could endure being abandoned by God if it did not result in his friends also turning against him. Their pity and understanding could have, to use Shakespeare's words, "shown the heavens more just." Job directly confronts Eliphaz, the first comforter, with the accusation: "You too have turned against me; my wretchedness fills you with fear." Job bitterly comprehends the irony that exacerbates the difficulty of human beings showing compassion and empathy for each other because need itself, affliction and wretchedness, appears as a form of ugliness, so that the greater the need for sympathy, the more the potential sympathizer is repelled. Thus Bildad's rebuke of Job can be seen as a psychological defense against offering sympathy that manifests itself as theological dogma: "God never betrays the innocent / or takes the hand of the wicked." With such rationalization in defiance of the obvious truth of Job's victimization by an impersonally hostile God (Job is afflicted only because of Satan's taunting of God), Bildad's betrayal of Job becomes a direct extension of God's betrayal of Job.

The model for proper moral behavior in Job's mind had earlier been established in the way God had treated him after his creation, and Job takes pains to remind God of his original care and solicitude:

> *Remember: you formed me from clay . . .*
> *clothed me in flesh and skin,*
> *knit me with bones and sinews.*
> *You loved me, you gave me life,*
> *you nursed and cared for my spirit.*

God had been both mother and father to Job, and it is precisely God's tender and sympathetic treatment of Job that—as Job claims later in the poem—has shaped Job's own compassionate attitude toward his fellow man:

> *Did I ever strike down a beggar*
> *when he called to me in distress?*
> *Didn't I weep for the wretched?*
> *Didn't I grieve for the poor?*

And so, in Job's mind, God's betrayal of him—God's undeserved and inscrutable withdrawal of mercy, pity, and protection—destroys the foundation of human connectedness and solidarity. Without a divine or a human bond of empathy, Job feels himself to be alone in nature (as Lear is spiritually alone on the heath) related only to the indifferent elements and the animals who lack moral consciousness:

I despair and can find no comfort;
I stand up and cry for help.
I am brother to the wild jackal,
friend to the desert owl.

And yet Job persists in his cry for help. No longer wishing to die or never to have been born, as he did at the beginning of the book, Job chooses to endure so that he can persevere in his demand that God answer his complaint and make clear His divine purposes. This choice defines Job and gives him his essential identity.

Like Job, Gloucester must overcome the temptation of suicide and, like Job, Lear must summon his utmost powers of will and determination to endure with patience. Lear, however, differs from Job, whose primary cry for justice is directed toward God, since Lear comes to expect no kindness from the worldly manifestation of God's elements, only from people, from family. If there is justice in Heaven, it will reveal itself only through human behavior:

Rumble thy bellyful! Spit fire! spout rain!
Nor rain, wind, thunder, fire, are my daughters.
I tax you not, you elements, with unkindness;
I never gave you kingdom, call'd you children,
You owe me no subscription. (III. ii. 14-18)

But this view, with its emphasis on human kindness in the face of the indifference of nature and the random cruelty of the elements, marks a radical change from Lear's earlier Job-like invocation to a rescuing divinity when he prays:

O Heavens,
If you do love old men, if your sweet sway
Allows obedience, if you yourselves are old,
Make it your cause. Send down and take my part! (II. iv. 90-93)

All the heavens send down, however, is rain and wind; if there is any meaning in natural destructiveness and disaster, it only can be found in the human will to endure and to resist and in the occasion such suffering provides for human introspection and self-judgment. Thus, when Lear says: "No, I will be the pattern of all patience. / I will say nothing," he is affirming in his despair the moral nothingness of a universe in which the heavens do not make human suffering their cause, a nothingness within which Lear will come to replace divine judgment with human judgment.

And so Lear's imagination, in rejection of absent gods, takes as its own the perspective of a wrathfully judgmental but just divinity who sees the corruption inherent in all human beings, and from this point of view Lear surveys the earth and sees sinfulness. Lear's only recourse is to cry for mercy:

> *Tremble, thou wretch,*
> *That hast within thee undivulged crimes*
> *Unwhipp'd of justice; hide thee, thou bloody hand,*
> *Thou perjur'd, and thou simular of virtue*
> *That art incestuous. Caitiff, to pieces shake,*
> *That under covert and convenient seeming*
> *Hast practiced on man's life. Close pent-up guilts,*
> *Rive your concealing continents, and cry*
> *These dreadful summoners grace.* (III. ii. 51-59)

(All the most fundamental violations of human morality, from incest, to hypocrisy, to the abuse of power, to murderousness are cataloged here.) Finally, the judgmental Lear turns these accusations against himself and confesses to them all and cries for grace, yet, astonishingly, declares that "I am a man / More sinned against than sinning." What Lear has in mind, no doubt, is the treatment he has received from Goneril and Regan, but his claim directs itself also against the unanswering heavens that betray human faith by refusing to take up the cause of human suffering. (In claiming, without rationalization or sentimentality, that he is "more sinned against than sinning," Lear places himself squarely with Job, who had not claimed absolute and impossible purity in confronting God: "Can't you forgive my sins / or overlook my mistakes?" Lear expresses the irrefutable truth of his own experience: the suffering of human beings does not exist in relation even to their admitted transgressions; there is no morally justifiable connection between one's behavior and one's necessary fate.)

The accusing and tormenting fool must be regarded as an aspect of Lear's mind—his conscience that functions at the border of madness—but also as a character who exists in his own right with his own emotions and needs. (Shakespeare often has one character represent some aspect of another.) It follows with inevitable logic that when Lear allows himself to feel some sympathy for himself, to acknowledge the measure of his own innocence as one "more sinn'd against than sinning," his empathy for the fool also should become manifest. Lear says to him, "Come, your hovel, / Poor fool and knave, I have one part in my heart / That's sorry yet for thee." The fool's song in response expresses Lear's own inner knowledge, so recently come upon, that the elements, representative of absent divinity, constitute the fortune of the human world that often is cruel beyond an individual's deserving:

> *He that has and a little tiny wit,*
> *With hey, ho, the wind and the rain,*
> *Must make content with his fortunes fit,*
> *For the rain it raineth every day.* (III. ii. 74-77)

Lear's reply to the fool's poignant song is simple, direct, and comprehensive: "True, my good boy," for it acknowledges that fortune and the moral nothingness of nature are what Lear must accept as inescapable absolutes.

Since fortune beyond human control defines the ongoing condition of nature, to understand the randomness of fortune is, paradoxically, to be able to see that one cannot see into the future, which is precisely what the fool reveals next in his elaborate non sequitur when he says "I'll speak a prophecy before I go":

> *When every case in law is right,*
> *No square in debt, nor no poor knight;*
> *When slanders do not live in tongues;*
> *Nor cutpurses come not to throngs;*
> *When usurers tell their gold i' th' field,*
> *And bawds and whores do churches build:*
> *Then shall the realm of Albion*
> *Come to great confusion.*
> *Then comes the time, who lives to see't,*
> *That going shall be us'd with feet.* (III. ii. 85-94)

The theme of the fool's prophecy is justice and virtue, and the rhetorical structure of the passage is to anticipate a time in the future when the vices of the world, represented by the nation of Albion, shall come to an end. All this anticipation leads, however, not to revelation, but to "confusion," for the prophecy ends with a crashing anticlimax: in the new age people will walk on their feet. (With the terrible forced rhyme of "see't" and "feet.") The point of this anticlimax is that the only thing that has been revealed is a non-revelation.

(The fool's comment about his own prophecy, which concludes the scene, is an amazing anachronism: "This prophecy Merlin shall make, for I live before his time." This is truly a mystical moment in the play. Living in "Prehistoric Britain," the fool nevertheless can see into the future of King Arthur's court where Merlin the king's magician served, and this future, for Shakespeare's audience, is, of course, the deep historical past. All time seems to be collapsed in the fool's mind, to exist in a single moment of insight, and the collapsing of historical periods occurs because what the fool envisions—the emptiness and nothingness of human existence, the failure of both human and divine justice—are unchanging and unchangeable conditions. The fool's anachronism is a parody of Jesus' remark, "Before Abraham was, I am" (John 8:58), since it replaces the abiding presence of divinity throughout time, transcending chronology, with an abiding absence: we have a prophecy of a prophecy that prophesies nothing. There is not yet a perspective from which a story of suffering and trial can be told.)

II The Whirlwind & the Storm

(The Book of Job and *King Lear* are profoundly alike in their basic themes. Both Job and Lear lose their children and property, suffer betrayals, endure great physical hardships, and confront the elements, which represent ambiguously answering or unresponsive divinity: Job encounters the whirlwind and Lear contends with the storm. Both The Book of Job and *King Lear* are filled with trial scenes and allusions to trials. Eliphaz says to Job: "If I were you, I would pray; / I would put my case before God." Job replies as if the trial already had taken place: "Man's life is a prison; he is sentenced to pain and grief." And after Bildad, assuming that Job's claim of innocence is both blasphemous and false, excoriates him with the presumed certainty that "Such is the fate of the impious, / the empty hope of the sinner," Job replies with rhetorical irony:

> *How can I prove my innocence?*
> *Do I have to beg him for mercy?*
> *If I testify, will he answer?*
> *Is he listening to my plea?*

Although deep in his heart, where his faith was once grounded, Job still hopes that God will intervene and explain himself, Job now knows with certainty—a certainty that has replaced his earlier belief in a just God—

that "He has punished me for a trifle; / for no reason he gashes my flesh." But Job goes further; he becomes God's accuser, putting God on trial in the courtroom of his own imagination as he recites the horrendous indictment: God "hands the earth to the wicked / and blindfolds its judges' eyes." Beyond this indictment of God's deeds, Job goes still further by impugning God's motives, castigating Him for hypocrisy. This is the ultimate in blasphemy:

> *For you keep pursuing a sin,*
> *trying to dig up a crime,*
> *though you* know *that I am innocent.*

Zophar tries to turn Job's questioning of God's justice and God's motives back onto Job, again placing Job in a courtroom where he is being cross-examined for a crime he is presumed to have committed:

> *But if God were to cross-examine you*
> *and turned up your hidden motives*
> *and presented his case against you*
> *and told you why he has punished you—*
> *you would know that your guilt is great.*

Job responds by linking Zophar in a conspiracy with God against him: "Will you lie to vindicate God? / Will you perjure yourselves for him?" In such a courtroom, as Job knows to his despair, he cannot receive justice or mercy at the hands of either God or man. In utter isolation, Job then ends his speech with a desperate plea to God to restore their former relationship when God treated Job as a loving father: "you would come to me and rejoice, / delighting in my smallest step / like a father watching his child." But having betrayed Job by abandoning him, God also has "destroy[ed] man's hope," and Job is left, cut off both from God and from man, trapped entirely in his own pain, without consolation or compassion, doomed therefore to mourn for himself and, still worse, to realize that, confined in the labyrinth of his own grief, his inward mourning must breed upon itself: "Only his own flesh hurts him, / and he mourns for himself alone."

Like Job, Lear is accused of a crime that seems both absurd and without justification. Regan says to him, "O, sir, you are old," and tells him that he owes Goneril an apology: "Say, you have wrong'd her." Appalled by the false accusation and Regan's attempt to intimidate him into making a hypocritical confession, Lear replies, "Ask her [Goneril's] forgiveness?" and then, with even more bitter irony, Lear acknowledges his supposed crime:

"Dear daughter, I confess that I am old. Age is unnecessary." This absurdity would seem to destroy any meaningfulness in the concepts of guilt and forgiveness, and supersede Lear's actual wronging of Cordelia. Lear, though innocent of Regan's charges, will have to acknowledge his need to ask for Cordelia's forgiveness even though, in the balance of the scale of justice, he is now "more sinn'd against than sinning." So, too, Job, though innocent of any specific legal or moral crime, nevertheless is guilty of insisting that God make himself understood in human terms: "I have spoken of the unspeakable / and tried to grasp the infinite." This presumption of being able to fathom divine mystery is the violation for which Job ultimately will repent, though it is uncertain whether any quest for knowledge (including Adam's) should be regarded as a crime. Yet there is something divine about this repentance since it is the same repentance that Yahweh himself confessed to when He ponders the evil of humankind, His own creation, before He starts all over after the flood: "And the Lord regretted having made the human on the earth and was grieved to the heart." (Genesis 6:6)

III Trial Scenes

There are two scenes in the play in which Lear in his madness fantasizes that he is presiding at a trial. In the first, Edgar is pretending that he has been possessed by the devil—"the foul fiend bites my back"—and, by virtue of this ironically reverse qualification, Lear selects him to be the judge at the trial of Goneril and Regan: "Thou robed man of justice, take thy place." Lear instructs the fool to take his place on the bench beside Edgar as "his yoke-fellow of equity" and orders the trial to begin. "Arraign her first," says Lear, and then he assumes the stand as the first witness against Goneril for the prosecution: "'Tis Goneril, I here take my oath before his honorable assembly, kicked the poor king her father." As if any worse assault by a daughter against a father were unimaginable, between bitter sarcasm and denial, Lear exhausts his testimony, except to add, "She cannot deny it," and the fool completes the parody of the legal issues of clemency versus justice by declaiming to the imagined Goneril, "Cry you mercy, I took you for a joint-stool." Lear then turns to the imagined figure of Regan, "And here's another, whose warp'd looks proclaim / What store her heart is made on," but immediately the trial comes to an end as Regan avoids conviction because of "corruption" in the court, and Lear says to Edgar in his role of judge: "False justicer, why hast thou let her 'scape?" Lear's thwarted longing for justice, for the exposure of true guilt, and for the meting out of meaningful punishment is perverted in his imagination, making him mad.

So, too, the world comes to seem mad to Job without a court of appeal in which to be heard by God: "If only I knew where to meet him / and could find my way to his court." Under such conditions, Job's testimony, like Lear's, becomes a convoluted perversion and a vain blasphemy: "I swear by God, who has wronged me / and filled my cup with despair."

In the second trial scene, the mad Lear meets the blinded Gloucester near the cliffs of Dover. Gloucester recognizes Lear by his voice, "Is't not the king?" and Lear responds by interpreting the main function of a king to be that of a judge. In this trial scene, however, Lear no longer plays the role of accuser, but the radically different role of pardoner: "I pardon that man's life. What was thy cause? Adultery? Thou shalt not die." In pardoning the anonymous figure in the above passage, Lear also is pardoning himself for, unconsciously, his daughters' betrayal of him carries the connotation of adultery; this accounts for his identification with the man on trial whose life Lear spares in his fantasy. The following speech about forbidden "copulation," ending with Lear's identification of the female genitals as "hell," testifies both to Lear's sense of his own guilt, his own incestuous wishes, and to his inner awareness of the need for pardon and forgiveness. Nevertheless, Lear, again like Job, despairs that justice cannot be counted on and must fail: "And the strong lance of justice hurtless breaks; / Arm it in rags, a pigmy's straw does pierce it." Job differs from Lear, however, because he continues to turn to God in his desperate wish for vindication—"Oh if only God would hear me, / state his case against me, / let me read his indictment," while Lear begins to take it upon himself to declare everyone, including himself, in the final balancing of the scales, to be innocent: "None does offend, none, I say none." Thus, in Lear's mind, the trial comes to an end, but what still remains to be resolved is Lear's forgiveness of himself, which cannot occur until forgiveness has been offered to him by Cordelia.

After Lear is rescued by Cordelia, we find him in a deep sleep in the French camp. Cordelia prays over his body, "O you kind gods, / Cure this great breach in his abused nature," and the attending doctor says that "in the heaviness of sleep, / We put fresh garments on him." Throughout the play the gods are merely a projection of the circumstances and nature of the person who calls upon them. The symbolism of dressing Lear anew suggests his return from spiritual and literal nakedness in the earlier scene when Lear, "Contending with the fretful elements," had been reduced to nothing. As described by the gentleman, Lear "Tears his white hair, / Which the impetuous blasts, with eyeless rage, / Catch in their fury and make nothing of." At the curative hands of Cordelia and the doctor who truly "shake the superflux" of their love and concern upon him, Lear, the "unaccommodated man," begins to become accommodated. It is deeply symbolic that Lear wakes from a heavy sleep, as if being reborn, so that he thinks that he has come back from death when he first sees Cordelia leaning over him: "You do me wrong to take me out of the grave." Lear does not yet feel sufficiently worthy of being treated with such solicitude, and, filled with guilt for having betrayed Cordelia by rejecting her, he says to her:

> *If you have poison for me, I will drink it.*
> *I know you do not love me, for your sisters*
> *Have (as I do remember) done me wrong.*
> *You have some cause, they do not.* (IV. vii. 71-74)

Cordelia's spontaneous response, "No cause, no cause," is the human equivalent of divine creation out of nothingness since the ordinary connections to be found in nature between cause and effect are replaced by a kind of magical leap that is the essence of the power of human volition. Cordelia offers her love to Lear beyond cause or causation, not as reward or in the fulfillment of duty, but as a gift that generates its own goodness and satisfaction. Her gift has a healing effect on Lear, and the doctor says: "Be comforted, good madam. The great rage, / You see, is cur'd in him." The immediate result of this cure is that Lear is released from the grip of his guilt and can now implore Cordelia to "forget and forgive," thus completing the movement from rage and the wish for vengeance toward tolerance and self-acceptance that began when Lear claimed that he was "a man more sinn'd against than sinning." Lear's new innocence, his ability to "forgive" and to receive forgiveness (since forgiveness implies that the past can be changed or redeemed by changing one's attitude toward the past) works as if by miracle. This restorative power, when love seemed lost, refutes Lear's opening statement that "Nothing will come of nothing" and begins to mitigate the betrayal both of himself and of his daughter.

IV Identity & Perspective

Earlier, the powerless Lear, whose identity had depended on his image of himself as king, had asked: "Who is it that can tell me who I am?" After Lear has been reunited with his daughter, the question of his identity returns, but in the most fundamental terms of the necessities of the human condition. The whole reunion scene is suffused with echoes and variants on the phrase "I am," beginning with Lear's metaphorical description of his tormented state: "I am bound / Upon a wheel of fire." It continues with his confusion as to where he actually is—"Where am I?"—and an assertion of his own victimization: "I am mightily abused." This is followed by a kind of breakthrough in self-perspective with the most humble yet objective statement Lear has so far been able to make: "I am a very foolish fond old man." Lear's gain in perspective and sanity deepens into the paradoxical awareness of his own mental instability, "I fear I am not in my perfect mind," and in his acknowledgment of his confusion, "I am doubtful," and "I am mainly ignorant." His speech concludes with the assertion of his simple humanity: ". . . as I am a man, I think this lady / To be my child Cordelia." Lear's grasp of his own basic, "I am," his fundamental identity, is met and affirmed by Cordelia's reply, "And so I am, I am"; the scene concludes with a resounding echo of Lear's earlier line of self-recognition: "Pray you now, forget and forgive. I am old and foolish." With this sense of himself within his deliberate possession, now free of pride and self-indulgent guilt, Lear at last can free himself from the constraints of merely trying to endure and the chains of unrealizable self-imposed silence: "No, I will be the pattern of all patience. / I will say nothing." Now Lear can both ask for and accept forgiveness. As if born anew as a child learning to walk when Cordelia asks him, "Will't please your highness walk?" Lear also has begun to learn a new language of restoration and humility.

    Having reconciled with Cordelia, Lear is literally in a state of ecstasy—he is outside of himself—and though this state resembles madness in its departure from ordinary reality, yet it is the opposite of madness for it assumes a higher, even divine, sanity. Although Lear and Cordelia are captured by the enemy forces, and Cordelia understands their predicament with exact and worldly irony—"We are not the first / Who with best meaning have incurr'd the worst," Lear's blissful mood remains unaffected as they are led off to prison, and Lear accepts his new fate, "Fortune's frown" as Cordelia gently calls it, as if his fate resulted from his own choice:

> *Come, let's away to prison.*
> *We two alone will sing like birds i' th' cage.*
> *When thou dost ask me blessing, I'll kneel down,*
> *And ask of thee forgiveness. So we'll live,*
> *And pray and sing, and tell old tales, and laugh*
> *At gilded butterflies, and hear poor rogues*
> *Talk of court news; and we'll talk with them too:*
> *Who loses and who wins, who's in, who's out;*
> *And take upon's the mystery of things,*
> *As if we were God's spies; and we'll wear out*

In a wall'd prison, pacts and sects of great ones
That ebb and flow by th' moon. (V. iii. 8-19)

Like Job, after God reveals himself in the whirlwind as the unfathomable creator whose creation is both beautiful and cruel, Lear now sees the world as a spectacle, a source of song and story, and he sees it as if not only from outside himself, but also from beyond the world, from a divine perspective: "As if we were God's spies." Neither Job nor Lear is given a vision of ultimate justice or the redemption of wrongs and suffering; rather, their visionary detachment is rewarded with the effusion of laughter. Political intrigue and struggle, "Who loses and who wins," no longer seem urgent or important, but merely become part of "the mystery of things," which are of no more significance, from this timeless perspective, than the image of "gilded butterflies." The worldly condition that makes such a vision possible for Lear, that connects his individual fortune to the impersonal transcendence of his fate, is his ability to exchange blessing and forgiveness with Cordelia. That ability alone, which is not dependent on events but on a willed attitude, can transfigure suffering into a kind of divine laughter. This moment of Lear's realization is like Hamlet's wish to become one who "in suffering all, that suffers nothing," and it is directly comparable to the jubilation in God's response to Job in recounting the origination of the created universe when "the morning stars burst out singing / and the angels shouted for joy!"

Cordelia and the fool have both served as curative forces within Lear's mind: Cordelia as the potentiality and power of forgiveness and the fool as Lear's inspired madness, his conscience. The fool vanishes mysteriously in the middle of the play, after having replied to Lear's line, "We'll go to supper i' th' morning," with the equally enigmatic, "And I'll go to bed at noon," suggesting that he knows his premature death is imminent. Since the fool has completed his cathartic work in the depths of Lear's mind, it is appropriate, however, that he be replaced by the soothing spiritual powers of Cordelia. And so when Cordelia dies, the figure of the fool—"And my poor fool is dead"—merges with her in Lear's mind as he symbolically bears witness to his own death as well, for both have been essential parts of Lear's own psyche. Because the deaths of the three of them are inextricably bound—and because Cordelia's death appears to Lear as a new and unanticipated betrayal of what should be the natural continuity of time in which children survive parents—Lear's ecstatic vision of himself and Cordelia safely outside of time and beyond worldly fortune is shattered. Thus, Lear responds to Cordelia's also premature death in terms of absolute negation:

And my poor fool is hang'd! No, no, no, life!
Why should a dog, a horse, a rat, have life,
And thou no breath at all? Thou'lt come no more.
Never, never, never, never, never! (V. iii. 303-6)

V Confronting Nothingness

The empty nothingness of time seen as unrestorative in which loss is absolute and eternal provokes the question Lear now asks of existence; this question is, in essence, identical to Job's wish to understand why God allows the "wicked to prosper" and the good to go unrewarded. As an unanswerable question, such inquiry exposes the moral nothingness at the foundation of Lear's universe. Immediately after the above lines, the interminable repetition of "Never," Lear asks Albany to undo a button on Cordelia's blouse because Lear's hands are trembling as he kneels over her breathless body:

Pray you, undo this button. Thank you, sir.
Do you see this? Look on her! look! her lips!
Look there, look there! O, O, O, O. (V. iii. 307-9)

Here, each "O" is filled with the emptiness of loss and the palpable love for his daughter who cannot be regained; the "O" that had earlier been an emblem of himself—"Now thou art an O without a figure" as the fool had declared—returns to the original silence that preceded human speech. We, the audience, are confronted with a nothingness more absolute than Cordelia's silence when she refused to respond with no more than the words, "Nothing, my Lord," to Lear's demand that Cordelia force her feelings of love into public declamation.

In another early scene that is comparable to the "Nothing, my lord," "Nothing will come of nothing" exchange between Cordelia and Lear, Edmund is "ostentatiously reading a letter" that supposedly his brother Edgar sent to him to suggest that the brothers plot together to kill their father in order to get his inheritance without further delay. Gloucester readily falls into the trap the treacherous Edmund has set for him and asks: "What paper were you reading?" Edmund, echoing Cordelia's words, replies: "Nothing my Lord." Gloucester's angry rejoinder reveals the same blindness of understanding that characterized Lear's response to Cordelia:

No? What needed then that terrible dispatch of it into your
pocket? The quality of nothing hath not such need to hide

itself. Let's see. Come! If it be nothing, I shall not need spectacles. (I. ii. 33-36)

At the end of the play, Edmund, faced with death and seemingly miraculously cured of his own hatefulness even, astonishingly, by the love of Goneril and Regan ("Yet Edmund was belov'd") as Lear is cured by Cordelia's love, Edmund attempts to redeem himself out of his own nothingness. In a reversal of character as radical as any Shakespeare ever offers his audience, Edmund, fully aware of his own transformation, cries out: "Some good I mean to do / Despite of mine own nature." But though Edmund has succeeded in redeeming himself (as had Cawdor in his death in *Macbeth*), he fails to prevent the death of Cordelia which he had ordered. Shakespeare's irony is immense. Even the reversal of nothing collapses back into nothing.

Faced with ultimate nothingness, Lear's heart, having endured so long, now breaks. And yet we, the audience, cannot tell for certain whether it is grief that kills Lear or—like the parallel moment in which Gloucester dies ("his flaw'd heart / . . . 'Twixt two extremes of passion, joy and grief, / Burst smilingly")—a joyous illusion that he sees movement on Cordelia's lips. At this culminating moment, everything and nothing appear as inseparable and interchangeable. If it is the illusion that Cordelia is alive that mercifully kills King Lear, we do not know whether to regard this illusion as the final irony of the play—as the ultimate failure of the hero of patience and reconciliation to endure the ultimate truth—or as a kind of triumph of the fictive imagination to impose itself upon mere reality. Lear's imagination asserts love here in the extremity of pain, like a work of art, in a universe of unheeding gods that begins and ends as a moral void. Like the epilogue of the Book of Job in which we are allowed a fantasy of restoration (new children cannot really replace children who have died), Lear, too, is relieved of having to die with the absolute certainty of Cordelia's death. We, the audience, exhausted ourselves from having to bear witness to what now surely feels like the ultimate betrayal of love by fortune or cruel destiny—whether sponsored by the gods or as a contingency of the indifference of nature—may wish to see Lear's last moment as one in which it is fitting that he enjoy Prometheus' gift to mankind of "blind hope." To Lear's earlier question to Edgar—"Coulds't thou save nothing?"—the answer at the play's conclusion would appear to rest for the survivors as an interpretation of an illusion, a willingness to accept a fiction as its own kind of truth.

The epilogue of the Book of Job returns the reader to the mythic, "Once upon a time" style of the Prologue, so different from the tough realism of the main body of the book, and offers the reader the fictive comfort of a happy restorative ending. Only in the realm of make-believe, however, can Job's new family truly replace the deceased former family. And there is a subtle but special irony, I believe, in Job's words acknowledging that he is made of dust, as they exactly echo the tactful words of Abraham to Yahweh, "Here, pray, I have presumed to speak to my Lord when I am but dust and ashes," after Abraham has confronted the Lord in their debate before Sodom and Gomorrah that so clearly prefigures Job: "Will you really wipe out the innocent with the guilty? Will not the Judge of all the earth do justice?" (Genesis 18:24) (4)

Statements about the power of fictional art, like the imagination which "gives to airy nothing / A local habitation and a name" (*A Midsummer Night's Dream*), appear in many of Shakespeare's plays, but none is more succinct and telling than Edgar's final response to having witnessed King Lear's agony: "The weight of this sad time we must obey; / Speak what we feel, not what we ought to say." Edgar's words, which emphasize the importance of connecting feeling—with its own reality—with speech so that language does not betray the shadings of meaning, directly echo the words of his father, Gloucester, in condemning the "lust-dieted Man" who "will not see / Because he does not feel," so that, at last, son and father are connected, and the son, in spirit and language, becomes the father's true inheritor. Thus seeing and feeling become one at last in contrast to the many forms of blindness that have been exposed throughout the play. As Edgar's words have echoed Gloucester's, so, too, have Gloucester's words,—"Heavens, deal so still! / Let the superfluous and lust-dieted man, / Because he does not feel, feel your power quickly. / So distribution should undo excess, / And each man have enough"—echoed Lear's most empathetic speech about the need for feeling: "Expose thyself to feel what wretches feel, / That thou mayst shake the superflux to them and show the heavens more just." In Edgar's final "Speak what we feel," then, all three of them are united in spiritual brotherhood and across the generations as a healthy version of the poisonous uniting of Goneril, Regan, and Edmund who, in the moment of death, confesses: "I was contracted to them both. All three / Now marry in an instant."

Art, as impassioned speech—speech that unifies motive and expression even at the abyss of nothingness—ultimately must be concerned with human endurance and survival. In so directing itself, felt speech must face and confront truths so terrible that they may seem to be unspeakable. And yet for both Job and Lear, the intractability of natural cruelty, seen as an inescapable aspect of creation itself—as if God's betrayal of mankind were the cause of the betrayals among brothers and friends, of children by parents which, in turn, generated the betrayal of parents by children— seems nevertheless to leave room for human invention, poetic art (illusion perhaps), to be created out of nothingness. For Job, that invention is the openness of wonder in the spirit of humble acceptance of the awesome magnificence of nature when no moral demands are made upon nature and its creator. For Lear, that invention is empathy, even more powerful because it exists only by virtue of the human will as an act of deliberate choice, for the suffering of others; thus empathy engenders love beyond self-love and the temptations of greedy betrayal. Edgar's assertion of the need for endurance to his own father: "Men must endure / Their going hence, even as their coming hither. / Ripeness is all," underlies his affirmation of honest human speech—speech felt and thus fictionalized—as a power that can enable vulnerable human beings to confront chaos and the original void with a ripeness that is not merely an analogy to harvest time and natural endings, but the consummation of the human imagination as it asserts itself by the recounting of the past, by storytelling, in the hopeless face of nothingness.

CHAPTER SEVEN

MACBETH: THE MORAL IMAGINATION

I Consequence

Macbeth differs from Hamlet, Othello, and King Lear in that Macbeth is a good man who decides to do evil and who succeeds, while the others are all good men whose intentions are to do good, but for the most part, fail. In compensation for their failures, Hamlet, Othello, and Lear learn something about what is precious in human life, but Macbeth is confirmed in what his conscience already knew: "We still have judgment here." To call Macbeth "a good man" is perhaps merely to call him a man, for Shakespeare's understanding of human nature is that—with certain exceptions like Iago—it is essentially moral since men and women contain within themselves their own heaven and hell; virtue is its own reward, and evil, its own punishment. Macbeth suffers not merely because he is a criminal, but because he is a good man committing evil deeds. Macbeth knows with absolute certainty that if he kills Duncan, since we "still have judgment here," he will be committing suicide; he will be commending "the ingredients of our poisone'd chalice / To our own lips." Every point Macbeth makes in his "If it were done when 'tis done, 'twere well / It were done quickly" speech, in which, perhaps unconsciously, he echoes Jesus' words to Judas who is about to betray him, "That thou doest, do quickly," (John 13:27)—a betrayal that parallels Macbeth's immanent betrayal of the saintly Duncan—argues forcefully against committing the crime. Macbeth's explanation, employing the concept of "vaulting ambition" is obviously unconvincing and insufficient, and shortly after Lady Macbeth enters the room, Macbeth says to her: "We will proceed no further in this business."

Why, then, does Macbeth perpetrate such a deed that violates the moral order and his own conscience, succumbing to some kind of impossibly perverse pride or some self-defeating ambition? Perhaps we need to assume that his ambition here goes far beyond the worldly wish to become king; perhaps at a much deeper level his ambition is a wish for immortality or even a wish to become God, like Adam's wish to eat of the other forbidden tree which God punishes with death. Macbeth's desire to control both nature and time strongly suggests that Macbeth's ambition surpasses the desire for political power. After some heated exchanges with his wife, Macbeth reverses his decision not to proceed further in the murder plot, and states bluntly "I am settled, and bend up / Each corporal agent to this terrible feat." One might argue that Macbeth has been persuaded by his wife, though it is difficult to see how her hysterical and questionable description of her hypothetical dashing the brains out of a nursing child should be persuasive to someone as morally clearheaded as is Macbeth at this early point in the play before he becomes divided against himself and loses what he calls "the single state of man." Rather, Shakespeare requires that his audience remain speculative about how human beings make choices since choice-making is the quintessence of our humanity.

So, too, even though their consequences may be fixed as inescapable guilt, are evil choices mysterious, beyond prediction or explanation; they follow no absolute psychological laws that make them inevitable since they are the product of a free will. Shakespeare knows that some limited good may come from evil—this is the wisdom we learn from all tragedy. Although Shakespeare accepts this paradox, he also embraces the further paradox that evil may be inevitable in a world of free men since free men, as history shows, sometimes make destructive choices; yet evil must be opposed as if tragic necessity is not absolute in its power of fatal determination. The model of Cawdor's repentance, which he chooses freely for its own sake, without any pragmatic hope that he might be spared from execution, remains in the audience's mind throughout the play as an option that is always there for Macbeth to choose also. Over and over, Macbeth willfully chooses to reject that option. When, for example, Macbeth asks the Doctor, "Can'st thou not minister to a mind diseased?" and the Doctor replies, "Therein the patient / Must minister to himself," Macbeth angrily rejects the Doctor's advice: "Throw physic to the dogs; I'll none of it," he says.

In Shakespeare's plays, the world, the state, and the individual are interrelated, macrocosm to microcosm. Any influence on one affects the others. A broken law in the affairs of men will be felt throughout the cosmos. The morning after Duncan's murder, Ross says:

> *Thou seest the heavens, as troubled with man's act,*
> *Threatens his bloody state: by the clock 'tis day,*
> *And yet dark night strangles the traveling lamp.* (II. iv. 5-7)

Animals no longer act according to their kind, but become strangely violent: a falcon is killed by a mousing owl, and Duncan's horses, "turn'd wild in nature," attack and eat each other. The world is in turmoil, the state is disrupted by the killing of the king, and, metaphorically, Macbeth has also killed the king—the father—within himself.

Hamlet both accepts and doubts the existence of a universal moral structure. He believes that by his actions Denmark can be cured of its ills, when he says "The time is out of joint. O cursed spite, / That ever I was born to set it right!" yet he finds that reason alone will not suffice in enabling him to render justice in a corrupt state. His unwillingness to avenge his uncle's murder of his father conceals both his innate repulsion against the convention of revenge and his unconscious Oedipal identification with Claudius. In a newly cynical state of mind, Hamlet undertakes to commit justice in a world that he fears may not be moral and may not sanction moral action. Hamlet's problem is not that he is unable to act, but that he is unable to do the significant act for fear that it will not prove to be meaningful in the fallen world of Denmark. Hamlet wants to do the right thing, in the right way, for the right reasons; since he finds this impossible, he questions all existence. Finally he acts, and there is a momentary desperate joy in the knowledge that his story will serve as a parable for those to come. Hamlet snatches the cup of poison from Horatio's lips and exhorts:

> If thou did'st ever hold me in thy heart,
> Absent thee from felicity awhile,
> And in this harsh world draw they breath in pain,
> To tell my story. (V. ii. 349-52)

Although the world is harsh, it is a world in which Hamlet desires to have his story told. By contrast, at the end, life for Macbeth seems "a tale / Told by an idiot, full of sound and fury, / Signifying nothing." For Hamlet, his own tale becomes that of man's quest for self-knowledge and a moral struggle with his own conscience, and Hamlet's tragic ecstasy is that he comes to know that even if he has failed to comprehend his own depth, to pluck out the heart of his own mystery, his attempt to do so has signified something worth recounting. The play ends with Horatio's effort to tell Hamlet's story, "And let me speak to the yet unknowing world / How these things came about," although the final irony is that Horatio will probably reduce Hamlet's story to its melodramatic components. One needs to be outside the historical moment through a willed act of artistic detachment, as is true only of Shakespeare himself, to be able to tell a complex story in its full complexity.

Othello also learns that the world is better than he had believed. What was his jealousy but a deep skepticism about love? Not until the very end does Othello fully realize that the world can include a faithful love. Like Hamlet, Othello feels called upon to commit justice and purge the world, and when Othello learns how he has been deceived by Iago, his instinct to set things right leads to his suicide in the name of love and lawful civilization. He kills himself for the sake of the state, as if still acting in an official capacity. Othello is elated as he plunges the knife into himself, for in his mind he has restored his lost identity symbolically. He loves Desdemona more fully, though not without some measure of rationalization and self-justification, in the moment of ultimate loss than he had before, knowing that his tale will be told and that, somehow, it will benefit all to hear it. He says to his audience before he dies:

> *I pray you, in your letters,*
> *When you shall these unlucky deeds relate,*
> *Speak of them as they are. Nothing extenuate,*
> *Nor set down aught in malice. Then must you speak*
> *Of one that lov'd not wisely but too well.* (V. ii. 340-44)

Even Lear, who undergoes the greatest suffering of these four tragic figures, does not renounce life, but desires it more intensely than ever, ripe with the awareness of the infinite value of Cordelia's love. Lear has passed through madness, forgiveness, and self-forgiveness, and has learned, at last, to experience a love that is beyond worldly possession; in this love, envisioned at the moment of his death, Lear is redeemed from his past failure to love Cordelia properly. Lear's final illusion of Cordelia's breathing—"Look on her! look! her lips! / Look there, look there!"—expresses the spiritual truth of his existence, for not pain but joy in love breaks his heart and frees him from the rack of the world. Lear's grief is more consoling to the audience than Macbeth's lack of feeling on learning of the death of his wife. Nature's ironic blessing is to make Lear's love most strongly felt in its loss, and, in the final moment of loss, Lear experiences the ecstasy of affirmation. The tragedy in *King Lear* begins with the hypocritical declarations of love for their father by Goneril and Regan, and it closes with the simple and honest statement by Edgar that Lear's story must be told truly, sad as it is, by speaking "what we feel." Macbeth, in contrast, chooses to fight his last battles, not because he desires to win, and not to achieve or gain something, but out of blind defiance. What remains of him is nothing but his hollow armor. Macbeth says, "Give me my armour," to which Seyton replies, "'Tis not needed yet," and then Macbeth blurts out, "I'll put it on," a rejoinder which is replete with typical Shakespearean irony. Of the protagonists whose perspectives at the end of their lives we have considered, only Macbeth feels that life is worthless and that his story is not worth telling.

II Punishment Versus Blessing

In Shakespeare's plays, reward, retribution, and punishment take place on earth and within the sphere of mortal life. Tragedy requires a world that is complete unto itself, its own end, not a means to another world. Reward, therefore, is not transcendence to a beatific state, nor is punishment imposed upon one in the afterlife like physical torture. The assuming of a burden or a responsibility must, in part, be its own reward: wisdom acquired through suffering, joy in right action, affirmation of moral values. And like reward, punishment must be essentially a state of conscience. Just as Hamlet realizes that "I could be bounded in a nutshell, and count myself a king of infinite space, were it not that I have bad dreams," so, too, Macbeth's mind becomes his own prison: "But now I am cabin'd, cribb'd, confined, bound in / To saucy doubts and fears."

Macbeth is a play about a man who violates the moral order within himself and is punished for having done so by his own conscience. No Dantean torture is imposed upon him to fit his crimes, though his beheading at the end symbolically reflects the split in himself between conscience and deeds; rather, the blessings of Macbeth's natural humanity fall from him one by one until he is deprived of all human ties, trust in friendship, empathy in marriage, even concern for himself. Macbeth's punishment for his Satanic choices is to lose those things that made up his "milk of human kindness," his humanity.

In this sense Macbeth recreates himself as his own antagonist. The entire moral order is reflected within his conscience as the functioning of his imagination, so that the great conflict of the play, despite its battle scenes, is primarily interior. Although Hamlet is opposed by Claudius; Othello, by Iago; Lear, by Regan, Goneril, and Edmund; their fates are at least partially determined by hostile, external forces. But Macbeth, though urged on by Lady Macbeth and the witches—all, in some sense, aspects of himself— can anticipate and calculate the results of his actions. Thus of all these protagonists he is distinct as being the freest and most deliberate master of his fate. He falls, not out of ignorance, foible, or weakness, but, like Satan, out of defiance and ambition to overthrow the order of nature, willingly and willfully embraced. Conscience, in all its vivid imagery of warning, is deliberately rejected by Macbeth, even to the point of absurdity, since Macbeth knows with absolute certainty that punishment and defeat are inevitable. Like John Milton's Satan who claims, "Each way I fly is hell; myself am hell," (1) Macbeth realizes that his character is his fate once he has chosen the deed that will define him in defiance of natural order: the murder of the saintly king, Duncan.)

When Macbeth kills the king, the entire structure of natural and moral order is disrupted, and, in this chaos, results can no longer be calculated from causes so that Macbeth is unable to read the signs of nature and is misled by appearances. Shakespeare describes this disorder by showing us storms, winds, wild seas, thunder, war, and witches, or in subtle ways as in the banquet scene when everybody enters in proper order (Macbeth says: "You know your own degrees; sit down: at first and last"), but exits in confusion (Lady Macbeth says: "You have displac'd the mirth, broke the good meeting, / With most admir'd disorder"). The "breach in nature" imagery is continuous: blood, sickness, predatory animals, dark overcoming light:

> *Light thickens, and the crow*
> *Makes wing to the rooky wood;*
> *Good things of day begin to droop and drowse,*
> *While night's black agents to their preys do rouse.* (III. ii. 50-53)

Macbeth is pictured as a man enveloped in a coat too large for him; he cannot properly wear the clothing of his usurped positions:

> *. . . now does he feel his title*
> *Hang loose about him, like a giant's robe*
> *Upon a dwarfish thief.* (V. ii. 20-23)

The reverberation of sounds echoing over vast regions suggests the incalculable and boundless effect and spread of evil issuing from a single source.

Perhaps, the most important of all the play's imagery is that of the symbol of Macbeth's ambition (like both Adam and Satan) to defy the laws of nature, redirect fate, and shape the future according to his own anarchic order. Macbeth determines his personal doom despite the fact that the control of the future, which the child represents in the image of the "naked new-born babe / Striding the blast" is beyond him. In wishing to usurp the power of nature to take its own course and thus to control the future, it is as if Macbeth desires to father himself, to perpetuate himself unto eternity as if he were God. (2) When the witches show Macbeth a vision of the future—a line of eight kings revealing the survival and triumph of Banquo's progeny—Macbeth cries out, "What! will the line stretch out to the crack of doom?" For Macbeth, a meaningful future can only be identified with himself, any other historical course will be seen by him only as "doom." The witches can predict the future, not because they control it, but because they see into the heart of Macbeth's character and therefore know the fate that will result from his stubbornly willed ambition, not merely to be king but to control the future. In their first speech, the witches speak the words that will come independently, so it seems, into Macbeth's mind, "Fair is foul, and foul is fair"; likewise, Macbeth's first words are "So foul and fair a day."

The order of Shakespeare's cosmos is never interrupted by the miraculous. Every extraordinary event takes place within the limits of natural law since Shakespeare's natural law includes spiritual, as well as material, reality. The witches, therefore, should not be regarded primarily as supernatural beings, but as objectifications of Macbeth's imagination, like the bloody dagger and Banquo's ghost, neither of which can be seen by anybody besides Macbeth. The apparent contradiction that Banquo also sees the witches is overcome by the fact that Banquo's mind has become tainted with the same evil ambition that has corrupted Macbeth. Banquo's ambition, too, is willing to seek its fulfillment by illegal or dubious means so that the witches have the same relation to Banquo as they do to Macbeth. Before he is murdered, Banquo has decided not to expose Macbeth as Duncan's murderer because he believes that Macbeth's advancement is the herald of his own familial enthronement:

> *Thou hast it now: King, Cawdor, Glamis, all,*
> *As the weird women promised; and, I fear,*
> *Thou play'dst most foully for't; yet it was said*
> *It should not stand in thy posterity*
> *But that myself should be the root and father*
> *Of many kings. If there come truth from them,—*
> *As upon thee, Macbeth, their speeches shine,—*
> *Why, by the verities on thee made good,*
> *May they not be my oracles as well,*
> *And set me up in hope?* (II. i. 1-10)

Shakespeare shows us the psychological similarity between Macbeth and Banquo even before the above scene. Banquo's corruption is intimated when earlier, he says to Fleance:

A heavy summons lies like lead upon me,
And yet I would not sleep: Merciful powers!
Restrain in me the cursed thoughts that nature
Gives way to in repose. (II. i. 6-9)

Banquo is sensitive to Macbeth's state of mind; thus, immediately after the witches' first prophecy that Macbeth will become king, Banquo says: "Good sir, why do you start, and seem to fear / Things that do sound so fair?" This, in addition to Lady Macbeth's question to her husband, "What made you break this enterprise to me?" makes it clear that Macbeth, not Lady Macbeth, initially conceived the idea of murdering for the crown. Banquo is not duped by the temptations of evil any more than is Macbeth; yet, he, too, succumbs in conscience and through his deliberate lack of action:

But 'tis strange:
And oftentimes, to win us to our harm,
The instruments of darkness tell us truths,
Win us with honest trifles, to betray's
In deepest consequence. (I. iii. 122-26)

Banquo might have saved his own life if he had acted according to this knowledge and opposed Macbeth after Duncan's murder, rather than hoping to ride to power by the forces that had prognosticated Macbeth's ascension to the throne.

Betrayal of one's wisest self also describes Macbeth's personal history. Macbeth conceives of the crime, knows the ultimate folly of committing it, but plunges into the ways of blood so that there is no return because he chooses to believe that he does not have the option of repentance. In effect, Macbeth goes on choosing again and again to repeat the same crime of setting himself against the natural order. Macbeth repeatedly creates his Satanic self. To assume that Macbeth is seduced into crime by Lady Macbeth when she argues that his reluctance is cowardice and that he is bound to a promise (that Lady Macbeth probably invented) is to underestimate Macbeth's intelligence and the clarity of his moral understanding at the play's beginning. Lady Macbeth, in the fervor of her own ambition, is entirely duped by her own false reasoning; she does not see the sword's other edge, as does her husband. Her convictions become Macbeth's rationalizations, for, inwardly in imagination he has already experienced the potentiality of the crime of regicide he will soon commit.

Before Macbeth begins his career in crime, he knows with absolute certainty—unlike Lady Macbeth—that punishment and judgment must follow. But what he does not fully realize—and herein lies his intellectual fallibility—is the means by which this punishment will be executed. The means, it turns out, are nature's means—nature working through Macbeth in the guilty forms taken by his imagination. Macbeth ceases to be able to tell the false from the true, the real from the illusory, and he is brought to his death as if nature—like the gods in classical mythology—could be active and determinative in plotting the affairs of men. Although Macbeth understands the workings of consequence, it is not likely that Macbeth comprehends the depth of his own motive of "ambition," his wish, like Satan's, to replace God's control over life and death with his own. What is certain, however, is that all the reasons Macbeth gives for why he should *not* kill Duncan cannot be outweighed with an explanation of ambition merely as worldly power.

III Male & Female Virtues

At the play's commencement, Macbeth exhibits a balance of hard and soft virtues: courage, bravery, strength, defiance, pride, and ambition; but also kindness and conscience. In the course of the play's unfolding, he loses the soft virtues, and we cease to feel sympathy for him, but he retains throughout the hard virtue of will itself. When we are in his presence, we are struck with awe; he is a spectacle of fixating horror, like Medusa. Because his strength is admirable, he is doubly dangerous, both for doing evil and for making evil secretly appealing. Like Satan, he is a fallen angel; as Malcolm says, "Angels are bright still, though the brightest fell." Shakespeare's art does not deny that evil has its attractive aspect; were this not so, evil would not flourish in the world. (Even Iago has an unmistakable charm and is thought honest by everyone around him, even his wife.) Yet Shakespeare wants to show how a human devil like Macbeth is destroyed, not merely by external punishment, but through the consequence of his choosing to act out of his own potential evil in defiance of his own moral virtues.

Satan—as depicted by Milton—was the first in an ongoing line of romantic rebels with Adam his initial inheritor through temptation not unlike that of Macbeth. Satan's evil was the result of his energy's lacking a creative goal of its own and thus becoming perversely misdirected in opposition to God's natural order. Adam's temptation to eat of the fruit of the Tree of Life and become immortal may be seen as the first act of rebellion against the limits nature imposes on humankind, as on all living creatures. Macbeth, seen as such a romantic, unwilling to accept limits, wishing to attain godlike powers, is not the creator but the destroyer, not the reformer but the anarchist. Because of an excess of selfish energy, Macbeth attempts to exploit even the forbidden possibilities of his life, and he tries to shape the order of nature to fit his own demands. The idea of Macbeth as Satan is suggested throughout the play in many forms and guises: the talk about rebels, abundant images of hell, numerous allusions to the devil himself. Lady Macbeth says to her husband before Duncan arrives: "Look like the innocent flower, / But be the serpent under 't." Macduff, describing Macbeth, claims that "Not in the legions / Of horrid hell can come a devil more damn'd / In evils to top Macbeth." Macbeth's evil, like the opposition of Milton's Satan—"better to reign in hell than serve in heaven"—is entirely self-generated. Hamlet, Othello, and Lear are provoked from without; they are trapped by extreme and extenuating circumstances. Partially out of ignorance, they are tempted into acting wrongly, and they suffer for it. They sin like Adam, who in defiance of limits and with imperfect understanding still was in the process of being created, but Macbeth sins like Satan— without essential provocation except his own ultimately inexplicable pride and super-worldly ambition.

Macbeth's crime is treason, and its execution is grounded in hopelessness. The absurdity of Macbeth's undertaking makes him ultimately difficult to comprehend. He knows, and we know, that he cannot succeed, and so we as audience are invited to perform the difficult if not impossible feat of imagining negation for the sake of negation, just as it is impossible ultimately to comprehend the mystery of the elusive Iago who invents his own motives yet, unlike Macbeth, enjoys doing evil. Macbeth, however, increases his misery with every crime he commits as his will does violence to the moral component of his nature.

The most important analogy between Satan and Macbeth is that they are both fully aware they are opposing an indestructible moral order, so that— absurd as it seems—they enter into crime aware of the inevitability of their punishment. Macbeth knows fully, even before the murder of Duncan, that crime has its fitting consequences, but nevertheless he proceeds, and directly after the murder, he exclaims: "Will all great Neptune's ocean wash this blood / Clean from my hand? No, this my hand will rather / The multitudinous seas incarnadine, / Making the green one red." Macbeth defies the repeated warnings of conscience and of his own knowledge and suffers a series of punishments, all consisting of deprivations, until at last he has lost what the poorest human being may possess—those most precious gifts of all—his humanity and his soul, "mine eternal jewel," which he has forfeited to Satan, "the common enemy of man."

Macbeth loses the ability to pray:

> MACBETH: *LISTENING THEIR FEAR, I COULD NOT SAY 'AMEN,'*
> *WHEN THEY DID SAY 'GOD BLESS US!'*
> LADY MACBETH: *Consider it not so deeply.*
> MACBETH: *But wherefore could I not pronounce 'Amen?'*
> *I had most need of blessing, and 'Amen'*
> *Stuck in my throat.* (II. ii. 29-33)

Macbeth loses the blessing of sleep:

> MACBETH: *Methought I heard a voice cry 'Sleep no more!*
> *Macbeth does murder sleep,' the innocent sleep . . .*
> *Balm of hurt minds, great nature's second course,*
> *Chief nourisher in life's feast,—* (II. ii. 35-39)

Macbeth loses his sense of the seriousness of life, making of his own ambition an ironic mockery:

> MACBETH: *Had I but died an hour before this chance,*
> *I had liv'd a blessed time; for, from this instant,*
> *There's nothing serious in mortality:*
> *All is but toys; renown and grace is dead,*
> *The wine of life is drawn, and the mere lees*
> *Is left this vault to brag of.* (II. iii. 98-103)

Macbeth loses his trust in even the men who work for him and sends a third murderer to watch after the first two:

> SECOND MURDERER: *He needs not our mistrust,*
> *since he delivers*
> *Our offices and what we have to do*
> *To the direction just.* (III. iii. 2-4)

He loses the power of rational thought and is trapped within his own fears and emotions:

MURDERER: *Most royal sir,*
Fleance is 'scaped.
MACBETH: *Then comes my fit again: I had else been perfect;*
Whole as the marble, founded as the rock,
As broad and general as the casing air:
But now I am cabin'd, cribb'd, confin'd, bound in
To saucy doubts and fears. (III. iv. 19-25)

Macbeth loses trust in his senses and is seized by madness. Banquo's ghost is not like the witches, but like the imaginary dagger, which can be seen only by Macbeth. Like distrust, madness separates men from their society:

LENNOX: *What is't that moves your Highness?*
MACBETH: *Which of you have done this?*
LORD: *What, my good lord?*
MACBETH: *(To Banquo's ghost who is sitting in*
Macbeth's chair.) Thou can'st not say I did it: never shake
Thy gory locks at me.
ROSS: *Gentlemen, rise; his highness is not well.* (III. iv. 48-52)

Macbeth loses all companionship, the comfort of family and society, and falls into terminal loneliness and isolation:

MACBETH: *I have liv'd long enough: my way of life*
Is fallen into the sear, the yellow leaf,
And that which should accompany old age,
As honour, love, obedience, troops of friends,
I must not look to have. (V. iii. 22-26)

Macbeth loses the power of compassionate feeling and cannot even grieve at the death of his wife:

SEYTON: *The queen, my lord, is dead.*
MACBETH: *She should have died hereafter;*
There would have been a time for such a word. (V. v. 16-18)

Macbeth loses love for everything and can take pleasure in nothing:

MACBETH: *Life's but a walking shadow, a poor player*
That struts and frets his hour upon the stage

And then is heard no more; it is a tale
Told by an idiot, full of sound and fury,
Signifying nothing. (V. v. 24-28)

Stripped of his humanity, Macbeth is left only with his will to oppose, reduced to animal defiance, fitting to the beast that he has become. His early knowledge in Act I, "I dare do all that may become a man; / Who dares do more is none," becomes a fact in Act V: "They have tied me to a stake: I cannot fly, / But bear-like I must fight the course."

Macbeth has violated nature's moral order and has thus become estranged from that order, so that to him the face of nature becomes a false one whose smiles are deceitful and whose warnings are misleading. As Macbeth has acted falsely, betraying his own nature as he had betrayed Duncan, so nature equivocates in its appearances, rendering Macbeth's punishment, the deprivation step by step of his humanity, to its culmination by means of the animated marching of Birnam Wood and Macduff's seemingly impossible birth which brings about Macbeth's defeat in battle and his downfall. As a result of his own deliberate choosing, the arc of Macbeth's career moves from hopeless defiance to the hopelessness of solitary and loveless death, and the final penalty of defying nature is to be separated from the medium of nature's unfolding—time—to be cut off from leaving an inheritance in the future. Macbeth cannot memorialize his wife, nor is he, unlike Banquo, left with a son who will succeed him and continue his line. Macbeth's claim that the reason he killed Duncan was for a son he does not have, "No son of mine succeeding," or children he has not spawned, "Only for them," is both pathetic and weirdly irrational.

IV *The Generations*

The theme of fathers and children is established early in the play when Lady Macbeth is unable to murder Duncan because he reminds her of her father: "Had he not resembled / My father as he slept I had done 't." There is no objective reason, however, to believe that Duncan did indeed resemble Lady Macbeth's father; rather, Lady Macbeth projects her ambivalent unconscious murderous wishes, once directed at her father, onto the figure of Duncan. Duncan's words to Lady Macbeth in Act I, "Give me your hand," remain in her mind, and later, when guilty and mad, she walks in her sleep like a child seeking her father in the night, she repeats those exact words, "Come, come, come, come, give me your hand," wishing from the depths of her being to undo the murder of Duncan and take his hand for paternal comfort. So, too, Duncan comes to represent Macbeth's father; Macbeth's words, "I have done the deed," follow immediately after Lady Macbeth's vision of Duncan as her father. Just as Macbeth's murder of Duncan is understood by Macbeth as a form of suicide when he says, "this even-handed justice / Commends the ingredients of our poison'd chalice / To our own lips," so, too, is Macbeth's murder of Duncan the psychological equivalent of murdering his own son—a thought made explicit by Lady Macbeth, who continues to represent an aspect of Macbeth when she imagines killing a hypothetical child of her own: "I would, while it was smiling in my face, / Have pluck'd my nipple from its boneless gums, / And dash'd the brains out." Throughout the play, Macbeth remains obsessed with the fact that he has no son, no inheritor, as when he comments on the witches' prophecy:

> They hailed him [Banquo] father to a line of kings.
> Upon my head they plac'd a fruitless crown,
> And put a barren scepter in my gripe,
> Thence to be wrench'd with an unlineal hand,
> No son of mine succeeding. (III. i. 60-64)

The theme of murderously contending fathers and sons is given its fullest expression, however, in symbolic form in Act IV, Scene 3, when the sonless father, Macduff, (he is soon to realize his condition) and the fatherless son, Malcolm, meet and test each other through verbal repartee to find out if the other can be trusted. The ostensible issue between them is the question of how a man should behave when dealing with grief. This central issue had been raised earlier in the play when Macbeth said, "I dare do all that may become a man; / Who dares do more is none." The exchange between Malcolm and Macduff begins with them taking opposite positions about manly behavior. Malcolm urges that first a man must express his emotions, and Macduff contrarily argues that a man must first seek appropriate action:

> MALCOLM: *Let us seek out some desolate shade, and there*
>   *Weep our sad bosoms empty.*
> MACDUFF *Let us rather*
> *Hold fast the mortal sword, and like good men*
>   *Bestride our down-fall'n birthdom . . .* (IV. iii. 1-4)

Soon, however, we see that each will learn from the other and incorporate the other's point of view into his own. Furthermore, Shakespeare will give us a parodic version of an extreme attempt to assume a manly response when he shows us Siward's reaction to the death of his son.

(After the initial exchange about the relative merits of emotional exorcism and pragmatic action, Malcolm begins to open up to Macduff by confessing his inner doubts about his own character. When Malcolm says, "I am young; but something / You may discern of him [Macbeth] through me," Macduff assumes that Malcolm's sole motive for comparing himself to Macbeth is to test Macduff by drawing out of him a similar confession. To this test Macduff responds with a flat denial: "I am not treacherous." Shakespeare's depiction of Malcolm, however, is more complex than Macduff's response to the young heir to the throne, for Shakespeare shows Malcolm to be functioning on two levels at the same time. Malcolm is suspicious of Macduff and is indeed testing him, but it is equally true that Malcolm does have doubts about himself; he needs to acknowledge his fears about his own potential for violent and lustful behavior and, hopefully, to exorcise his own demonic impulses through a ritualized confession with Macduff playing the role of an attending priest. Furthermore, this confession must take place at the same time that Malcolm suspects Macduff of the crime of betraying his own family.)

Malcolm confronts Macduff directly with the fact that Macduff has left his wife and son at home unprotected. Macduff's behavior has genuinely puzzled Malcolm, but he does not want to make a premature and damning assessment of Macduff, so he waits to see if he can detect sincerity in Macduff's reply. Macduff repeats his disclaimer, "I would not be the villain that thou think'st / For the whole space that's in the tyrant's grasp, / And the rich East to boot." There is an urgency and directness in Macduff's words that must seem persuasive to Malcolm, and so he changes the subject from Macduff's leaving home to the plight of the country under the tyranny of Macbeth: "I think our country sinks beneath the yoke; / It weeps, it bleeds, and each new day a gash / Is added to her wounds." Malcolm evokes the image of a protective and benevolent father, the King of England, who has offered help, "And here from gracious England have I offer / Of goodly thousands," but he turns to the other subject that troubles him—his doubts about his own character: "When I shall tread upon the tyrant's head, / Or wear it on my sword, yet my poor country / Shall have more vices than it had before."

At this point, Macduff is confused by the turn in the conversation. Although he knows that his own behavior is properly suspect, Macduff has no reason to be suspicious of Malcolm, and so Macduff, baffled by Malcom's allusion to himself as a man of vices, innocently asks, "What should he be?" Malcolm's depiction of himself as a would-be tyrant, even worse than Macbeth, becomes more explicit in Malcolm's response to Macduff's question:

> It is *myself I mean; in whom I know*
> *All the particulars of vice so grafted,*
> *That, when they shall be open'd, black Macbeth*
> *Will seem as pure as snow, and the poor state*
> *Esteem him as a lamb, being compar'd*
> *With my confineless harms.* (IV. iii. 50-55)

Macduff misses the point and cannot take in the fact that Malcolm is talking about himself, so he gets caught up in an irrelevant argument, the technicality of whether anyone could be worse than Macbeth: "Not in the legions / Of horrid hell can come a devil more damn'd / In evils to top Macbeth." But Malcolm will not relent in the portrayal of himself as pre-eminent in his capacity for greed and lust:

> *I grant him* [Macbeth] *bloody,*
> *Luxurious, avaricious, false, deceitful,*
> *Sudden, malicious, smacking of every sin*
> *That has a name; but there's no bottom, none,*
> *In my voluptuousness: your wives, your daughters,*
> *Your matrons, and your maids, could not fill up*
> *The cistern of my lust; and my desire*
> *All continent impediments would o'erbear*
> *That did oppose my will; better Macbeth*
> *Than such an one to reign.* (IV. iii. 58-66)

Malcolm's motive in making such extreme claims—puzzling no doubt even to the audience—about his own potentiality for evil continue to be strategic because he wants to see if Macduff will make a similar acknowledgment. It must be equally stressed that this speech also constitutes a genuine confession—not of crimes that Malcolm has committed, but of crimes that Malcolm, having seen what he has seen of human nature, fears he also might be capable of committing. After all, Malcolm has already borne witness to the treason of the rebels, Macdonwald and Cawdor, and, even more astonishing, to Duncan's betrayal by the seemingly loyal Macbeth. It is not entirely surprising, therefore, that Malcolm should suspect that all men, including himself, are susceptible to the temptations of the devil.

Malcolm can barely control himself when he begins to enumerate all the weaknesses he fears he may possess, and the very excess of his rhetoric, his imagining of himself as diabolical, suggests the fantasy and anxiety that characterize what, in effect, becomes a confession of what Malcolm fears may be inherent in his own nature:

> *Nay, had I power, I should*
> *Pour the sweet milk of concord into hell,*
> *Uproar the universal peace, confound*
> *All unity on earth.* (IV. iii. 96-100)

Macduff takes Malcolm's words at face value, for he still does not realize that Malcolm, perhaps at an unconscious level, is testing himself by admitting his fears about his own potential evil, as well as testing Macduff's loyalty, so Macduff angrily claims that someone with the characteristics Malcolm claims for himself is not "Fit to govern. / No, not to live."

The turning point in what by now appears to be a hopeless exchange of mutual suspicion and misunderstanding comes when, in desperation, Macduff summons up the image of Malcolm's parents:

> *Thy royal father*
> *Was a most sainted king; the queen that bore thee,*
> *Oft'ner upon her knees than on her feet,*
> *Died every day she lived. Fare thee well!*
> *These evils thou repeat'st upon thyself*
> *Have banish'd me from Scotland. O my breast,*
> *Thy hope ends here!* (I. iii. 108-111)

This urgently despairing speech by Macduff conclusively persuades Malcolm of Macduff's honesty and loyalty to the realm, but it also serves to assuage Malcolm's fears about himself by reminding him of the goodness and holiness of his own parentage. Malcolm is reassured that the saintly Duncan is his true father, not Lucifer, and that there are other models besides Macbeth and treachery to which he can turn. When in relief Malcolm then says, "Macduff, this noble passion, / Child of integrity, hath from my soul / Wip'd the black scruples, reconcil'd my thoughts / To thy good truth and honor," Malcolm now links himself to Macduff. Just as Macduff had reminded Malcolm of the honesty of his parents, so, too, Malcolm calls Macduff a "child of integrity"—as if psychologically they were part of the same family.

But the familial imagery of Malcolm and Macduff immediately undergoes a significant modulation. Since Macduff is older and experienced and Malcolm a mere youth, Malcolm must turn for help to the more mature Macduff as a father. For even now, Malcolm says, "I put myself to thy direction, and / Unspeak my own detraction." Confessing further that he has not committed any of the crimes of lust or aggrandizement that seemingly he has boasted about, that he in fact is "Unknown to woman" and "would not betray the devil to his fellow," Malcolm makes a unifying offer to Macduff: "What I am truly, / Is thine and my poor country to command."

This scene of reconciliation and healing in which a fatherless son and a sonless father confess and take cause with one another prefigures the restoration of Scotland that will take place at the play's end after the overthrow of Macbeth. It is symbolically fitting that the scene should culminate with the conjuring of the coming arrival of Edward, the good king of England, who appears like a reincarnation of Duncan, a holy ruler who possesses miraculous powers: "at his touch, / Such sanctity hath heaven given his hand / They presently amend." Because of this healing power, Malcolm can look to the future as a time of restoration, rather than the perpetuation of violence, rebellion, and disorder:

> To the succeeding royalty he leaves
> The healing benediction. With this strange virtue,
> He hath a heavenly gift of prophecy,
> And sundry blessings hang about his throne
> That speak him full of grace. (IV. iii. 154-159)

The reconciliation between Malcolm and Macduff, however, is not yet fully complete, and a future time of blessing and grace is still to be realized. Ross enters the scene with devastating news for Macduff: "Your castle is surpris'd; your wife and babes / Savagely slaughtered." Macduff reacts with shock and disbelief: "My children too? . . . My wife kill'd too?" so that Macduff's grief will later reveal through contrast how hollow and unfeeling is Macbeth's response to the death of his own wife. Malcolm tries to assuage Macduff's agony with the thought of revenge: "Be comforted: / Let's make us medicines of our great revenge, / To cure this deadly grief," but Macduff remains inconsolable: "All my pretty ones? / Did you say all?" Malcolm's next reply, "Dispute it like a man," is the reversal of what Malcolm had said at the beginning of the scene before he subjected himself to Macduff's influence. Only a grief ago, Malcolm had articulated the need for the expression of sorrow: "Let us seek out some desolate shade, and there / Weep our sad bosoms empty." Now it is Macduff who acknowledges that feeling must be given its expression, so that his immediate rejoinder to Malcolm's, "Dispute it like a man," is "But I must also feel it as a man." In defining manliness as taking action, Malcolm, too, has reversed himself and adopted Macduff's earlier position, "Let us rather / Hold fast the mortal sword, and like good men / Bestride our down-fall'n birthdom." Rather than thinking that each of them has contradicted himself and taken the other's position, however, it would be more accurate to imagine that each has learned from the other and incorporated the other's half of a larger truth: manliness requires the full expression of powerful feelings, as well as action. United then as political allies, as father and son—like Odysseus and Telemachus ready to contend with the suitors—complete in their complementary manliness, Malcolm and Macduff are now prepared to confront Macbeth. Malcolm says, "This tune goes manly. / Come, go we to the king; our power is ready."

Shakespeare makes it abundantly clear that Malcolm has learned deeply and well the lesson that manliness must include an affective or feminine aspect—the very femininity that Lady Macbeth had fatally repressed in herself—as well as demonstrate physical assertiveness and courage. As a result, his humanity, transcending mere male and female attributes, has been enlarged. At the end of the play, young Siward is slain in battle by Macbeth. The news of his death is delivered to his father by Ross:

> Your son, my lord, has paid a soldier's debt:
> He only liv'd but till he was a man;
> The which no sooner had his prowess confirm'd
> In the unshrinking station where he fought,
> But like a man he died. (V. vii. 68-72)

Siward, the father, asks with cold succinctness, "Then he is dead?" and Ross, assuming that Siward's brief reply indicates extreme shock (as earlier such abrupt questioning had indicated disbelief in Macduff) attempts to console Siward by acknowledging that such sorrow cannot be glibly expressed: "Your cause of sorrow / Must not be measur'd by his worth, for then / It hath no end." But Ross has misunderstood Siward, who only wants to know if his son has died honorably, in military terms, with wounds on the front of his body. When Siward is assured that his son has died bravely as a soldier, he is satisfied, and, from his military point of view, no grieving is necessary. Siward's words, with his grim and inappropriate pun on "hairs" as heirs, are brutally conclusive:

Why then, God's soldier be he!
Had I as many sons as I have hairs,
I would not wish him to a fairer death:
And so, his knell is knoll'd. (V. vii. 76-79)

Malcolm is repelled by Siward's lack of sentiment, his failure to acknowledge the emotional reality of grief, and he admonishes Siward: "He's
worth more sorrow, / And that I'll spend on him," thus replacing Siward as
a failed father with his own fatherly expression of manifest sorrow. In doing
so, Malcolm has come into his own maturity, his own humane manliness,
capable of both judicious and compassionate political leadership.

V Repulsion & Compassion

By the end of the play, we have lost the empathy for Macbeth that we
had at the beginning when he was struggling with his own guilt and remorse. Now he evokes in us only fear and horror and awe. Since Macbeth
has, in effect, ceased to be human, negating himself both as father and as
son, the most we can feel for him is an abstract pity; we are not sorry for
him because of the fate he suffers, but we are sorry that in our human world
such corruption can and does take place, and that such power of potential
goodness can release what is terrible and dark in political affairs.

Our pity and sympathy for Hamlet, for Othello, and for Lear increase
as their tragedies direct them to ends that, in part, are beyond their control.
The necessity of their suffering binds us in empathy. With our knowledge
of their losses, we recognize the inevitability of our own losses; and since
to understand loss, to feel the weight of suffering through it, is also to understand that which has been lost, we recognize that through the suffering
of loss our affirmation of life is expressed and strengthened in tragic awareness. This is the knowledge by which, at the times of their deaths, Hamlet,
Othello, and Lear accept their own fates while affirming the goodness of
life and feel love most strongly out of the depths of their losses.

Macbeth does not make such an affirmation; in dying, he does not affirm
the moral order, or spiritual love, or any force of life, but the natural world
affirms itself, revealing its own inherent morality, in the way it has punished
and destroyed him. Natural morality, according to Shakespeare in this play,
is an order by means of which its opponents are punished by the very
fact of their opposition to that order, so Macbeth suffers commensurately
with his power to defy moral laws. Out of the same necessity that makes
suffering a means to the recognition of the good comes the reestablishment

of harmony, of "measure" and "grace," affirmed by Malcolm after the defeat of the forces of evil. The ending of *Macbeth*, with the ascension of Malcolm to the throne bodes for the future more reason for optimism than we are left with in the other great tragedies, though Shakespeare leaves hanging the ominous question of why Macolm's brother, Donaldbain, is not to be seen at Malcolm's coronation. So, too, just as a little earlier at the battlefield, Donaldbain is noticeably absent as Caithness observes, "Who knows if Donaldbain be with his brother?" to which Lennox makes an understated reply, "For certain, sir, he is not."

Does this bode more conflict between brothers that we see so often in Shakespeare's plays? Nevertheless, compared to the future for Denmark, which looks particularly grim as the tyrant and dictator, Fortinbras, takes control in *Hamlet*, there is reason to be optimistic that the compassionate Malcolm will be a good king.

If, in the course of the play, our feelings for Macbeth move from sympathy and admiration to horror and awe, our feelings for Lady Macbeth move in an opposite way: from horror and revulsion to pity and sympathy. At the beginning, she is unable to understand Macbeth, mistaking conscience for cowardice, and she is therefore unable to help or to advise him wisely. At the end, Macbeth—having chosen to oppose and reject his own conscience—can no longer sympathize with his wife or assist her when she suffers the extreme recriminations of her guilty conscience. Macbeth knows before he acts to commit regicide that the rhythm that leads from deed to consequence is a rhythm established in the stars, not to be changed by human manipulation: "If it were done when 'tis done then 'twere well / It were done quickly." But Lady Macbeth does not learn this lesson until temptation is chronicled in action: "What's done cannot be undone." Shakespeare's repetition of the words "done" and "do" throughout the play, reveals an inevitability that leads Macbeth to his fate as a necessary result of his initiating choice—a choice made over and over to violate the moral order.

Macbeth's greatness of will, Shakespeare shows so vividly, is opposed to his goodness: he is able to accomplish feats of destruction beyond the powers of ordinary men. His will enables him to detach himself from his own natural humanity and act against the dictates of his own knowledge and his own conscience. Macbeth refused to be himself—the self Lady Macbeth described as being "too full of the milk of human kindness;" rather, he creates a Satanic identity no matter what the outcome, and without remorse or regret. This defiance of nature constitutes a fantastic spectacle, one that Lady Macbeth thinks she too can emulate, but at which she fails miserably.

Macbeth, by his success, wins our hatred; Lady Macbeth, by her failure, wins our pity. It is an ironic and paradoxical ascent that Lady Macbeth travels, for she is destroyed by the inner goodness of her moral nature, by her conscience which has continued to flourish on the level of her unconscious mind. Not by strength of will does she repent; her nature repents for her even though she must be driven mad in order for her conscience to be released and find its definitive expression as guilt in madness.

Lady Macbeth undertakes the murder of Duncan because she thinks that any resulting consequences will be entirely social, and her ambition is willing to assume this calculated risk. She does not acknowledge what the consequences of crime and conscience will be. But she is abysmally wrong in thinking that "A little water clears us of this deed." Her inability to act on discovering that Duncan resembles her father ironically reverses her disavowal of parental feeling, "I have given suck, and know / How tender 'tis to love the babe that milks me: / I would, while it was smiling in my face, / Have plucked my nipple from his boneless gums, / And dashed the brains out," and so her weakness to act derives, though unwillingly, from natural goodness in the form of innate conscience and the capacity to feel appropriate guilt and remorse.

It becomes increasingly obvious that Lady Macbeth's repentance, as well as her guilt, is instinctual and not cognitively considered. Because of this dichotomy in her personality, she sinks into madness in which she acts out her symbolic penances, and in such a way is her humanity made manifest. In this madness she attempts to shut out the darkness of her corrupted rational mind, so that the light of her innermost being can reveal her in those gestures of submission to the natural order that she has violated and perhaps make her in some mysterious way eligible for the "forgiveness" that the doctor prescribes. Her own darkness has corrupted her, and she must pitifully seek for the light that will redeem her:

> DOCTOR: *How came she by the light?*
> GENT: *Why, it stood by her: she has light by her continually; 'tis her command.* (V. i. 24-26)

This is the darkness of spilled blood and of the grave, so her gesture of repentance is one of washing to remove the sooty blackness that she now perceives to be upon her:

> DOCTOR: *Look, how she rubs her hands.*
> GENT: *It is an accustomed action with her, to seem*

thus washing her hands. I have known her
to continue this a quarter of an hour.
LADY MACBETH: *Yet here's a spot.* (V. i. 29-34)

At her death, Lady Macbeth has lost all will to oppose the dictates of her moral nature which become manifest in the form of guilt and conscience. She ends in the weakness of utter submission to nature's superior power, and the doctor who has tended her has no prescription for her but forgiveness:

> *Unnatural deeds*
> *Do breed unnatural troubles; infected minds*
> *To their deaf pillows will discharge their secrets;*
> *More needs she the divine than the physician.*
> *God, God, forgive us all!* (V. i. 72-82)

That the doctor should ask "all" to be forgiven suggests implicitly that he identifies with Lady Macbeth; thus, Lady Macbeth receives a response that perhaps returns her to the fellowship of human sympathy in the hearts of the play's actual audience, according to the Doctor's prescription, though not to Malcolm who, not having heard the doctor's imploring words, dismisses her as a "fiend-like queen."

VI Greatness Versus Goodness

Greatness is an attribute of will. Goodness, as Shakespeare portrays it in *Macbeth*, is an attribute of the natural heart. Will either may be in opposition to goodness or may embrace it, so that moral action, in this play, exists in this freedom of choice: sin is opposition to the natural order, and virtue is acceptance of its limits since human beings are not designed for immortality or with the power to control the future. Nature in this play does not present itself as impersonal and indifferent as it does in *King Lear*. Though greatness in itself is not a moral virtue, greatness always is fascinating because it reveals the power of will by which people are capable of either affirming or destroying themselves. People are alike in their instinctual goodness (Iago, of course, is an exception), but they are unique in their greatness. Thus, goodness is a social and moral force, while greatness primarily makes itself manifest through the individual assertion of self, through anarchic defiance or self-overcoming as when Cordelia is described as being a "queen over her passion."

The emptiness and futility of the willful defiance of one's human nature, whether as father, mother, son or daughter, is ultimately and fully revealed in Macbeth's last words: "Lay on, Macduff, / And damn'd be him that first cries, 'Hold, enough!'" The immense irony here is that Macbeth is the first one to cry, "Hold, enough!"—these words issue from his own mouth—and thus he himself proclaims his own damnation even as he had foreseen. This proclamation fulfills what he, knowingly, well understood earlier in the play when he accurately analyzed the consequences of the contemplated act of murder of the good king Duncan as bringing forth "even-handed justice / [which] Commends the ingredients of our poisoned chalice / To our own lips."

The heroes of Shakespearean tragedy are often depicted as men who first desire an order that their selfish wishes would impose upon the world. Ultimately, their greatness and their goodness must be reconciled if they are to accept the natural order as one imposed by a vaster and more encompassing power than their own. So, too, their individuality must be subsumed within a collective sense of what it means to be mortal and human, a man or a woman—different, yet alike in their fundamental humanity. As Cleopatra says in describing herself, "No more, but e'en a woman, and commanded / By such poor passion as a maid that milks / And does the meanest chares." Richard II expresses a similar sentiment: "I live with bread like you, feel want, / Taste grief, need friends: subjected thus, / How can you say to me I am a king?" Prospero, in giving up his magic powers, acknowledges his finitude and the limits of his mortal nature. Macbeth is Shakespeare's exception; he is anarchic and individualistic to the end, unwilling to "subject himself" or bow to any order other than his own. The penalties follow; for him there is no recovery, no pardon, no tender memory by his successors.

The will opens the final door to overt behavior as one steps from the threshold of moral contemplation into the arena of social action. Causality, then, operates in this way in Macbeth's universe: there is free choice of action, but the consequences following from action are fixed. The punishments that our moral nature impose on us are implicit in the sinful actions that violate this order, so that the very violation contains within itself the means by which the harmony of moral order subsequently may be restored. Ambition on its deepest psychological level inevitably exceeds the possibilities of satisfaction. The most potent meaning of peace is as a goal that never may be permanently reached, and, if attained for the moment, must be again sought, and again momentarily attained. Thus, success is a kind of failure, for it is always partial, and failure can be transformed into a kind of success, for it speaks most truly of the limitations of what men can achieve and thus may inspire needed humility and the compassion for others.

We accept lady Macbeth in the pathos of her failure. Macbeth succeeds to the end, with gargantuan irony, in remaining willfully defiant in the face of natural limits, but at the ultimate price of negating his humanity. Macbeth's realization of who he has become is so grim and nihilistic that he considers his life to be a story not worth telling. What does remain worth telling, however, is the story of Macbeth's fate in which he is revealed as someone who comes to the end, as the result of his own choosing, without wishing to have his story told—the story, as Malcolm says in his final speech, "Of this dead butcher." This recounting will enable Malcolm to move on to other matters of state, "what needful else / That calls upon us," and he vows to do exactly that in declaring: "We will perform in measure, time, and place" in order to restore "the grace of Grace." The divine blessing inherent in nature, if not violated, that we saw embodied earlier as "heaven's breath" in the air where the temple-haunting martlet made its "procreant cradle," signifies the sweetness of life, the exact opposite of Macbeth's fatal choice to turn himself before our appalled eyes into "nothing."

CHAPTER EIGHT

THE TEMPEST: SELF-MASTERY AND FREEDOM

I An Exceptional Day

Miranda is right when she says to Ferdinand about Prospero, her father, that "Never till this day / Saw I him touched with anger so distempered." It is for good reason, however, that Prospero is in such an untypical distempered mood. For twelve years Prospero has been preparing for this day of reckoning with his perfidious brother, Antonio. Although that reckoning will indeed take place, on this day Prospero will lose everything he most loves and prizes: he will relinquish possession of Miranda to Ferdinand— "for / I have lost my daughter;" he will abnegate his magical powers by breaking his "staff" and drowning his "book;" he will set free and say farewell to his beloved Ariel; and he will prepare himself to return to Milan "where / Every third thought shall be my grave," in the full acknowledgment of his mortality and the impotence of old age. One might speculate that to think of death in old age only in every third thought is the mark of an optimist, yet the weight of the word "grave" at the end of Prospero's speech seems to emphasize death's decisive finality over which human beings have no control. This for Prospero is indeed the climactic day of relinquishments and losses. Prospero must accept ceasing to be in godlike control of the weather or the lives of others. The freedom that Prospero will exercise on this day is the willed acceptance of the limiting conditions of reality. Agreeing to tell his story and setting Ariel free are the other final choices that he is free to make.

In a larger Shakespearean context, fathers are rarely able to relinquish their daughters gracefully and with good will. Polonius holds on to Ophelia even though it becomes quite clear that Hamlet's wooing of her is honorable; Brabantio feels betrayed by Desdemona when she tells him she has married Othello even though earlier Brabantio had befriended Othello; Lear demands total love from Cordelia; Egeus would rather have his daughter Helena die or go to a convent than select a mate of her own choice. Certainly, Shakespeare views Prospero's acceptance of Miranda's replacing him with Ferdinand as an emotionally heroic triumph, a rare feat of willed generosity. Prospero is being remarkably honest when, acknowledging the constraints of human egotism, he says: "So glad of this as they, I cannot be

/ Who are surpris'd withal; but my rejoicing / At nothing can be more." In the end, Prospero's capacity for empathy, with much strain, triumphs over fundamental selfishness and fatherly possessiveness. As it is crucial to regard this play from the perspective of Prospero's acceptance of his losses, so, too, it is imperative to read the entire play as a "dream" of power from which Prospero must awaken. In reality, no one (except the biblical God) can will a storm into being for private purposes. All Prospero's magic is like the "pageant" that Prospero conjures up to please Miranda and Ferdinand: "for I must / Bestow upon the eyes of this young couple / Some vanity of mine art" as a vision of "marriage blessing" and of the earth as a place of "harvest." Love requires some concept of the ideal that physical desire can aspire to, and Ferdinand, even though he had earlier been treated harshly by Prospero, is indeed inspired by this "majestic vision" and grateful to Prospero for having provided it: "Let me live here ever, / So rare a wonder'd father and a wise, / Makes this place paradise." But the visionary world of Prospero's dreaming art, just as Ferdinand's wish to live in "paradise," must give way to the dangers of reality, represented at this moment by the threat posed by Caliban's plot to murder Prospero. And so Prospero must dispel the dancing figures he has conjured up, just as he soon will relinquish his magic altogether; he must acknowledge that humans are creatures with the need to dream, "We are such stuff / As dreams are made on," and wake himself to the reality that human beings can neither control nature nor evade the finality of death.

II Multiple Selves

In many of Shakespeare's plays, individual characters and their particular fates are most fully understood by regarding other characters as representing an aspect of them. For example, Macbeth and Lady Macbeth contain antithetical features of each other, differing in their definitions of what constitutes manliness; the fool can be seen as King Lear's conscience and the emerging into consciousness of his sense of guilt and culpability; and in *Henry IV*, after Hal has been summoned to see his father, Falstaff and Hal exchange roles by creating an imaginary scene in which Falstaff plays the King and Hal plays himself, then Hal plays the king and Falstaff plays Hal. Characters, at least in their imaginations, are different versions of each other.

In *The Tempest*, though both Caliban and Ariel are presented as characters with their own identities, they also represent aspects of Prospero's nature and psychological makeup. In a reductive sense, Caliban can be seen as a projection of Prospero's instinctual self, his Freudian id and his Darwinian drive to reproduce his genes. When Prospero confronts Caliban with the charge that he has tried to rape Miranda, Caliban cannot even feign remorse or contrition; rather, he cries out in delight at the thought of the intended rape: "Oh ho! Oh ho!—would it had been done! / Thou did'st prevent me; I had peopled else / This isle with Calibans." Only the idea of replicating himself, without any allusion to Miranda, animates Caliban's thinking. Caliban is a fuller dramatization of human egotism, the center of the drive for survival, than even what we saw at the play's opening when the idealistic Gonzalo exhorts the Boatman to honor his social obligation to the king in the priority of his concerns, "remember whom thou hast aboard," to which the Boatman unhesitatingly replies, "None that I more love than myself." The fullness of human potentiality can be achieved only with the overcoming of such self regard.

The reader or spectator of this play should be on guard not to sentimentalize Caliban: he is a would-be rapist and murderer. (Later, I will return to the question of whether he is capable of learning or reforming in any way.) The reader also must realize that Shakespeare presents Caliban as that aspect of Prospero, in the most primal sense, that he must choose to control in himself, including his repressed incestuous wishes toward his own daughter. Prospero acknowledges the Caliban within him when he confesses: "This thing of darkness I acknowledge mine." Prospero might as well have said, "This thing of darkness I acknowledge 'me.'" This acknowledgment raises the question of whether Prospero will take Caliban back to Milan or whether he will leave him on the island. This question—though it must remain in the realm of conjecture—is raised by Shakespeare when he has Stephano imagine selling Caliban: "If I can recover him, and keep him tame . . . he shall pay for him that hath him," and, with even more comic irony, when Antonio considers selling Caliban on the Milan fish market—an appropriate ironic fate for a cannibal to be himself eaten. My own surmise is that since Caliban is an aspect of Prospero's own unconscious urges, he must go with Prospero wherever Prospero goes. He is the beast within us all, as described by Plato:

> *The Wild Beast in us, full-fed with meat and drink,*
> *becomes rampant and shakes off sleep to go in quest*
> *of what will gratify its own instincts. As you know,*
> *it will cast off all shame and prudence at such mo-*
> *ments and stick at nothing. In phantasy it will not*
> *shrink from intercourse with a mother or anyone*

else, man, god, or brute, or from forbidden food or
any deed of blood. It will go to any lengths of shame-
lessness or folly. (The Republic 9: 571) (1)

The pleasure-seeking aspect of the instinctual self, however, should not be thought of only in negative terms or in the context of moral issues. Much of the goodness of life comes from creaturely enjoyment, from the gratification of our senses and appetites. In this respect, Caliban also represents fundamental human capacities for spontaneous love and for learning about nature for practical purposes. He says to Prospero: "I lov'd thee / And show'd thee all the qualities o' th' isle. / The fresh springs, brine-pits, barren place, and fertile." Unfortunately, his love will turn to murderous hatred when Caliban, lusting for Miranda, comes into Oedipal conflict with Prospero. Caliban's delight in his senses, however, culminating in his appreciation for music, will relate him to other characters in the play who share this capacity for being affected by music. Ferdinand, for example, hears island music, which consoles him when thinking of his presumedly dead father: "This music crept by me upon the waters, / Allaying both their fury, and my passion, / With its sweet air," and Alonso and Gonzalo exchange appreciative remarks on hearing the music: "What harmony is this? my good friends, hark!" queries Alonso, to which Gonzolo replies: "Marvelous sweet music!"

Caliban's expression of his delight in music, which epitomizes the enjoyment to be had in response to nature, constitutes the basis for a general "sense of the sublime," as Darwin himself believed. This delight, which Darwin dates back to our "half human ancestors," is given its fullest lyric articulation by Caliban, despite the fact that earlier Caliban had cursed Prospero for teaching him language: "You taught me language, and my profit on't / Is I know how to curse: the red plague upon you / For learning me your language." But in response to music, Caliban forgets that he thinks language is a curse and rises to high celebratory expression:

Be not afeard: the isle is full of noises,
Sounds and sweet airs, that give delight, and hurt not.
Sometimes a thousand twangling instruments
Will hum about my ears; and sometimes voices,
That, if I then had wak'd after long sleep,
Will make me sleep again: and then, in dreaming,
The clouds methought would open and show riches
Ready to drop upon me; that, when I wak'd,
I cried to dream again. (III. iii. 147-154)

In Caliban's mind, music and dreaming are linked, and together they suggest some visionary state, similar to Ferdinand's response to Prospero's artistic pageant, which Ferdinand believes "Makes this place paradise."

The symmetry between Caliban's speech about dreaming and Prospero's later speech about dreaming is remarkable, suggesting further that some aspects of these two characters, according to Shakespeare's design, reflect each another. In addition to the central focus on the power and prevalence of dreaming in human nature, both passages contain visions of the heavens. Caliban says that "The clouds methought would open and show riches / Ready to drop upon me," and Prospero says that "the great globe itself, / Yea, all which it inherit, shall dissolve / And, like this insubstantial pageant faded, / Leave not a rack [cloud] behind." Despite this symmetry of image and theme, however, the interpretation of these themes by Caliban and Prospero is antithetical. Caliban wishes to go on dreaming forever; Prospero, though acknowledging the human need to dream, argues that we must wake from our dreams and artistic visions to confront reality and its dangers, such as the threat Prospero faces from Caliban's murder plot. Caliban's naive vision of heaven is that divine blessing is possible and immanent, while Prospero's mature vision is of everything dissolving and vanishing.

Caliban's enjoyment of music links him most closely to Ariel, who is the main source of music on the island, so that Prospero's highest self— the moral Ariel self that is capable of art, reason, and forgiveness—is inextricably linked to his lowest instinctual self. The acceptance of this linkage is synonymous with Prospero's acknowledgment of his mortality, which is symbolized by his freely giving up his magical powers. In effect, Prospero is saying that the control of nature and of other humans is a dream, an illusion. Thus this play, much like *A Midsummer Night's Dream*, must be viewed as an inextricable mixture of dream and reality in a most paradoxical way since Prospero is enacting the illusion of being in control of nature, including his own, and, simultaneously, is aware of this illusion as such. Shakespeare represents him as both being awake to the need of realizing human limitations and also indulging in artistic dreaming.

Before Prospero can return to his fully vulnerable human self, he must rehearse his dream of power one last time, though he might just as well be describing his visionary poetic art as if he had written this very play:

I have bedimm'd
The noontide sun, call'd forth the mutinous wind,
And 'twixt the green sea and the azur'd vault
Set roaring war: to the dread-rattling thunder

Have I given fire and rifted Jove's stout oak
With his own bolt: the strong-bas'd promontory
Have I made shake; and by the spurs pluck'd up
The pine and cedar: graves at my command
Have wak'd their sleepers, op'd, and let them forth
By my most potent art. (V. i. 41-50)

The godlike powers that Prospero describes—his control of natural forces like sun and wind, thunder and fire, and the ability to raise the dead—belong in part to pagan mythology; indeed, Prospero here overtly compares himself to Zeus. But although Zeus may be a sky god, he is not "heavenly" in the sense that Ariel is heavenly in being able to evoke in Prospero the powers of reason and forgiveness. However, Prospero must relinquish the Zeusian image of himself as the product of "rough magic" as he goes on to say, "But this rough magic / I here abjure," and replace it with the higher inspiration of "heavenly music." What follows from this momentous decision, this most radical of all Prospero's free choices, is represented by Prospero's breaking of his staff and drowning of his book.

The significance of Prospero's decision to "break my staff" can best be understood if we compare Prospero with Moses after Moses calls on Yahweh for help in providing the complaining Israelites with water. Yahweh says: "Take the staff and assemble the community, you and Aaron your brother; and you shall speak to the rock before their eyes, and it will yield water." (Numbers 28:8) Moses fails, however, to follow Yahweh's instructions explicitly: "And Moses raised his hand and struck the rock with his staff twice and abundant water came out; and the community with its beasts drank." (Numbers 20:12) As a result, astonishing though it may seem, "Yahweh severely punishes Moses and Aaron by not allowing them to enter the promised land: "And the Lord said to Moses and to Aaron, 'Inasmuch as you did not trust *me* before the eyes of the Israelites, even so you shall not bring this assembly to the land that I have given to them.'" (Numbers 20:12) (2)

Prospero does not make the mistake that Moses makes—of counting on magic, rather than on ordinary speech; thus he "abjures" the "rough magic" that his staff symbolizes. The staff is put back into the "earth," the medium of mortality, the element out of which Adam was taken, and to which, realistically, Prospero also must return to be buried. Just as Prospero must divest himself of his staff, so, too, must he choose to give up the other source of supernatural power, his "book," and he will replace supernatural control quite simply with the telling of his life's story. To Alonso's request, "I long / To hear the story of your life," Prospero replies: "I'll deliver all."

The book is "drowned," restoring, as it were, all those who appeared to have been shipwrecked and rescued by Prospero's magic art. In this way, too, reality is given its necessary and inevitable recognition. Prospero's culminating choice must be to accept and affirm that necessity.

Prospero's speech in which he renounces the magical powers of his staff and book follows his climactic exchange with Ariel (to which I will shortly return), in which Ariel advises Prospero on how to enhance his humanity, so it is now timely to explore Ariel as an aspect of Prospero as I have discussed Caliban as the representative of Prospero's instinctual self. To see Ariel as a depiction of the Freudian superego as symmetrical to seeing Caliban as id or instinct, however, creates problems of interpretation, particularly in exploring Shakespeare's representation of the theme of freedom which will culminate at the play's end when Prospero gives Ariel his promised freedom. Setting Ariel free—since Ariel represents Prospero's imagination and moral conscience—cannot mean that Prospero reverts entirely to his instinctual Caliban self, nor can it mean that Prospero no longer needs to exercise his power of will, his freedom to control his baser instincts.

III The Stings of Conscience

Freud's depiction of the superego is usually one of harshness in summoning guilt to control and override instincts, predominantly those of sexual desire and aggression, as we see them revealed in Caliban. Freud states: "The superego torments the sinful ego with the feelings of anxiety and is on the watch for opportunities of getting it punished by the external world." (3) Although we do see such harshness in Prospero's treatment of both Caliban and Ferdinand through the agency of Ariel, when Prospero has Caliban pinched or knotted with cramps and Ferdinand is confined to menial work, Ariel's main service is to inspire Prospero in the ways of reconciliation and forgiveness. Prospero's anger and severity toward Ariel, in Freudian terms, is a projection and reversal of ego and super-ego; it is a reversal that seems to have a cathartic effect since Prospero is able to express his fundamental love for Ariel as the acceptance of his own conscience in its most benevolent form by the play's end. When Ariel asks, "Do you love me master?" Prospero replies unequivocally, "Dearly, my delicate Ariel." Lear's fool more closely than Ariel represents the superego, or the stings of guilty conscience, in his deliberate attempts to bring Lear to acknowledge his sinful and stupid behavior than Ariel does in guiding Prospero.

There is also an alternative and less harsh aspect of the superego that Freud elucidates in his late essay "Humour" (1928) (4) in which

[handwritten margin note: I see Ariel as the feminine side of Pros. The Yin/Yang]

Freud tells us that in humor the superego speaks "words of comfort to the intimidated ego." [*of art (a play)*] This is a remarkable statement since Freud usually portrays the superego, which "inherits the parental function," as severe, chastising, and constraining. In the case of humor, however, it is as if the father, the superego, allows the son, the ego, a moment of play exempt from the strictures of reality. Freud calls this holiday from the demands of the reality principle "a rare and precious gift," a description that fits Ariel perfectly. Freud articulates a distinction between the holiday from reality that humor makes possible in the momentary feeling of triumph that comes in laughter and the unreality of dreams. Humor carries within it a knowledge of the path back to reality, the world in which the self is limited by the constrictions of nature. This gift of the father to the son, interiorized as a benevolent dynamic between the superego and the ego, is a form of inner grace, much like that interim when we allow ourselves to inhabit the timeless world of a poem, a musical composition, or a dream. Although the superego, according to Freud, is a "stern master," its tough sense of reality paradoxically includes the knowledge that we cannot endure reality all the time; we require the respite of temporary illusion in the form of play or art, as embodied in the actions of Prospero and *The Tempest* itself as a comprehensive dream. Given this tolerance, the superego can remain true to its disciplining function even though, as Freud says, it may "wink at affording the ego a little gratification."

In *The Tempest* the equivalent of humor, as Freud describes it, may be thought of as Ariel's music since both offer a hiatus and bring relief in the form of pleasure from stressful situations. This relief is felt on a much higher level than that offered by the crude (excremental) humor in the play, as in the scene where Trinculo, having come upon Caliban, whom at first he takes to be a fish, hides from the storm by getting under Caliban's "gabardine" with him. Drunken Stephano discovers them together and thinks he has found an island monster with four legs. Trinculo identifies himself and, given his position relative to Caliban, Stephano then assumes that Trinculo is the shit of Caliban: "How can'st thou to be the siege of this moon-calf? Can he vent Trinculos?" Humorous as is this image, it surely does not fit Freud's high-minded description of providing comfort to the "intimidated ego." Stephano's speculation that he could make money by exhibiting Caliban back in Milan, "If I can recover him, and keep him tame, I will not take too much for him: he shall pay for him that hath him, and that soundly," is on a much lower level of concern than Prospero's later remark: "This thing of darkness I acknowledge mine," and such broad farce obviously does not approach the comfort offered by Ariel's sublime advice to Prospero to forgive his brother.

All relationships in this play, even those that are not strictly familial, can be seen as having their family analogues, such as brother and brother or father and daughter. From one perspective, for example, both Caliban and Ferdinand may be seen as Prospero's surrogate sons and Ariel can be seen as Prospero's androgenous daughter (whom he also must set free) in addition to Miranda. Prospero has raised Caliban, cared for him, instructed him, and Caliban acknowledges that at one time he loved Prospero. But this phase of their relationship ends when Caliban tries to rape Miranda and becomes murderously competitive with Prospero.

In a symbolic sense, Prospero gives birth to Ariel in releasing her/him from the tree in which he was contained, and Ariel, as the good son (or daughter) who remains faithful to Prospero in contrast to Caliban, becomes an aspect or extension of Prospero's power and magic. In another sense Ariel and Prospero reverse roles so that Ariel can be seen in a fatherly (or motherly) relationship to Prospero, as when she/he instructs Prospero in the art of forgiveness. In this instance, Ariel extends Prospero's humanity through increased tenderness into a new realm of maturity which includes Prospero's acceptance of Ferdinand who acknowledges that Prospero has become a father to him, "of whom I have / Receiv'd a second life; and second father / This lady [Miranda] makes him to me." Ferdinand's father, Alonso, replies to his son, "I am hers," meaning that he now is also father to Miranda as the result of her betrothal to Ferdinand. Further, Alonso sees his role in relationship to Ferdinand in another reversal, as if psychologically he has become Ferdinand's son, when he says: "But O! how oddly it will sound that I / Must ask my child forgiveness." Just as Prospero has been instructed in the ways of forgiveness by Ariel, so, too, Alonso learns the need for forgiveness from his son—as if his son has become his father.

The dramatic climax of the play in which a family relationship is transformed and redefined can be regarded as the moment when Prospero, with much hostility and resentment still in his heart, chooses to forgive his treacherous brother, Antonio, rather than indulge in the primal pleasure of revenge. In this moment Prospero must will himself to rise above emotional inclination, and although Prospero has been preparing himself for a long time to rise above his "fury," this self-transcendence will not come easily or without ambivalence. Prospero is only able to make this noble choice, however, with the help and gentle prodding of Ariel, whose very name (air—aria) invokes the spirit of music:

> ARIEL: *Your charm so strongly works them,*
> *That if you now beheld them, your affections*
> *Would become tender.*

PROSPERO: *Dost thou think so, spirit?*
ARIEL: *Mine would, sir, were I human.*
PROSPERO: *And mine shall.*
Hast thou, which art but air, a touch, a feeling
Of their afflictions, and shall not myself,
One of their kind, that relish all as sharply,
Passion as they, be kindlier mov'd than thou art?
Though with their high wrongs I am struck to the quick,
Yet with my nobler reason 'gainst my fury
Do I take part: the rarer action is
In virtue than in vengeance. (V. i. 17-25)

The magical power of self-overcoming that Prospero will next exhibit, inspired by Ariel, is not, however, physical or supernatural, but moral and emotional—it is entirely human, provided that one regards Ariel as an aspect of Prospero's imagination which dwells in the realm of ideas and moral reasoning.

Before his disillusionment, because of the death of his father and the hasty remarriage of his mother, Hamlet had viewed human nature as possessing divine attributes. Hamlet recounts his lapsed belief: "How noble in reason! how infinite in faculties! in form and moving how express and admirable! in action how like an angel! in apprehension how like a god!" Prospero, in danger of falling into a similar state of despair as expressed by Hamlet's current view, "Man delights not me," due to his own disappointments, his brother's betrayal and his banishment from Milan, nevertheless resists the temptation of disillusionment caused by defeated idealism, such as Hamlet's. In Prospero's realization of the angelic potential that Ariel proffers, much like Hamlet's earlier optimism about human nature as quoted above, he is open to the appeal of Ariel's subtle persuasion: "your charm so strongly works them, / That if you now beheld them, your affections / Would become tender." Prospero immediately seizes this potential for tenderness as an alternative to revenge, "Does thou think so, spirit?" augmenting his own humanness with Ariel's spirituality, as Ariel replies, "Mine would, sir, were I human." We witness at this astounding moment the manifestation of Prospero's humanity as the result of the incarnation of an idea that seems to come right out of the air—an idea whose quality is that of harmonious music.

Prospero's idealism, his choice of the morality of forgiveness, is grounded both in reason and in reality. Unlike the sweet-tempered Gonzalo, whose vision of society as a "commonwealth" is contrary to human nature in its denial of innate human lust and greed, Prospero is fully aware of Caliban's instinctual desires—which are also his own at an unconscious level—his brother's treachery of years ago, and the various murder plots of the present moment on the island. Gonzalo's utopian vision in which everyone is equal and there is "No occupation; all men idle, all; / And women too, but innocent and pure; No sovereignty" is contrary to reason in its very self-contradiction, which even Sebastian can readily perceive as he ironically replies, "Yet he [Gonzalo] would be king on't," to which Antonio sarcastically adds, "The latter end of his commonwealth / Forgets the beginning." Prospero's reason, however, does not forget the beginning—a beginning that lies in the human proclivity toward "fury" and violence. There is much remembering and reenacting that needs to be accomplished before the grace and the relief of forgetting, due to the moral magic of forgiveness, will become possible, before Prospero will be able to say to Alonso: "Let us not burden our remembrances / With a heaviness that's gone."

IV Remembrance & Volition

The whole play is an effort of remembrance to bring back the past and to redeem the past by taking a different attitude to what happened and thus changing it through forgiveness. In this way, a different course for the future is set in which the pangs of memory are assuaged. The past is brought back under different conditions—conditions in which Prospero is now temporarily in control, no longer victim but agent. This therapeutic process of remembering begins with Prospero recounting to Miranda the circumstances under which they were banished from Milan and set adrift at sea. Prospero wishes to evoke in Miranda even her dim recollections: "rather like a dream than an assurance / That my remembrance warrants." Prospero prods her memory even further: "What see'st thou else / In the dark backward and abysm of time?" Yet Prospero is also aware of how memory can be self-deceiving as a rationalization for past behavior for which one feels guilt. This is how he explains his usurping brother Antonio's warping of memory: "like one, / Who having into truth, by telling it, / Made such a sinner of his memory, / To credit his own lie,—he did believe / He was indeed the duke." And Ariel believes that he has to continue to remind Prospero of what he has done for him: "Remember, I have done thee worthy service." Painful memory does not come easily and needs to be reinforced in the telling to achieve its therapeutic effect.

Prospero recognizes the fundamental dichotomy in human nature between emotion, "fury," and "reason," and therefore he knows that nobility requires self-control. Just as Cordelia in *King Lear* is described as being queen over herself, "It seemed she was queen / Over her passion, who most rebel-like / Sought to be king o'er her," Prospero must freely exercise his will to be king over himself, over his furious passion for long-contemplated revenge, and in this civilizing enterprise he needs Ariel's help. In exercising his will, it is not necessary (or possible) that negative emotion be entirely dissipated, only that it be mastered. And it is reasonable to exercise reason ("Yet with my nobler reason 'gainst my fury / Do I take part: the rarer action is / In virtue than in vengeance,") because the alternative to such reasoned virtue is the perpetuation of the violent cycle of retaliation and reenergized fury. Furthermore, there is also the sense, derived from the Ariel aspect of himself, that virtue for Prospero is in part its own reward since it graces its possessor with a feeling of nobility, which itself exists only as idea, made from air, and yet achieves its own actuality and its own kind of power as the word "virtue" implies.

The choice to take control of one's passions, to be king over oneself, is a form of freedom, or even more accurately, the creation of freedom. The theme of what constitutes freedom suffuses the entire play and is portrayed in its various aspects from Caliban to Ferdinand to Prospero to Ariel. Shakespeare explores the different meanings of servitude and freedom in bodily, psychological, and social terms, and he makes precise distinctions to show when servitude and when freedom are the appropriate conditions for particular characters. Caliban feels antagonism toward Prospero, sees him as a tyrant, because Prospero demands that Caliban carry wood for the fire. But this is useful work which must be done by someone within any social structure. We are shown how Caliban misuses and misjudges freedom in seeking to replace Prospero's authority with that of a drunken fool. First, Caliban seeks to serve Trinculo, drunkenly singing, "Ban, Ban—Ca—Caliban, / Has a new master—Get a new man," and celebrates what he now misperceives as his liberation: "Freedom, high-day! high-day, freedom! freedom! high-day, freedom!" Later, deciding that Trinculo is not "valiant," Caliban quickly switches his allegiance to the drunken Stephano, who he has taken to be a god, making himself subservient and prostrating himself, saying, "Let me lick thy shoe." Caliban, even without compulsion, chooses his own servitude.

Through Ferdinand, Shakespeare depicts doing menial work as not in itself demeaning, and, in contrast to Caliban's objection to doing such necessary work, Shakespeare shows us how Ferdinand regards being given the same task of carrying logs. Ferdinand says, "some kinds of baseness / Are nobly undergone," because, he correctly reasons, they serve some practical or higher purpose: "The mistress which I serve," continues Ferdinand, "quickens what's dead / And makes my labors pleasures;" further, he rhapsodizes that "these sweet thoughts [of Miranda whom he serves] do even refresh my labours." The experience of labor is determined by his state of mind. The paradox of choice and commitment—which in romantic terms limits the choice of whom one might freely love—is lucidly articulated by Ferdinand in response to Miranda's questioning his marital intentions, "My husband then?" to which Ferdinand replies: "Ay, with a heart as willing / As bondage e'er of freedom: here's my hand."

Ferdinand's pledge confirms his earlier claim in which he expresses the paradox of freedom's being essentially an attitude, a happy commitment to a wise and loving choice, as when he says:

> *Might I but through my prison once a day*
> *Behold this maid: all corners else o' the earth*
> *Let liberty make use of; space enough*
> *Have I in such a prison.* (I. i. 487-490)

This is the same insight, reversed into the positive, that the distraught Hamlet possessed (having been rejected by Ophelia) when he states: "I could be bounded in a nutshell, and count myself a king of infinite space, were it not that I have bad dreams." For Ferdinand, on the contrary, Miranda is a dream realized through the making of a marriage vow and a permanent commitment as the lovers seek to do in *A Midsummer Night's Dream*. Prospero's emphasis on Miranda's remaining chaste must be understood not as a puritanical aversion to sexuality, but as the demonstration of Ferdinand's and Miranda's capacity for self-control, for being king and queen over their desires, and therefore capable of future fidelity.

Just as Ferdinand and Miranda must master their lust, which Caliban cannot do, Prospero must not only master his own desire to keep Miranda to himself, but he must also overcome his wish to retain possession of Ariel, whom he also truly loves. "Do you love me, master?" asks Ariel in wonderment whether love can take a non-carnal form (an idea that Sycorax cannot comprehend), to which Prospero appropriately replies in recognition of Ariel's spiritual quality: "Dearly, my delicate Ariel." Prospero's love for Miranda and for Ariel, as much as he treasures them, can, however, offer only a substitution, since they are not love objects which permit sexual expression or fulfillment that is simultaneously bodily and spiritual. Prospero's wife died a long time ago and was replaced, so Miranda recalls, by "Four or five women once that tended me." Prospero has interjected the lost wife/mother into himself and has become both mother and father in relation not only to Miranda but also to Ariel. His love for Miranda, as he expresses it to Ferdinand, "for I / Have given you here a third of mine own life, / Or that for which I live," allows us to see most poignantly how difficult it must be for Prospero to lose her, and why it is so important for him to test Ferdinand's worthiness. (Good marriages are not to be taken for granted as we are reminded by the coerced marriage of Claribel and the tragic marriage of Dido.)

Shakespeare makes clear that Caliban's good qualities, such as his ability to perform useful work like carrying logs, will only be made manifest when he is under the control of a proper master since he himself is not capable of self-control. Otherwise, Caliban, as we see in his conspiracy with Stephano and Trinculo to kill Prospero, will give in to his penchant for destructive wildness in the form of rape and murder. Servitude in the name of love is a good thing, as when Ferdinand accepts servitude willingly on behalf of Miranda in obeying Prospero's order to carry logs. Shakespeare is suggesting that Ferdinand must pass through a Caliban-like stage, after which he will be able to recognize and articulate the psychological paradox of freedom in accepted servitude as a form of commitment. Just as one person may properly serve another who merits authority, so, too, must the head or reason rule over the basic passions—genital desire and the aggressive instincts. We see such instincts under proper civilized control (control through sublimation) when Prospero suddenly comes upon Ferdinand and Miranda playing chess, in which they act out and resolve the potential conflicts of who has what powers that reside in any love relationship:

> MIRANDA: *Sweet lord, you play me false.*
> FERDINAND: *No, my dearest love,*
> *I would not for the world.*
> MIRANDA: *Yes, for a score of kingdoms you should wrangle,*
> *And I would call it fair play.* (V. i. 170-173)

Miranda and Ferdinand can sublimate and express competitive feelings within the safe confines of a game of chess, and, on a larger scale, they can find their freedom within the constraints of an exclusive commitment which contains inevitable emotional ambivalence. Ariel, in contrast, can only find freedom in release from bondage imposed from without. As the spirit of nature and as a symbol of the human capacity for creation out of "airy nothing," (Shakespeare's phrase defining the imagination in *A Midsummer Night's Dream*), Ariel was imprisoned by <u>Sycorax</u>, Caliban's witch mother, before the action of the play begins. In releasing

Ariel from imprisonment, Prospero shows himself ultimately as an agent of freedom. Sycorax, unlike Ariel, is not a native of the island; rather, she is a castoff from human civilization, and, in this particular ironic sense, she is the counterpart of the banished Prospero. She represents the destructiveness of the fallen world and of nature corrupted. Prospero's releasing of Ariel from the "cloven pine; within which rift / Imprison'd, thou did'st painfully remain / A dozen years," where Ariel remained after the death of Sycorax, prefigures the setting free of Ariel by Prospero at the play's conclusion. The imprisonment of Ariel has psychological as well as a physical import since Sycorax, we are appalled to learn, attempted to seduce Ariel but could not succeed because "thou wast a spirit too delicate / To act her earthy and abhorr'd commands, / Refusing her grand hests." Here the implication is that one is only free when acting according to one's highest nature, both sexually, as when Miranda and Ferdinand control their desire for one another in pledging fidelity, and morally when Prospero chooses forgiveness of his brother over revenge.

Ariel's freedom is closely related to Prospero's acceptance of the fact that nature both precedes and follows human art. Prospero's final words to Ariel, "then to the elements / Be free, and fare thou well!" indicate that Ariel, as the highest manifestation of elemental nature, must, in some symbolic sense, ultimately be free of human imposition. It is right for Prospero to control Caliban, but it is not right for Prospero to attempt to exercise permanent control over Ariel. If Ariel, like Caliban, represents not only some aspect of original nature, but also some aspect of Prospero's human nature, then Ariel's freedom must indicate some final liberation from the burden of consciousness back into inorganic matter, back into the materials out of which all life emerged and eventually evolved into human cognition and ingenuity. Language in this play is seen both as a curse and as a blessing, but like Prospero's visionary pageant, the manifestation of his art, words must "dissolve" back into air, Ariel's original element, out of which they came, "into air, into thin air." Art, imagination, and consciousness must return to inorganic nature out of which they evolved. The island, having become a stage, must return to being only an island, but this metamorphosis must be remembered in the retelling of the story of transformation for which the island and the surrounding sea constitute the symbolic setting.

V Emergence

With the evolutionary emergence of human consciousness and human art, the capacity to think in symbolic terms, causation becomes complex in the arena of human motivation. Although Shakespeare represents human character as having a fatalistic aspect—as if one must behave according to what one is (a kind of genetic determinism)—there is always something unknowable, some possible exercise of free will that can enable a character to transcend what he or she has been previously. With willful effort Prospero will be able to master his hostility toward Ferdinand (whom he sometimes treats harshly), and Prospero's ability to resist the temptation of revenging himself against his brother will require the intervention of Ariel, an act which also can be seen as Prospero's willed transcendence of himself.

Two other instances in which Shakespeare represents the mystery and elusiveness of human motivation and the capacity for self-willed change are evident. Prospero's judgment of Caliban assumes that he is incapable of any reformation:

> A devil, a born devil, on whose nature
> Nurture can never stick; on whom my pains,
> Humanely take, all, all lost, quite lost. (IV. i. 188-191)

But Prospero is probably wrong in this assessment as seen in Caliban's remarks of startling self-recognition in response to Prospero's command that Caliban return to Prospero's "cell:"

> Ay, that I will; and I'll be wise hereafter,
> And seek for grace. What a thrice-double ass
> Was I, to taken this drunkard [Stephano] for a god,
> And worship this dull fool! (V. i. 295-298)

Although Caliban's motivation is not entirely clear—perhaps being "wise" does not indicate a sincere wish for grace, but is merely a pragmatic social tactic—Caliban has learned something important about his own credulity that is based on a idolatrous wish. And even more mysterious, in the climactic scene in which Prospero, still struggling to overcome his fury, nevertheless pardons his brother with the words, "I do forgive thy rankest fault." Antonio, in response, says absolutely nothing. This moment of prolonged silence is surely the most shocking moment in the entire play. Antonio has only one brief remark to make through the remainder of the play. In response to Sebastian's question about what kind of creature Caliban is and whether he might be sold for money, Antonio crudely replies, "one of them / Is a plain fish" and thus, no doubt, marketable. The lowliness of Antonio's character is again revealed and the uncertain effect of Prospero's forgiveness is given its final troubling emphasis.

In addressing Antonio, Prospero makes the accusation, "Unnatural though thou art," and since earlier Prospero had described Caliban as one on "whose nature / Nurture can never stick," some clarification is needed to explain how Shakespeare uses the terms, "nature" and "unnatural." Not only in this play, but throughout Shakespeare's works, we see the recurrence of enmity and treachery between brothers, what Claudius calls "the primal eldest crime," in comparing his murder of Hamlet's father with Cain's murder of Abel. Although this primal pattern is inherent in human behavior, as is lust and aggression endemic in Caliban's, and in this sense can be considered natural, Shakespeare nevertheless calls such behavior "unnatural." With the emergence of civilized morality, it ceases to be natural to behave naturally; some higher form of nature is now demanded of human nature. This is the essential paradox in the nature-nurture debate as presented by Shakespeare in this play. It is no longer natural, Shakespeare shows, to behave as we naturally are (or were), and therefore the failure of will to exercise its freedom and choose one's Ariel-self over one's Caliban-self is to be castigated and condemned. By nature, we are designed to learn and are thus to be held responsible for whom we have chosen or have failed to choose to be.

So how might Antonio's silence be interpreted? There are two antithetical possibilities, which cannot be resolved: either Antonio, now completely under Prospero's control, is so astonished and moved by Prospero's generosity that he is dumbfounded and for a moment, untypical of him, can find no appropriate words to utter, or, alternatively, Antonio's hatred for Prospero—hatred perhaps exacerbated by Prospero's goodness—is so extreme that he dare not attempt even to offer some perfunctory or hypocritical remark lest he reveal his unmitigated antagonism. We simply cannot know with certainty, nor does Prospero, for whatever self-protecting reason, attempt to penetrate his brother's silence. Prospero is now most concerned with the telling of "the story of my life" and, turning to the audience, having just set Ariel free, he makes the request to all onlookers that he, too, be set free, thus linking Ariel's freedom to his own.

When Prospero seeks repose, like the Sabbath that followed creation, we are reminded that the model for such needed rest is to be found in the Bible, as suggested by Ariel when he responds to Prospero's question, "How's the day?" with the cryptic remark: "On the sixth hour; at which time, my lord, / You said our work should cease." The analogy here is to God's resting after six days of creation, nature having been completed through God's verbal commands. When Prospero decides to abjure his "rough magic," and to replace it with "heavenly music," he withdraws his controlling hand and returns nature to its original condition of wilderness. While Prospero's magic prevails, no one in the play drowns, but now that he must "drown" his book, a storm, once again, will be a storm; nature will return to its original state that preceded human existence, independent of human needs or wishes.

Having deposed himself of his magical powers, which in the context of the entire play were in a sense only a dream from which he has necessarily awakened, Prospero returns to his wholly human identity to confront the fact of his mortality and his innate sinful proclivities, as suggested by the Caliban within him. As Prospero has released Ariel, now he, too, asks the audience—which is another version of self-awareness (his being spectator of himself)—"to release me from my bands / With the help of your good hands." What earlier had been the moral magic of forgiveness, now becomes the power of prayer, not prayer to a specific god, but to Prospero's own power of self-overcoming within the human community as represented by the audience. The foundation for the human community is the common recognition of the need for artistic fictions that reveal our frailty and vulnerability as Prospero's very last couplet makes explicit: "As you from crimes would pardon'd be, / Let your indulgence set me free." Another aspect of freedom, then, in this play that has explored the varieties and nuances of freedom so deeply, is the freedom that derives from our mutual dependence on and acceptance of one another.

VI Humility

The Tempest is Shakespeare's most comprehensive work of the power of the human imagination to depict the rival claims of responding to nature's power and beauty in the spirit of dread and awe and of taking dominion over nature, including one's own nature, to cultivate and control it. The storm in The Tempest is like the sea in Homer's Odyssey (5) or the whirlwind in The Book of Job as an agent both of destruction and renewal, and Prospero's power of goodness derives from his artful ability to simulate a storm, temporarily take dominion over the island and its inhabitants, and finally relinquish that dominion. Like Job, Prospero's humility (meaning "of the earth," from the Latin, humilis) comes from the acknowledgment that he himself is of the earth and must accept this fact as the basis for his shared bond with all fellow humans (and perhaps monsters if we elect to put Caliban in that category.) Miranda, at the beginning of the play, does not understand Prospero's uses of nature. In saying, "Had I been any god of power, I would / Have sunk the sea within the earth," she reveals her wish to eliminate the destructive element of nature, which is an element that

Prospero himself can transform only by employing nature's own power.

To comprehend Shakespeare's balanced attitude toward nature in this play, we must consider, in addition to the imagery of the storm, Shakespeare's depiction of Ariel and Caliban, the two surviving inhabitants of the island before Prospero's arrival. Both can be regarded as symbolizing primal forces in human as well as in external nature, but we need to recall that Caliban's witch-like mother, Sycorax, when pregnant with Caliban, was banished from "Argier" (Algiers) and deposited on the island by sailors. Unlike Ariel, Sycorax is not an original inhabitant of the island, and Shakespeare's Platonic implication is that Ariel's music, whose "numbers" may be seen as the underpinning of physical reality, precedes natural beauty—which even Caliban can appreciate—as the originating and self-organizing force of the universe. (6) In modern terms, we might say that the necessary emergence of complexity, as represented by human art, is inherent as potentiality in inorganic nature from the very beginning.

Although Ariel can be thought of as a projection of Prospero's conscience or his imaginative capacity to apprehend ideas and act according to them, in contrast to Caliban who mainly represents murderous and sexually rapacious instinct, Shakespeare's metaphorical structure, I believe, presents both Caliban and Ariel as aspects of primal, as opposed to socially conditioned, human nature. Their significant linkage is to be found in the main virtue that Caliban possesses—his appreciation of the island's natural beauty and music. Caliban is not capable of moral understanding or empathy; for him Miranda—even though he can appreciate her beauty—is merely a vehicle for populating the island with more Calibans. Still, Caliban does have an innate capacity for taking delight in the sensuous beauty of the island. The music that moves him so deeply is Ariel's music, which Prospero, in freeing Ariel, has put to his own moral and aesthetic uses. Ariel thus represents a beauty and harmony inherent in nature, more fundamental even than his role as moral imagination, and even more fundamental than Calibanian lust and aggression.

The power of art—as Shakespeare reveals it in *The Tempest* through Prospero's book and Ariel's music—is not merely the human imposition of order upon chaotic force, but the human ability (as if by magic) to exploit and redirect natural forces for human purposes. Shakespeare's illuminating paradox is that human beings cannot transcend nature without the aid of nature, whereby what may begin as a curse, nature's violence, ends as a blessing, nature's transfiguration through human art. Despite Prospero's power over the elements and over his own innate drives, as represented by both Ariel and Caliban, Prospero's ultimate and consummating magic—

which he achieves only through an extreme effort of willed choice—lies in the moral enterprise of forgiving his treasonous brother. Forgiveness, as in many of Shakespeare's plays, is exemplary of the transforming power of moral goodness, which possesses a kind of magic of its own. The full realization of this paradox can be seen in Ferdinand's response to Ariel's music: "Where should this music be? i' th' air, or th' earth? / It sounds no more;—and sure, it waits upon / Some gods o' th' island." As Ferdinand is able to recognize the redemptive power of the music, so, too, he can express wonder at the potential of stormy nature to bring about reconciliation and opportunity: "Though the seas threaten, they are merciful: / I have cursed them [as Miranda had earlier] without cause." To this realization the kindly Gonzalo replies: "Now all the blessings / Of a glad father compass thee about!"

On one level this is a play about restoration in which "all losses are restored and sorrows end," but mainly in the sense that everyone believed dead turns out to be alive. Though teetering at the brink of tragedy in which more potential murderous violence might be let loose, the play is resolved in the spirit of comedy with the imminent wedding of Miranda and Ferdinand (in contrast to Claribel's forced and choiceless marriage, described by Sebastion as "between loathness and obedience.") Alonso sums up all the restorations, including, significantly, the restoration of many of the characters' senses of themselves, their most admirable identities:

> *In one voyage*
> *Did Claribel her husband find at Tunis,*
> *And Ferdinand, her brother, found a wife*
> *Where he himself was lost; Prospero his dukedom*
> *In a poor isle; and all of us ourselves,*
> *Where no man was his own.* (V. i. 208-213)

Beneath the joyousness of all these restorations, however, lies the deep awareness of Prospero's wisdom—wisdom that he has made bearable through self-mastery—that everything "dissolves," that "our little life / Is rounded with a sleep." What a well-chosen word is "little," suggesting the preciousness of what that "little" has to offer when we humans are at our "tender" best.

The play ends with both Ariel and Prospero, each according to the needs of his own nature, being set free. Prospero, having taught Caliban language, is now responsible for him. He fully accepts this condition when he says, "This thing of darkness / I acknowledge mine," and so, I assume, Prospero will have to take Caliban back to Milan with him, where Caliban can be controlled (but not sold on the fish market) like the other rebellious and murderous forces that are part of every human psyche beneath the veneer of civilization. In taking Caliban back to Milan (but not to be exhibited for money as a freak as Antonio thinks), Prospero will be leaving the island in its natural state, as it was before the interventions of Sycorax and of Prospero himself, to Ariel alone, who will de-evolve back into inchoate matter. Ariel's freedom is closely related to Prospero's acceptance of the fact that nature both precedes and follows human art. Prospero's final words to Ariel, "then to the elements / Be free, and fare thou well!" indicate that Ariel, as elemental nature, must, in some final sense, be free of human imposition, and this account of nature's ultimate indifference to human wishes and aspirations is part of the story to be told.

The quintessential argument for the human need for wilderness as a reminder of original chaos is expressed in Shakespeare's dramatic vision of our little lives being "rounded with a sleep." We only can make sense of human life and human values when we perceive them as a temporary effulgence of nature. Thus, it is to nature that we must give our equally deep allegiance, as well as to what we, in passing, make of nature through human volition even in its manifestation of storytelling and art. Without wilderness, as exemplified by the tempest itself (as it was in the whirlwind that addresses Job), our humanity is diminished because we fail to perceive the poignant beauty inherent in our ephemerality; we fail to acknowledge ourselves as creatures among other creatures, among other evolving and vanishing forms, and we are unable to attain Hamlet's wished-for consummation: to be "as one, in suffering all, that suffers nothing," words that might easily be a further fitting expression of Prospero's capacity for acceptance.

When Prospero abjures his "rough magic" at the play's end, declaring "I'll drown my book," he makes a heroic and significant choice—the choice to accept the limits nature imposes upon him, including his own mortality, and to relinquish his attempt to take ultimate dominion over nature. Prospero's final freedom, then, in giving up "Spirits to enforce" is the freedom from human arrogance and pride which seek the overthrow of nature in order to replace natural fecundity with human contrivance and human art. All dreams, including artistic visions—our most representative capacity to know ourselves from the stories we tell about ourselves—must turn back into thin air. And so Prospero's final words to the audience, words which express his sense of their mutual bond and interdependence, "As you from crimes would pardon'd be / Let your indulgence set me free," acknowledge the play's ultimate paradox: human power must be exercised to acknowledge the limits of the use of human power. The mastery of nature must find its culmination in the freedom that comes from our mastery of ourselves, as so richly exemplified by Prospero's renunciations, and, finally, in the acceptance of the vanishing even of that mastery.

EPILOGUE

I Prospero's Three Thoughts

Although Prospero's final decision is to set Ariel free, to keep his word as he had pledged to do, his penultimate choice before departing from the island is to tell his story. Since the whole play is a plot of his own making—his own contrivance and creation—he is promising to tell the story about his telling his story. This doubling of story upon story is Shakespeare's complex and rich metaphor for human consciousness itself—for the way the human mind works, for human thought, particularly when it is made manifest as fictive art. Prospero claims that on his return to Milan, when he is back in ordinary, not magical, reality, "Every third thought shall be my grave." But this third thought of personal demise, his awareness of personal mortality itself, must be seen in relation to the other two-thirds of Prospero's thinking as his life rounds to its end and becomes his story; these other thoughts mitigate the severity of the thought of the grave though they do not deny it. The fundamental requirement of reality is the acceptance of death.

Surely, one of those other thoughts will be Miranda about whom Prospero, speaking in the metaphor of the tripartite mind, has said to Ferdinand, "for I / Have given you a third of mine own life, / Or that for which I live." In thinking about Miranda, Prospero can well be gratified by the inheritance he leaves behind as made manifest in the values of love, devotion, and sacrifice that his teaching has instilled in his daughter as exemplified in her choice and commitment to Ferdinand.

The other third of Prospero's mind, it is reasonable to assume, focuses on Ariel, the most spiritual aspect of Prospero's love and the main agent of his art. When Ariel asks Prospero, "Do you love me, master? no?" Prospero responds without hesitation, "Dearly, my delicate Ariel." Death and love, appropriately, constitute Prospero's ultimate concerns.

Setting Ariel free to return to the "elements" at the play's conclusion, then, may be imagined as an alternative way of thinking about death to the seemingly mundane and gloomy, "Where every third thought shall be my grave." Since the basic elements include water and air, Ariel's song in Act I, which gives expression to Ferdinand's fearful assumption that his father has drowned, nevertheless offers a consoling, even ecstatic, vision of death. Ferdinand acknowledges that Ariel's music alleviates his grief, "allaying . . . my passion, / With its sweet air." Ariel's visionary depiction of death by drowning as part of the natural process is remarkably impersonal and aesthetically beautiful; Ariel himself (or herself as the complement of Prospero's motherly aspect) articulates the strangeness—in its meaning of wonder or astonishment of this exquisite transformation caused by death:

> *Full fathom five thy father lies;*
> *Of his bones are coral made:*
> *Those are pearls that are his eyes:*
> *Nothing of him that doth fade,*
> *But doth suffer a sea change*
> *Into something rich and strange.* (I. ii. 391-399)

How soothingly lovely these lines are, how delightful are the images of coral and pearl, which can be thought of as nature's own works of art. Death is not rendered here as grotesque or sorrowful, but as transfigurative, and the word "suffer" is suggestive of Hamlet's visionary lines about "one, in suffering all, who suffers nothing." The fact that drowning is described aesthetically may well explain Prospero's choice to "drown my book," the book with which he has so deeply identified—the book of magic that will be replaced by Prospero's ultimate willingness to overcome the social proprieties that constitute his reluctance to tell his story.

When Alonso inquires of Prospero, "When did you lose your daughter?" not realizing that Prospero is speaking metaphorically, Prospero begins to respond by recounting the narrative of the tempest itself, "In this last tempest," but he soon interrupts his narrative:

> *I am Prospero and that very duke*
> *Which was thrust forth of Milan; who most strangely*
> *Upon this shore, where you were wrack'd, was landed*
> *To be the lord on't. No more yet of this;*
> *For 'tis a chronicle of day by day,*
> *Not a relation for a breakfast nor*
> *Befitting this first meeting.* (V. 1. 159-165)

Here, Shakespeare emphasizes the importance Prospero gives to the storytelling, to the conditions of when and under what circumstances the story should be told, and what details it should encompass. Prospero also makes the significant claim about how "strangely" the past events unfolded with the implication that the story itself would challenge credulity, picking up on the very word "strange" that Ariel had used earlier to describe death as "a sea change."

Soon after, however, Prospero will change his mind when he assures Alonso that he will recite "the story of my life, / And the particular accidents gone by / Since I came to this isle." In agreeing to do this, Prospero has overcome his earlier ambivalent recalcitrance, his remaining qualms about who is to be trusted, in his willingness to take upon himself what Lear called, "the mystery of things." When Alonso responds enthusiastically to Prospero's offer to tell his story by saying, "I long / To hear the story of your life, which must / Take the ear strangely," Prospero seems to quicken in reaction to Alonso's use of the word "strangely," by committing himself to the story-telling; "I'll deliver all," he says. In doing so, Prospero leaves behind his will and testament (and maybe Shakespeare's as well).

Immediately after Prospero has made this commitment, he releases Ariel to the elements with the charge—"Be free"—but Shakespeare leaves it to the audience to speculate about the meaning of this freedom. It suggests freedom from the evolved complexity of organic life and thus from thought itself and the tangles of guilt and conscience; or perhaps it is the choice to reaffirm that part of the human mind that transcends personal concerns with universal principle. Prospero, earlier, transcends his desire to revenge himself for the crimes committed against him by his brother ("Yet with my nobler reason 'gainst my fury / Do I take part") at Ariel's urging. Maybe the freedom—represented by Ariel as the spirit of art and music— lies in story-telling itself, what imaginative art adds to reality. In the face of inescapable mortality, over which humans have no choice except in the attitude they take toward that reality, whether or not to make the willful choice to tell a story of human finitude and human striving remains open.

II Ending as Prologue

Although *The Tempest* is a comedy and ends with the assumed marriage of Miranda and Ferdinand, there is a melancholy feeling associated with the vanishing of the musical Ariel and with a number of matters that remain uncertain or unresolved. We do not know for sure whether Prospero's brother, Antonio, will accept Prospero's forgiveness or contrive another plot against him. And we do not know whether Prospero, without his magic, will be able to rule successfully in Milan. As the epilogue reveals, he is burdened with some nameless sense of guilt, "As you [including himself] from crime would pardoned be," as well as the awareness of his approaching death.

From the conclusion of *The Tempest*, it is difficult to project the possibilities for the immediate future; ironically, these prospects are not nearly as upbeat and optimistic as are those at the end of *Macbeth* with the ascent of Malcolm to the throne. Malcolm has been tried and tested and is now filled with the "grace of Grace" and with self-knowledge (unlike Duncan his innocent and naïve father). Malcolm is fully aware of the potential for evil in all men, including himself. His experience and self-awareness make him ready to rule, and nature, which in this play is not neutral or indifferent, has reasserted a moral order seemingly inherent in the heavens and the earth. The one disquieting note may be the absence of Donalbain at Malcolm's coronation, but all the nobility have been promoted, which seems like a judicious first political move considering what Malcolm knows now about human ambition.

To keep the idea of future prospects in perspective, however, we can surely assert that *The Tempest* is not as certainly forboding in its prospects for the future as is *Hamlet* with the dictator and tyrant Fortinbras usurping control in Denmark and with Horatio's inappropriately melodramatic description of Hamlet's life as one of "accidental judgments, casual slaughters, / Of deaths put on by cunning and forc'd cause" as if Hamlet's story were nothing more than a tragedy of revenge lacking the mystery and inwardness of Hamlet's character. The play does not conclude with the possible meanings of "silence" and "rest," but with the blatant noise of soldiers shooting.

At the end of *King Lear*, the trustworthy Albany requests that Kent and Edgar "Rule in this realm, and the gor'd state sustain," but Kent declines with the assumption that he will soon follow his master Lear in the "journey" to death. Edgar, who has proven his loyalty and devotion to his father, and is, unlike Kent, still young, nevertheless seems so exhausted and depleted that we must wonder if he is capable of ruling: "The oldest hath borne most," he says; "we that are young / Shall never see so much or live so long." And unlike in *Macbeth*, nature remains totally indifferent to human suffering; there is no Birnam wood that comes to restore order and grace.

The rulers in charge in *Othello* are all decent people. The Duke, for example, is a model of fairness and freedom from bias and prejudice as we see when he rejects Brabantio's charge that Othello has bewitched Desdemona. "To vouch this is no proof," he asserts, and he sums up with the pithy and admirable remark about Othello: "If virtue no delighted beauty lack, / Your son-in-law is far more fair than black." Lodovico's final words to the lord governor, Montano, give orders of what to do with Iago: "the censure of this hellish villain, / The time, the place, the torture. O, enforce it! / Myself will straight aboard, and to the state / This heavy act with heavy heart relate." The difference between the similar phrases, Malcolm's "measure, time, and place," and Lodovico's "the time, the place, the torture," make manifest the mood of vengeance and the inadequacy even of torture in the face of unfathomable evil with which the play concludes. Perhaps Lodovico's relating of Othello's betrayal of his own values, his belief in love even under unlikely circumstances, will serve to prevent future tragedy, but Iago's silence, his refusal to speak at the end, leaves the audience with a skeptical feeling about the sufficiency of human intelligence to resist the diabolical forces in the world.

The multiple marriages at the conclusion of *A Midsummer Night's Dream*, and, in particular, the willingness of the lovers to make marital vows when they are not under some spell or the influence of drugs, indeed bodes well. And the fact that marriage looks forward to a future which includes the "blessing" of having healthy children removes love from the realm of dreaming into the world of reality. The wounds caused by romantic desire seem to have healed as Robin in his last couplet claims that he "shall restore amends." When Shakespeare wants to present us with a happy conclusion with good prospects, he knows exactly how to do it.

But my reading of the ending of *The Tempest* need not be as melancholy as I have suggested. "The story of my life" that Prospero will tell keeps alive in memory the music of Ariel and the moral magic of Prospero's forgiveness of his brother. And it is even possible that Caliban is not entirely trapped in his "nature," that he is sincere in saying, "I'll be wise hereafter, / And seek for grace." The future remains open since the final contingency is left to the imagination of the audience; after all, it is the applause of the audience— our choice—that will determine whether or not Prospero will be set free.

Notes

CHAPTER I: INTRODUCTION: WILL, CHOICE, AND STORYTELLING

1. All quotations from Shakespeare's plays are taken from individual volumes of *The Yale Shakespeare* (New Haven: Yale University Press, 1947).
2. Ernst Jones, *Hamlet and Oedipus* (New York: W.W. Norton, 1976).
3. Sophocles, *Oedipus Rex*, translated by Dudley Fitts and Robert Fitzgerald (New York: Harcourt Brace, 1977).
4. Heinz Pagels, *The Cosmic Code* (New York: Bantam Books, 1984), p. 77.

CHAPTER II: HAMLET: THE HEART OF THE MYSTERY

1. Allen Johnson and Douglass Price-Williams, *Oedipus Ubiquitous* (Stanford: Stanford University Press, 1996), pp.6-7.
2. Sophocles, *Oedipus Rex*, p. 51.
3. Sophocles, *Oedipus Rex*, p. 72.
4. Tacitus, *The Annals, 109 A.C.E.*, translated by Alfred John Church & William Jackson Brodribb, in *The Complete Works of Tacitus*, ed. Moses Hadas (New York: Modern Library, 1942).
5. *The New English Bible*, Oxford Study Edition (New York: Oxford University Press, 1976).

CHAPTER III: MEASURE FOR MEASURE: WHAT WILL ISABELLA DECIDE?

1. *The New English Bible*.
2. *Exodus*, translated by Robert Alter, *The Five Books of Moses* (New York: W.W. Norton, 2004).

CHAPTER IV: OTHELLO: INCREDULITY AND THE POSSIBLE

1. David Buss, *The Evolution of Desire* (New York: Basic Books, 1994), p. 126.
2. Charles Darwin, *The Origin of the Species*, edited by Philip Appleman (New York: W.W. Norton, 1975). See Darwin on the "struggle for existence" (p. 41), particularly as it pertains to "one individual with another of the same species." This connects with Darwin's other main thesis of "sexual selection," the competitive attempt of each individual to get his genes into the next generation (pp.50, 106).
3. Richard Dawkins, *The Selfish Gene* (New York: Oxford University Press, 1976), p. vi.

CHAPTER V: A MIDSUMMER NIGHT'S DREAM: FROM LUNACY TO PROSPERITY

1. Sigmund Freud, *Introductory Lectures on Psychoanalysis*, translated and edited by James Strachey (New York: Liveright, 1966), p. 550.

2. Janet Malcolm, *Psychoanalysis: The Impossible Profession* (Northvale, N.J.: Jason Aranson, 1994), p. 6.
3. Jared Diamond, *The Third Chimpanzee* (New York: Harper Perennial, 1992), pp. 104-05.
4. Ernst Mayr, *This Is Biology* (Cambridge, Mass.: The Belknap Press, 1997), p. 75.
5. George Bernard Shaw, *Man and Superman* (Baltimore: Penguin Books, 1964), p. 212.

CHAPTER VI: BETRAYAL AND NOTHINGNESS: THE BOOK OF JOB AND KING LEAR

1. The Book of Job, translated with an introduction by Stephen Mitchell (San Francisco: North Point Press, 1987).
2. *Darwin*, selected and and edited by Philip Appleman (New York: W.W. Norton, 1979), pp. 200-01. Darwin emphasizes repeatedly the importance of the "distinct emotion of sympathy" as the basis for human community.
3. The Five Books of Moses, translated by Robert Alter.
4. The Five Books of Moses, translated by Robert Alter.

CHAPTER VII: MACBETH: THE MORAL IMAGINATION

1. John Milton, *Paradise Lost*, edited by Scott Elledge (New York: W.W. Norton, 1975), p. 80.
2. Sigmund Freud, *Collected Papers*, vol. 4, translated by Joan Riviere (New York: Basic Books, 1959), p. 201. Freud describes the ultimate impossible fantasy as follows: "All the instincts, the loving, the grateful, the sensual, the defiant, the self-assertive and independent—all are gratified in the wish to be the father of (oneself)."

CHAPTER VIII: THE TEMPEST: SELF-MASTERY AND FREEDOM

1. Plato, *The Republic*, translated by B. Jowett, in *The Dialogues of Plato* (New York: Random House, 1937).
2. The Five Books of Moses, translated by Robert Alter.
3. Sigmund Freud, *Civilization and Its Discontents*, translated and edited by James Strachey (New York: W.W. Norton, 1989), p. 86.
4. Sigmund Freud, "Humor" in *Character and Culture*, edited by Philip Rieff (New York: Collier Books, 1963), p. 268.
5. Homer, *The Odyssey*, trans. Stanley Lombardo (Indianapolis: Hackett, 2000). Christian de Duve, *Vital Dust* (New York: Basic Books, 1995), p. xviii. De Duve argues that the evolution of highly organized complexity, including life, was inherent in matter, "vital dust, from the very beginning."

Index of Themes

Index of Authors, Works, and Characters